2005 SUPPLEMENT

FEDERAL COURTS AND THE LAW OF FEDERAL–STATE RELATIONS

FIFTH EDITION

by

PETER W. LOW
Hardy Cross Dillard Professor of Law
University of Virginia

JOHN C. JEFFRIES, JR.
Emerson Spies Professor of Law
Arnold H. Leon Professor and Dean of the Law School
University of Virginia

FOUNDATION PRESS
NEW YORK, NEW YORK
2005

Foundation Press, of Thomson/West, has created this publication to provide you with accurate and authoritative information concerning the subject matter covered. However, this publication was not necessarily prepared by persons licensed to practice law in a particular jurisdiction. Foundation Press is not engaged in rendering legal or other professional advice, and this publication is not a substitute for the advice of an attorney. If you require legal or other expert advice, you should seek the services of a competent attorney or other professional.

© 2004 FOUNDATION PRESS
© 2005 By FOUNDATION PRESS
        395 Hudson Street
        New York, NY 10014
        Phone Toll Free 1–877–888–1330
        Fax (212) 367–6799
        fdpress.com
Printed in the United States of America

ISBN 1–58778–861–6

PREFACE

It may seem odd that the Fifth Edition, published only last year, would require a substantial Supplement, but the casebook went to press when the 2003–2004 term of the Supreme Court was barely underway. As it happened, both the 2003–2004 and the 2004–2005 terms of the Supreme Court were unusually productive for students of Federal Courts. In consequence, we offer a substantial supplement to a relatively new edition.

Specifically, the 2005 Supplement includes eight main cases:

Sosa v. Alvarez-Machain (2004)—Perhaps the most important of these decisions is *Sosa v. Alvarez-Machain*, where the Supreme Court narrowed, but did not eliminate, private liability for violations of international law under the Alien Tort Statute. *Sosa* has been added to a new section, included for the first time in the Fifth Edition, on the power of the federal courts to enforce customary international law. The section begins with *Filartiga v. Pena-Irala* (2nd Cir. 1980), which launched the revivification of the Alien Tort Statute, and now closes with Sosa, which curtailed it.

Elk Grove Unified School District v. Newdow (2004)—Elk Grove rejected, on grounds of standing, an Establishment Clause challenge to public school recitation of "under God" in the Pledge of Allegiance. The Court ruled that a non-custodial father did not have a right to complain of the patriotic exercises conducted in his daughter's school, at least so long as the daughter and her mother did not support his position. Interestingly, Elk Grove was explicitly based on prudential standing rather than on the requirements of Article III. As it's the first modern standing decision to rest on that ground, we've included it as a main case.

Vieth v. Jubelirer (2004)—*Vieth v. Jubelirer* refused to accept a constitutional challenge to a political gerrymander. A plurality of four Justices rested this decision on the ground that political gerrymanders are nonjusticiable political questions. *Vieth* is now the centerpiece of a completely revised section on this topic. Previously, we used *Nixon v. United States* (1992) as the main case on political questions. *Vieth* has the advantage of presenting the political question doctrine in a context of immediate controversy and importance and in a context where nonjusticiability is most plausibly distinguished from the merits.

Grable & Sons Metal Products, Inc. v. Darue Eng. & Mfg. (2005)—In *Grable & Sons*, the Supreme Court unanimously approved removal to federal court of an action to quiet title despite the absence of a federal cause of action. The defendant claimed title from a federal tax sale, and the Court found the federal interest sufficiently substantial to justify removal jurisdiction.

Exxon Mobil Corp. v. Allapattah Services, Inc. (2005)—*Exxon Mobil Corp. v. Allapattah Services, Inc.* answered a question that had divided the lower courts since the adoption of the supplemental jurisdiction statute, 28 U.S.C. § 1367. Zahn v. International Paper Co., 414 U.S. 291 (1973), held that every member of a plaintiff class in a diversity class action had to satisfy the jurisdictional minimum of 28 U.S.C. § 1332. The question was whether that rule survived the adoption of § 1367, which broadly authorized supplemental jurisdiction. In Exxon Mobil the Court held that, so long as one named plaintiff satisfies the jurisdictional minimum, the claims of other plaintiffs can be heard under supplemental jurisdiction, regardless of the amount in controversy.

Hibbs v. Winn (2004)—By a five-four vote, the Court concluded that the Tax Anti-Injunction Act, 28 U.S.C. § 1341, does not bar an Establishment Clause challenge to a state system of income-tax credits for funding for private schools. *Hibbs* is included as a new main case in the materials on abstention.

Dretke v. Haley (2004)—*Dretke v. Haley* concerned the "actual innocence" exception to the "cause" and "prejudice" requirements for raising defaulted claims via federal habeas corpus. At issue was whether the "actual innocence" exception reached procedural default of objections to non-capital sentencing enhancements under habitual or repeat offender statutes. By a vote of six to three, the Court refused to allow immediate relief from an unauthorized sentence but required prior consideration of other possible avenues of relief.

Brosseau v. Haugen (2004)—*Brosseau* is the Court's most recent pronouncement on qualified immunity under § 1983. On that issue, the Court divided eight-one in favor of the defendant, with only Justice Stevens dissenting. Interestingly, however, Justice Breyer, joined by Justices Scalia and Ginsburg, concurred to ask for reconsideration of the rule requiring adjudication of the merits before reaching questions of qualified immunity. Partly for that reason, *Brosseau* has been added to the materials on § 1983.

Additionally, the Supplement provides substantial note treatment of a remarkable burst of Supreme Court activity that resulted in six (!) decisions in 2005 on statute-of-limitations questions under the Antiterrorism and Effective Death Penalty Act of 1996. Collectively, these note cases replace

Pliler v. Ford (2004), which had appeared as a main case in the 2004 Supplement.

In addition to these cases, the 2005 Supplement includes note treatment of other decisions and references to recently published secondary literature.

PERMISSION TO DUPLICATE

There are many intersections between **Federal Courts and the Law of Federal-State Relations** (5th ed. 2004) and Jeffries, Karlan, Low & Rutherglen, **Civil Rights Actions: Enforcing the Constitution** (4th ed. 2000). Occasionally, a teacher using one book may wish to use material from the other book or its supplement. To facilitate such borrowings, we authorize teachers who have adopted either book to duplicate limited portions of the other or its annual supplement for distribution to their students. We are grateful to Foundation Press for agreeing to make this option available.

PWL

JCJ<small>JR</small>

Charlottesville, Virginia
July 2005

TABLE OF CONTENTS

Supplement Page

PREFACE iii
TABLE OF CASES xi
TABLE OF SECONDARY AUTHORITIES xvii

PART I. FEDERALISM AND SEPARATION OF POWERS: THE BASIC STRUCTURE

CHAPTER I. CHOICE OF LAW IN THE FEDERAL SYSTEM

Casebook Page

Section 1: State Law in Federal Court
16	*Virginia v. Maryland*	2
19	Additional Citation	2
23	Additional Citations	2

Section 2: Federal Law in State Court
69	Additional Citation	2

Section 3: Supreme Court Review of State Court Decisions
102	Additional Citation	3

CHAPTER II. THE POWER OF THE FEDERAL COURTS TO CREATE FEDERAL LAW

Section 2: Implied Rights of Action to Enforce Federal Statutes
176	Additional Citation	4

Section 5: Customary International Law
234	*SOSA v. ALVAREZ-MACHAIN*	4

vii

CHAPTER III. CONGRESSIONAL CONTROL OF THE FEDERAL COURTS

Casebook Page		Supplement Page
	Section 2: The Power to Expand Federal Jurisdiction	
277	Additional Citation	24
277	Addition to Note 3	24

CHAPTER IV. JUSTICIABILITY

	Section 1: Standing	
414	*ELK GROVE UNIFIED SCHOOL DISTRICT v. NEWDOW*	26
	Section 3: The Political Question	
459	Omit Pages 459–75 and Substitute:	
	Introductory Notes on the History of the Doctrine	26
	1. *Luther v. Borden*	35
	2. *Baker v. Carr*	36
	3. *Powell v. McCormack*	37
	4. *Nixon v. United States*	39
	VIETH v. JUBELIRER	39
	Additional Notes on the Political Question	56
	1. Questions and Comments on Vieth v. Jubelirer	56
	2. The Political Question Doctrine in Foreign Affairs: *Goldwater v. Carter*	56
	3. The Political Question Doctrine and Judicial Review	57
	4. Bibliography	59

PART II. THE JURISDICTION OF THE FEDERAL COURTS

CHAPTER V. SUBJECT MATTER JURISDICTION

	Section 1: Federal Question Jurisdiction	
479	Additional Citation	60
493	Additional Citation	68
511	*Aetna Health Inc. v. Davila*	68
	Section 2: Diversity Jurisdiction	
527	Additional Citation	68
528	Additional Citation	69
528	*Grupo Dataflux v. Atlas Global Group, L.P.*	69
545	Additional Citations	69

CHAPTER VI. ABSTENTION

Casebook Page		Supplement Page
	Section 1: General Principles	
641	The *Rooker-Feldman* Doctrine: *Exxon Mobil Corporation v. Saudi Basic Industries Corporation*	93
660	*San Remo Hotel, L.P. v. City and County of San Francisco*	95
661	Additional Citation	96
	Section 4: Anti-Injunction Act	
736	*HIBBS v. WINN*	96

PART III. FEDERAL COURT ENFORCEMENT OF FEDERAL RIGHTS

CHAPTER VII. HABEAS CORPUS

	Section 1: The Scope of Review	
739	Additional Citation	114
739	Add a new Note:	
	3. Challenges to Executive Detention: The "Enemy Combatant" Cases	
	(i) *Hamdi v. Rumsfeld*	114
	(ii) *Rumsfeld v. Padilla*	117
	(iii) *Rasul v. Bush*	117
773	Additional Citation	118
796	*Yarborough v. Gentry, Mitchell v. Esparza, Yarborough v. Alvarado, Holland v. Jackson,*	118
799	*Beard v. Banks, Schriro v. Summerlin*	118
801	*Tennard v. Dretke*	119
802	Additional Citations	119
	Section 3: Exhaustion of State Remedies and Repetitive Applications	
870	*Castro v. United States*	119
883	*PLILER v. FORD*	120
	Section 4: Claims of Innocence	
916	Additional Citation	141
926	*DRETKE v. HALEY*	141

CHAPTER VIII. STATE SOVEREIGN IMMUNITY AND THE 11TH AMENDMENT

Casebook Page		Supplement Page
	Section 1: Nature of the Limitation	
931	Additional Citations	149
	Section 2: Consent and Congressional Abrogation	
966	Additional Citation	149
1026	*Tennessee v. Lane*	149
1036	Additional Citation	152
	Section 3: Does Ex parte Young Survive?	
1047	Additional Citation	152
1047	*Frew v. Hawkins*	152

CHAPTER X. REMEDIAL INTERACTIONS

	Section 1: Relation of § 1983 to Habeas Corpus	
1336	*Nelson v. Campbell*	166
1336	Add new notes:	
	Notes on Subsequent *Preiser* Litigation	
	1. *Edwards v. Balisok*	166
	2. *Wilkinson v. Dotson*	166
	3. *Nelson v. Campbell*	168
	4. Res Judicata	172

APPENDIX B. SELECTED FEDERAL STATUTES

APPENDIX C. JUDICIAL REVIEW

C–10	Additional Citation	175

TABLE OF CASES

Principal cases are in bold type. Non-principal cases are in roman type. References are to Pages.

ACLU of Louisiana v. Bridges, 334 F.3d 416 (5th Cir.2003), 105
Aetna Health Inc. v. Davila, 542 U.S. 200, 124 S.Ct. 2488, 159 L.Ed.2d 312 (2004), 68
Alaska Packers Ass'n v. Industrial Acc. Com'n, 294 U.S. 532, 55 S.Ct. 518, 79 L.Ed. 1044 (1935), 1
Aldinger v. Howard, 427 U.S. 1, 96 S.Ct. 2413, 49 L.Ed.2d 276 (1976), 72, 73
Alexander v. Sandoval, 532 U.S. 275, 121 S.Ct. 1511, 149 L.Ed.2d 517 (2001), 10
Allen v. Wright, 468 U.S. 737, 104 S.Ct. 3315, 82 L.Ed.2d 556 (1984), 28, 29, 32, 173
Almendarez–Torres v. United States, 523 U.S. 224, 118 S.Ct. 1219, 140 L.Ed.2d 350 (1998), 146
Alvarez–Machain, United States v., 504 U.S. 655, 112 S.Ct. 2188, 119 L.Ed.2d 441 (1992), 4, 5
American Well Works Co. v. Layne & Bowler Co., 241 U.S. 257, 36 S.Ct. 585, 60 L.Ed. 987 (1916), 67, 68
Anderson v. Creighton, 483 U.S. 635, 107 S.Ct. 3034, 97 L.Ed.2d 523 (1987), 156, 158
Ankenbrandt v. Richards, 504 U.S. 689, 112 S.Ct. 2206, 119 L.Ed.2d 468 (1992), 29, 32, 33
Apprendi v. New Jersey, 530 U.S. 466, 120 S.Ct. 2348, 147 L.Ed.2d 435 (2000), 119, 146
Arkansas v. Farm Credit Services of Cent. Arkansas, 520 U.S. 821, 117 S.Ct. 1776, 138 L.Ed.2d 34 (1997), 102
Artuz v. Bennett, 531 U.S. 4, 121 S.Ct. 361, 148 L.Ed.2d 213 (2000), 121, 124, 125, 127, 128
Ashwander v. TVA, 297 U.S. 288, 56 S.Ct. 466, 80 L.Ed. 688 (1936), 28
Atlee v. Richardson, 411 U.S. 911, 93 S.Ct. 1545, 36 L.Ed.2d 304 (1973), 56

Baker v. Carr, 369 U.S. 186, 82 S.Ct. 691, 7 L.Ed.2d 663 (1962), 36, 37, 38, 39, 41
Banco Nacional de Cuba v. Sabbatino, 376 U.S. 398, 84 S.Ct. 923, 11 L.Ed.2d 804 (1964), 10, 12
Beard v. Banks, 542 U.S. 406, 124 S.Ct. 2504, 159 L.Ed.2d 494 (2004), 118, 119
Bivens v. Six Unknown Named Agents of Federal Bureau of Narcotics, 403 U.S. 388, 91 S.Ct. 1999, 29 L.Ed.2d 619 (1971), 15, 17
Black & White Taxicab & Transfer Co. v. Brown and Yellow Taxicab & Transfer Co., 276 U.S. 518, 48 S.Ct. 404, 72 L.Ed. 681 (1928), 9
Board of Trustees of University of Alabama v. Garrett, 531 U.S. 356, 121 S.Ct. 955, 148 L.Ed.2d 866 (2001), 149, 150
Bob Jones University v. Simon, 416 U.S. 725, 94 S.Ct. 2038, 40 L.Ed.2d 496 (1974), 100
Boerne, City of v. Flores, 521 U.S. 507, 117 S.Ct. 2157, 138 L.Ed.2d 624 (1997), 149, 150, 151
Bowen v. Massachusetts, 487 U.S. 879, 108 S.Ct. 2722, 101 L.Ed.2d 749 (1988), 34
Brockett v. Spokane Arcades, Inc., 472 U.S. 491, 105 S.Ct. 2794, 86 L.Ed.2d 394 (1985), 34
Brosseau v. Haugen, 543 U.S. ___, 125 S.Ct. 596, 160 L.Ed.2d 583 (2004), **154,** 159, 163
Brown v. Allen, 344 U.S. 443, 73 S.Ct. 397, 97 L.Ed. 469 (1953), 143
Brown v. Board of Ed. of Topeka, Shawnee County, Kan., 347 U.S. 483, 74 S.Ct. 686, 98 L.Ed. 873 (1954), 96, 105
Bunting v. Mellen, 541 U.S. 1019, 124 S.Ct. 1750, 158 L.Ed.2d 636 (2004), 157, 163
Burford v. Sun Oil Co., 319 U.S. 315, 63 S.Ct. 1098, 87 L.Ed. 1424 (1943), 95

California v. Grace Brethren Church, 457 U.S. 393, 102 S.Ct. 2498, 73 L.Ed.2d 93 (1982), 101, 102, 103, 110, 111
California v. Rooney, 483 U.S. 307, 107 S.Ct. 2852, 97 L.Ed.2d 258 (1987), 164
Castro v. United States, 540 U.S. 375, 124 S.Ct. 786, 157 L.Ed.2d 778 (2003), 119
Caterpillar Inc. v. Lewis, 519 U.S. 61, 117 S.Ct. 467, 136 L.Ed.2d 437 (1996), 69, 78
Chicago v. International College of Surgeons, 522 U.S. 156, 118 S.Ct. 523, 139 L.Ed.2d 525 (1997), 77, 78, 90

Christianson v. Colt Industries Operating Corp., 486 U.S. 800, 108 S.Ct. 2166, 100 L.Ed.2d 811 (1988), 62

City of (see name of city)

Clark v. Paul Gray, Inc., 306 U.S. 583, 59 S.Ct. 744, 83 L.Ed. 1001 (1939), 72, 74, 77, 79, 85, 86, 88, 90, 92

Cole v. Bone, 993 F.2d 1328 (8th Cir.1993), 157

Colegrove v. Green, 328 U.S. 549, 66 S.Ct. 1198, 90 L.Ed. 1432 (1946), 36, 37

Colorado River Water Conservation Dist. v. United States, 424 U.S. 800, 96 S.Ct. 1236, 47 L.Ed.2d 483 (1976), 29, 33, 94

Committee For Public Ed. & Religious Liberty v. Nyquist, 413 U.S. 756, 93 S.Ct. 2955, 37 L.Ed.2d 948 (1973), 105

Connecticut Nat. Bank v. Germain, 503 U.S. 249, 112 S.Ct. 1146, 117 L.Ed.2d 391 (1992), 136

Correctional Services Corp. v. Malesko, 534 U.S. 61, 122 S.Ct. 515, 151 L.Ed.2d 456 (2001), 10, 17

County of (see name of county)

Crockett v. Reagan, 720 F.2d 1355 (D.C.Cir. 1983), 56

Custis v. United States, 511 U.S. 485, 114 S.Ct. 1732, 128 L.Ed.2d 517 (1994), 129, 130

Daniels v. United States, 532 U.S. 374, 121 S.Ct. 1578, 149 L.Ed.2d 590 (2001), 130, 131

Davis v. Bandemer, 478 U.S. 109, 106 S.Ct. 2797, 92 L.Ed.2d 85 (1986), 40, 41, 42, 43, 44, 46, 47, 48, 50, 51

District of Columbia Court of Appeals v. Feldman, 460 U.S. 462, 103 S.Ct. 1303, 75 L.Ed.2d 206 (1983), 72, 93, 94, 95

Dodd v. United States, 545 U.S. ___, 125 S.Ct. 2478 (2005), 136

Doremus v. Board of Ed. of Borough of Hawthorne, 342 U.S. 429, 72 S.Ct. 394, 96 L.Ed. 475 (1952), 32

Dretke v. Haley, 541 U.S. 386, 124 S.Ct. 1847, 158 L.Ed.2d 659 (2004), **141**

Duncan v. Walker, 533 U.S. 167, 121 S.Ct. 2120, 150 L.Ed.2d 251 (2001), 121, 128

Dunn v. Carey, 808 F.2d 555 (7th Cir.1986), 103

Edwards v. Balisok, 520 U.S. 641, 117 S.Ct. 1584, 137 L.Ed.2d 906 (1997), 166, 171

Edwards v. Bates County, 163 U.S. 269, 16 S.Ct. 967, 41 L.Ed. 155 (1896), 88

Elk Grove Unified School Dist. v. Newdow, 542 U.S. 1, 124 S.Ct. 2301, 159 L.Ed.2d 98 (2004), **26**

England v. Louisiana State Bd. of Medical Examiners, 375 U.S. 411, 84 S.Ct. 461, 11 L.Ed.2d 440 (1964), 96

Engle v. Isaac, 456 U.S. 107, 102 S.Ct. 1558, 71 L.Ed.2d 783 (1982), 147, 148

Erie R. Co. v. Tompkins, 304 U.S. 64, 58 S.Ct. 817, 82 L.Ed. 1188 (1938), 1, 10, 11, 12, 16, 18, 19, 21

Estate of (see name of party)

Estelle v. Gamble, 429 U.S. 97, 97 S.Ct. 285, 50 L.Ed.2d 251 (1976), 169

Ex parte (see name of party)

Exxon Mobil Corp. v. Allapattah Services, Inc., 545 U.S. ___, 125 S.Ct. 2611 (2005), **69**

Exxon Mobil Corp. v. Saudi Basic Industries Corp., 544 U.S. ___, 125 S.Ct. 1517, 161 L.Ed.2d 454 (2005), 93

Fair Assessment in Real Estate Ass'n, Inc. v. McNary, 454 U.S. 100, 102 S.Ct. 177, 70 L.Ed.2d 271 (1981), 102, 111

Fay v. Noia, 372 U.S. 391, 83 S.Ct. 822, 9 L.Ed.2d 837 (1963), 144

Federal Election Com'n v. NRA Political Victory Fund, 513 U.S. 88, 115 S.Ct. 537, 130 L.Ed.2d 439 (1994), 112

F. Hoffman–La Roche Ltd. v. Empagran S.A., 542 U.S. 155, 124 S.Ct. 2359, 159 L.Ed.2d 226 (2004), 22

Filartiga v. Pena–Irala, 630 F.2d 876 (2nd Cir.1980), 9, 12, 13, 17

Finley v. United States, 490 U.S. 545, 109 S.Ct. 2003, 104 L.Ed.2d 593 (1989), 71, 72, 73, 74, 78, 80, 81, 83, 84, 85, 86, 89

Franchise Tax Bd. of Cal. v. Construction Laborers Vacation Trust for Southern California, 463 U.S. 1, 103 S.Ct. 2841, 77 L.Ed.2d 420 (1983), 62

Francis v. Henderson, 425 U.S. 536, 96 S.Ct. 1708, 48 L.Ed.2d 149 (1976), 144

Frew v. Hawkins, 540 U.S. 431, 124 S.Ct. 899, 157 L.Ed.2d 855 (2004), 152

Galletti, United States v., 541 U.S. 114, 124 S.Ct. 1548, 158 L.Ed.2d 279 (2004), 99, 100, 107

GASH Associates v. Village of Rosemont, 995 F.2d 726 (7th Cir.1993), 95

Gates v. Collier, 501 F.2d 1291 (5th Cir. 1974), 160

General Dynamics Land Systems, Inc. v. Cline, 540 U.S. 581, 124 S.Ct. 1236, 157 L.Ed.2d 1094 (2004), 99

Gideon v. Wainwright, 372 U.S. 335, 83 S.Ct. 792, 9 L.Ed.2d 799 (1963), 130

Gilligan v. Morgan, 413 U.S. 1, 93 S.Ct. 2440, 37 L.Ed.2d 407 (1973), 38

Gillis, In re, 836 F.2d 1001 (6th Cir.1988), 105

Goldwater v. Carter, 444 U.S. 996, 100 S.Ct. 533, 62 L.Ed.2d 428 (1979), 56, 57

Gomez v. United States Dist. Court for Northern Dist. of California, 503 U.S. 653,

112 S.Ct. 1652, 118 L.Ed.2d 293 (1992), 171
Gonzaga University v. Doe, 536 U.S. 273, 122 S.Ct. 2268, 153 L.Ed.2d 309 (2002), 165
Gonzalez v. Crosby, 545 U.S. ___, 125 S.Ct. 2641 (2005), 121
Grable & Sons Metal Products, Inc. v. Darue Engineering & Mfg., 545 U.S. ___, 125 S.Ct. 2363 (2005), **60**
Graham v. Broglin, 922 F.2d 379 (7th Cir. 1991), 167
Graham v. Connor, 490 U.S. 386, 109 S.Ct. 1865, 104 L.Ed.2d 443 (1989), 156
Great Lakes Dredge & Dock Co. v. Huffman, 319 U.S. 293, 63 S.Ct. 1070, 87 L.Ed. 1407 (1943), 102
Griffin v. School Bd. of Prince Edward County, 377 U.S. 218, 84 S.Ct. 1226, 12 L.Ed.2d 256 (1964), 104, 105
Grupo Dataflux v. Atlas Global Group, L.P., 541 U.S. 567, 124 S.Ct. 1920, 158 L.Ed.2d 866 (2004), 69
Gully v. First Nat. Bank, 299 U.S. 109, 57 S.Ct. 96, 81 L.Ed. 70 (1936), 62, 68

Hagans v. Lavine, 415 U.S. 528, 94 S.Ct. 1372, 39 L.Ed.2d 577 (1974), 113
Hamdi v. Rumsfeld, 542 U.S. 507, 124 S.Ct. 2633, 159 L.Ed.2d 578 (2004), 114
Hans v. Louisiana, 134 U.S. 1, 10 S.Ct. 504, 33 L.Ed. 842 (1890), 149
Harlow v. Fitzgerald, 457 U.S. 800, 102 S.Ct. 2727, 73 L.Ed.2d 396 (1982), 158, 161
Hartford Underwriters Ins. Co. v. Union Planters Bank, N.A., 530 U.S. 1, 120 S.Ct. 1942, 147 L.Ed.2d 1 (2000), 139
Hays, United States v., 515 U.S. 737, 115 S.Ct. 2431, 132 L.Ed.2d 635 (1995), 48
Heck v. Humphrey, 512 U.S. 477, 114 S.Ct. 2364, 129 L.Ed.2d 383 (1994), 167, 171
Hibbs v. Winn, 542 U.S. 88, 124 S.Ct. 2276, 159 L.Ed.2d 172 (2004), **96**
Hilton v. Braunskill, 481 U.S. 770, 107 S.Ct. 2113, 95 L.Ed.2d 724 (1987), 168
Holland v. Jackson, 542 U.S. 649, 124 S.Ct. 2736, 159 L.Ed.2d 683 (2004), 118
Holmes Group, Inc. v. Vornado Air Circulation Systems, Inc., 535 U.S. 826, 122 S.Ct. 1889, 153 L.Ed.2d 13 (2002), 60
Home Ins. Co. v. Dick, 281 U.S. 397, 50 S.Ct. 338, 74 L.Ed. 926 (1930), 1
Hope v. Pelzer, 536 U.S. 730, 122 S.Ct. 2508, 153 L.Ed.2d 666 (2002), 158, 159
Hopkins v. Walker, 244 U.S. 486, 37 S.Ct. 711, 61 L.Ed. 1270 (1917), 61, 63, 64

IIT v. Vencap, Ltd., 519 F.2d 1001 (2nd Cir. 1975), 6
In re (see name of party)

Jackson v. Virginia, 443 U.S. 307, 99 S.Ct. 2781, 61 L.Ed.2d 560 (1979), 143, 145, 146
Jefferson County v. Acker, 527 U.S. 423, 119 S.Ct. 2069, 144 L.Ed.2d 408 (1999), 100
Johnson v. De Grandy, 512 U.S. 997, 114 S.Ct. 2647, 129 L.Ed.2d 775 (1994), 44, 51
Johnson v. United States, 544 U.S. ___, 125 S.Ct. 1571, 161 L.Ed.2d 542 (2005), 129, 130

Kadic v. Karadzic, 70 F.3d 232 (2nd Cir. 1995), 20
Karcher v. Daggett, 462 U.S. 725, 103 S.Ct. 2653, 77 L.Ed.2d 133 (1983), 51
Kravitz v. Homeowners Warranty Corp., 542 F.Supp. 317 (E.D.Pa.1982), 65

Laing v. United States, 423 U.S. 161, 96 S.Ct. 473, 46 L.Ed.2d 416 (1976), 99, 106
Lanier, United States v., 520 U.S. 259, 117 S.Ct. 1219, 137 L.Ed.2d 432 (1997), 158, 160
L.A. Tucker Truck Lines, Inc., United States v., 344 U.S. 33, 73 S.Ct. 67, 97 L.Ed. 54 (1952), 112
Liddell v. Missouri, 731 F.2d 1294 (8th Cir. 1984), 104
Lorillard v. Pons, 434 U.S. 575, 98 S.Ct. 866, 55 L.Ed.2d 40 (1978), 106
Lujan v. Defenders of Wildlife, 504 U.S. 555, 112 S.Ct. 2130, 119 L.Ed.2d 351 (1992), 28, 29, 32
Luther v. Borden, 48 U.S. 1, 7 How. 1, 12 L.Ed. 581 (1849), 35, 36

Malley v. Briggs, 475 U.S. 335, 106 S.Ct. 1092, 89 L.Ed.2d 271 (1986), 162
Marbury v. Madison, 5 U.S. 137, 2 L.Ed. 60 (1803), 41, 58
Marriage of (see name of party)
Mayle v. Felix, 545 U.S. ___, 125 S.Ct. 2562 (2005), 120
McClellan v. Carland, 217 U.S. 268, 30 S.Ct. 501, 54 L.Ed. 762 (1910), 94
McCleskey v. Zant, 499 U.S. 467, 111 S.Ct. 1454, 113 L.Ed.2d 517 (1991), 144
McDonnell Douglas Corp. v. Green, 411 U.S. 792, 93 S.Ct. 1817, 36 L.Ed.2d 668 (1973), 51
McGlotten v. Connally, 338 F.Supp. 448 (D.D.C.1972), 101, 109
Mentry, In re Marriage of, 142 Cal.App.3d 260, 190 Cal.Rptr. 843 (Cal.App. 1 Dist. 1983), 31, 34
Merchants' Ins. Co. v. Ritchie, 72 U.S. 541, 18 L.Ed. 540 (1866), 112
Merrell Dow Pharmaceuticals Inc. v. Thompson, 478 U.S. 804, 106 S.Ct. 3229, 92 L.Ed.2d 650 (1986), 61, 64, 65, 66, 67, 68

TABLE OF CASES

Metropolitan Life Ins. Co. v. Taylor, 481 U.S. 58, 107 S.Ct. 1542, 95 L.Ed.2d 55 (1987), 68
Miller v. Johnson, 515 U.S. 900, 115 S.Ct. 2475, 132 L.Ed.2d 762 (1995), 43
Miller–El v. Cockrell, 537 U.S. 322, 123 S.Ct. 1029, 154 L.Ed.2d 931 (2003), 119
Mills v. Maryland, 486 U.S. 367, 108 S.Ct. 1860, 100 L.Ed.2d 384 (1988), 119
Missouri v. Jenkins, 495 U.S. 33, 110 S.Ct. 1651, 109 L.Ed.2d 31 (1990), 104
Mitchell v. Esparza, 540 U.S. 12, 124 S.Ct. 7, 157 L.Ed.2d 263 (2003), 118
Monell v. Department of Social Services of City of New York, 436 U.S. 658, 98 S.Ct. 2018, 56 L.Ed.2d 611 (1978), 165
Monge v. California, 524 U.S. 721, 118 S.Ct. 2246, 141 L.Ed.2d 615 (1998), 146
Moore v. Chesapeake & O. Ry. Co., 291 U.S. 205, 54 S.Ct. 402, 78 L.Ed. 755 (1934), 65
Mueller v. Allen, 463 U.S. 388, 103 S.Ct. 3062, 77 L.Ed.2d 721 (1983), 105, 173
Murga, In re Marriage of, 103 Cal.App.3d 498, 163 Cal.Rptr. 79 (Cal.App. 4 Dist. 1980), 31, 34
Murray v. Carrier, 477 U.S. 478, 106 S.Ct. 2639, 91 L.Ed.2d 397 (1986), 141, 144, 145
Murray v. Charming Betsy, the, 6 U.S. 64, 2 L.Ed. 208 (1804), 22

National Private Truck Council, Inc. v. Oklahoma Tax Com'n, 515 U.S. 582, 115 S.Ct. 2351, 132 L.Ed.2d 509 (1995), 102, 111
Nelson v. Campbell, 541 U.S. 637, 124 S.Ct. 2117, 158 L.Ed.2d 924 (2004), 168
Newdow v. United States Congress (Newdow III), 328 F.3d 466 (9th Cir.2003), 28
Newdow v. United States Congress (Newdow II), 313 F.3d 500 (9th Cir.2002), 28, 30, 33
Newdow v. United States Congress (Newdow I), 292 F.3d 597 (9th Cir.2002), 27, 33
Norfolk Southern Railway Co. v. Kirby, 543 U.S. ___, 125 S.Ct. 385, 160 L.Ed.2d 283 (2004), 2
Northern Pac. Ry. Co. v. Soderberg, 188 U.S. 526, 23 S.Ct. 365, 47 L.Ed. 575 (1903), 64
Northern Pipeline Const. Co. v. Marathon Pipe Line Co., 458 U.S. 50, 102 S.Ct. 2858, 73 L.Ed.2d 598 (1982), 25

Ort v. White, 813 F.2d 318 (11th Cir.1987), 161
Owen Equipment & Erection Co. v. Kroger, 437 U.S. 365, 98 S.Ct. 2396, 57 L.Ed.2d 274 (1978), 71, 73, 75, 80, 83, 89, ,CH

Pace v. DiGuglielmo, 544 U.S. ___, 125 S.Ct. 1807, 161 L.Ed.2d 669 (2005), 124
Pacific States Telephone & Telegraph Co. v. Oregon, 223 U.S. 118, 32 S.Ct. 224, 56 L.Ed. 377 (1912), 36

Palmore v. Sidoti, 466 U.S. 429, 104 S.Ct. 1879, 80 L.Ed.2d 421 (1984), 29
Parsons Steel, Inc. v. First Alabama Bank, 474 U.S. 518, 106 S.Ct. 768, 88 L.Ed.2d 877 (1986), 95
Pennhurst State School and Hosp. v. Halderman, 465 U.S. 89, 104 S.Ct. 900, 79 L.Ed.2d 67 (1984), 153
Powell v. McCormack, 395 U.S. 486, 89 S.Ct. 1944, 23 L.Ed.2d 491 (1969), 37, 38
Preiser v. Rodriguez, 411 U.S. 475, 93 S.Ct. 1827, 36 L.Ed.2d 439 (1973), 166, 167

Railroad Commission of Tex. v. Pullman Co., 312 U.S. 496, 61 S.Ct. 643, 85 L.Ed. 971 (1941), 95
Ramirez de Arellano v. Weinberger, 745 F.2d 1500 (D.C.Cir.1984), 56
Rancho Palos Verdes, City of v. Abrams, 544 U.S. ___, 125 S.Ct. 1453, 161 L.Ed.2d 316 (2005), 165
Rasul v. Bush, 542 U.S. 466, 124 S.Ct. 2686, 159 L.Ed.2d 548 (2004), 117
Republican Party of North Carolina v. Hunt, 77 F.3d 470 (4th Cir.1996), 42
Republican Party of North Carolina v. Martin, 980 F.2d 943 (4th Cir.1992), 42
Republican Party of North Carolina v. North Carolina State Bd. of Elections, 27 F.3d 563 (4th Cir.1994), 42
Reynolds v. Sims, 377 U.S. 533, 84 S.Ct. 1362, 12 L.Ed.2d 506 (1964), 37, 46
Rhines v. Weber, 544 U.S. ___, 125 S.Ct. 1528, 161 L.Ed.2d 440 (2005), 121, 126
Richardson v. United States, 526 U.S. 813, 119 S.Ct. 1707, 143 L.Ed.2d 985 (1999), 136
Ring v. Arizona, 536 U.S. 584, 122 S.Ct. 2428, 153 L.Ed.2d 556 (2002), 119
R.M.S. Titanic, Inc. v. Haver, 171 F.3d 943 (4th Cir.1999), 17
Rodgers, United States v., 461 U.S. 677, 103 S.Ct. 2132, 76 L.Ed.2d 236 (1983), 63
Rompilla v. Beard, 545 U.S. ___, 125 S.Ct. 2456 (2005), 118
Rooker v. Fidelity Trust Co., 263 U.S. 413, 44 S.Ct. 149, 68 L.Ed. 362 (1923), 93, 94, 95
Rose v. Lundy, 455 U.S. 509, 102 S.Ct. 1198, 71 L.Ed.2d 379 (1982), 121, 123, 127
Rosewell v. LaSalle Nat. Bank, 450 U.S. 503, 101 S.Ct. 1221, 67 L.Ed.2d 464 (1981), 102, 103, 111
Rumsfeld v. Padilla, 542 U.S. 426, 124 S.Ct. 2711, 159 L.Ed.2d 513 (2004), 117

Sacramento, County of v. Lewis, 523 U.S. 833, 118 S.Ct. 1708, 140 L.Ed.2d 1043 (1998), 164
Sanchez–Espinoza v. Reagan, 770 F.2d 202 (D.C.Cir.1985), 56

San Remo Hotel, L.P. v. City and County of San Francisco, 545 U.S. ___, 125 S.Ct. 2491 (2005), 96, 172

Saucier v. Katz, 533 U.S. 194, 121 S.Ct. 2151, 150 L.Ed.2d 272 (2001), 154, 156, 157, 163, 164

Sawyer v. Whitley, 505 U.S. 333, 112 S.Ct. 2514, 120 L.Ed.2d 269 (1992), 141, 144

Schriro v. Summerlin, 542 U.S. 348, 124 S.Ct. 2519, 159 L.Ed.2d 442 (2004), 119

Semtek Intern. Inc. v. Lockheed Martin Corp., 531 U.S. 497, 121 S.Ct. 1021, 149 L.Ed.2d 32 (2001), 92

Shaw v. Reno, 509 U.S. 630, 113 S.Ct. 2816, 125 L.Ed.2d 511 (1993), 43, 48, 49

Shoshone Mining Co. v. Rutter, 177 U.S. 505, 20 S.Ct. 726, 44 L.Ed. 864 (1900), 64, 65

Shulthis v. McDougal, 225 U.S. 561, 32 S.Ct. 704, 56 L.Ed. 1205 (1912), 62, 63, 65

Singleton v. Wulff, 428 U.S. 106, 96 S.Ct. 2868, 49 L.Ed.2d 826 (1976), 30

Slack v. McDaniel, 529 U.S. 473, 120 S.Ct. 1595, 146 L.Ed.2d 542 (2000), 119

Smith v. Freland, 954 F.2d 343 (6th Cir. 1992), 157

Smith v. Kansas City Title & Trust Co., 255 U.S. 180, 41 S.Ct. 243, 65 L.Ed. 577 (1921), 61, 62, 64, 65, 66, 67, 68, 156

Snyder v. Harris, 394 U.S. 332, 89 S.Ct. 1053, 22 L.Ed.2d 319 (1969), 88

Sosa v. Alvarez–Machain, 542 U.S. 692, 124 S.Ct. 2739, 159 L.Ed.2d 718 (2004), **4**

South v. Peters, 339 U.S. 276, 70 S.Ct. 641, 94 L.Ed. 834 (1950), 36

South African Apartheid Litigation, In re, 238 F.Supp.2d 1379 (Jud.Pan. Mult.Lit.2002), 13

South Carolina v. Regan, 465 U.S. 367, 104 S.Ct. 1107, 79 L.Ed.2d 372 (1984), 110, 113

Starks, Estate of v. Enyart, 5 F.3d 230 (7th Cir.1993), 157

State Farm Fire & Cas. Co. v. Tashire, 386 U.S. 523, 87 S.Ct. 1199, 18 L.Ed.2d 270 (1967), 71

Strawbridge v. Curtiss, 7 U.S. 267, 2 L.Ed. 435 (1806), 71

Strickland v. Washington, 466 U.S. 668, 104 S.Ct. 2052, 80 L.Ed.2d 674 (1984), 118, 144

Supreme Tribe of Ben Hur v. Cauble, 255 U.S. 356, 41 S.Ct. 338, 65 L.Ed. 673 (1921), 80, 82, 84, 86

Swift v. Tyson, 41 U.S. 1, 16 Pet. 1, 10 L.Ed. 865 (1842), 1, 16

Syngenta Crop Protection, Inc. v. Henson, 537 U.S. 28, 123 S.Ct. 366, 154 L.Ed.2d 368 (2002), 90

Tax Analysts and Advocates v. Shultz, 376 F.Supp. 889 (D.D.C.1974), 101, 109

Taylor v. Beckham, 178 U.S. 548, 20 S.Ct. 890, 44 L.Ed. 1187 (1900), 36

Teague v. Lane, 489 U.S. 288, 109 S.Ct. 1060, 103 L.Ed.2d 334 (1989), 119, 138

Tennard v. Dretke, 542 U.S. 274, 124 S.Ct. 2562, 159 L.Ed.2d 384 (2004), 119

Tennessee v. Garner, 471 U.S. 1, 105 S.Ct. 1694, 85 L.Ed.2d 1 (1985), 155, 156, 158

Tennessee v. Lane, 541 U.S. 509, 124 S.Ct. 1978, 158 L.Ed.2d 820 (2004), 150

Texas Industries, Inc. v. Radcliff Materials, Inc., 451 U.S. 630, 101 S.Ct. 2061, 68 L.Ed.2d 500 (1981), 16

Textile Workers v. Lincoln Mills of Ala., 353 U.S. 448, 77 S.Ct. 912, 1 L.Ed.2d 972 (1957), 10

The Paquete Habana, 175 U.S. 677, 20 S.Ct. 290, 44 L.Ed. 320 (1900), 12, 14

Thompson v. Louisville, 362 U.S. 199, 80 S.Ct. 624, 4 L.Ed.2d 654 (1960), 146

Troy Bank v. G.A. Whitehead & Co., 222 U.S. 39, 32 S.Ct. 9, 56 L.Ed. 81 (1911), 87, 88

Tyler v. Cain, 533 U.S. 656, 121 S.Ct. 2478, 150 L.Ed.2d 632 (2001), 139

United Mine Workers v. Gibbs, 383 U.S. 715, 86 S.Ct. 1130, 16 L.Ed.2d 218 (1966), 70, 71, 72, 73, 76, 80

United States v. _____ (see opposing party)

Verizon Maryland, Inc. v. Public Service Com'n of Maryland, 535 U.S. 635, 122 S.Ct. 1753, 152 L.Ed.2d 871 (2002), 152

Vieth v. Jubelirer, 541 U.S. 267, 124 S.Ct. 1769, 158 L.Ed.2d 546 (2004), **39, 56**

Vieth v. Pennsylvania, 195 F.Supp.2d 672 (M.D.Pa.2002), 55

Virginia v. Maryland, 540 U.S. 56, 124 S.Ct. 598, 157 L.Ed.2d 461 (2003), 2

Wainwright v. Sykes, 433 U.S. 72, 97 S.Ct. 2497, 53 L.Ed.2d 594 (1977), 144, 147

Ware v. Hylton, 3 U.S. 199, 3 Dall. 199, 1 L.Ed. 568 (1796), 7

Warth v. Seldin, 422 U.S. 490, 95 S.Ct. 2197, 45 L.Ed.2d 343 (1975), 29

Washington v. Davis, 426 U.S. 229, 96 S.Ct. 2040, 48 L.Ed.2d 597 (1976), 49, 52

Weinberger v. Ramirez de Arellano, 471 U.S. 1113, 105 S.Ct. 2353, 86 L.Ed.2d 255 (1985), 56

Wesberry v. Sanders, 376 U.S. 1, 84 S.Ct. 526, 11 L.Ed.2d 481 (1964), 46

West Virginia Board of Education v. Barnette, 319 U.S. 624, 63 S.Ct. 1178, 87 L.Ed. 1628 (1943), 27

Whitley v. Albers, 475 U.S. 312, 106 S.Ct. 1078, 89 L.Ed.2d 251 (1986), 159

Wilkinson v. Dotson, 544 U.S. ___, 125 S.Ct. 1242, 161 L.Ed.2d 253 (2005), 166

Will v. Michigan Dept. of State Police, 491 U.S. 58, 109 S.Ct. 2304, 105 L.Ed.2d 45 (1989), 113

Williams v. Taylor, 529 U.S. 362, 120 S.Ct. 1495, 146 L.Ed.2d 389 (2000), 118

Williamson County Regional Planning Com'n v. Hamilton Bank of Johnson City, 473 U.S. 172, 105 S.Ct. 3108, 87 L.Ed.2d 126 (1985), 173

Wilson v. Layne, 526 U.S. 603, 119 S.Ct. 1692, 143 L.Ed.2d 818 (1999), 164

Wilson Cypress Co. v. Pozo, 236 U.S. 635, 35 S.Ct. 446, 59 L.Ed. 758 (1915), 64

Winn v. Killian, 321 F.3d 911 (9th Cir.2003), 107

Winship, In re, 397 U.S. 358, 90 S.Ct. 1068, 25 L.Ed.2d 368 (1970), 146

Yarborough v. Alvarado, 541 U.S. 652, 124 S.Ct. 2140, 158 L.Ed.2d 938 (2004), 118

Yarborough v. Gentry, 540 U.S. 1, 124 S.Ct. 1, 157 L.Ed.2d 1 (2003), 118

Young, Ex parte, 209 U.S. 123, 28 S.Ct. 441, 52 L.Ed. 714 (1908), 152, 153

Younger v. Harris, 401 U.S. 37, 91 S.Ct. 746, 27 L.Ed.2d 669 (1971), 32, 95

Zahn v. International Paper Co., 414 U.S. 291, 94 S.Ct. 505, 38 L.Ed.2d 511 (1973), 72, 73, 74, 77, 79, 80, 81, 82, 84, 85, 86, 88, 90, 92

Zarvela v. Artuz, 254 F.3d 374 (2nd Cir. 2001), 123

TABLE OF SECONDARY AUTHORITIES

Achtenberg, Taking History Seriously: Municipal Liability under 42 U.S.C. § 1983 and the Debate over Respondeat Superior, 73 Fordham L. Rev. 2183 (2005)--p. 165

Althouse, Vanguard States, Laggard States: Federalism and Constitutional Rights, 152 U. Pa. L. Rev. 1745 (2004)--p. 152

Bandes, The *Rooker-Feldman* Doctrine: Evaluating Its Jurisdictional Status, 74 Notre Dame L. Rev. 1175 (1999)--p. 94

Barkow, More Supreme Than Court? The Fall of the Political Question Doctrine and the Rise of Judicial Supremacy, 102 Colum. L. Rev. 237 (2002)--p. 59

Bassett, The Hidden Bias in Diversity Jurisdiction, 81 Wash. U.L.Q. 119 (2003)--p. 68

Beermann, Comments on *Rooker-Feldman* or Let State Law Be Our Guide, 74 Notre Dame L. Rev. 1209 (1999)--p. 94

Bellia, Jr., Article III and the Cause of Action, 89 Iowa L. Rev. 777 (2004)--p. 68

Bellia, Jr., State Courts and the Making of Federal Common Law, 153 U. Pa. L. Rev. 825 (2005)--p. 1

Berkowitz, Error-Centricity, Habeas Corpus, and the Rule of Law as the Law of Rulings, 64 La. L. Rev. 477 (2004)--p. 141

Bickel, The Supreme Court, 1960 Term—Foreword: The Passive Virtues, 75 Harv. L. Rev. 40, 46 (1961)--p. 58

Blumoff, Judicial Review, Foreign Affairs and Legislative Standing, 25 Ga. L. Rev. 227 (1991)--p. 59

Bonfield, The Guarantee Clause of Article IV, Section 4: A Study in Constitutional Desuetude, 46 Minn.L.Rev. 513 (1962)--p. 36

Bradley & Goldsmith, Customary International Law as Federal Common Law: A Critique of the Modern Position, 110 Harv. L. Rev. 815, 824 (1997)--p. 16

Brown, When Political Questions Affects Individual Rights: The Other *Nixon v. United States*, 1993 Sup. Ct. Rev. 125--p. 39

Casto, The Federal Courts' Protective Jurisdiction Over Torts Committed in Violation of the Law of Nations, 18 Conn. L. Rev. 467, 479, 480 (1986)--pp. 7, 17

Champlin and Schwarz, Political Question Doctrine and Allocation of the Foreign Affairs Power, 13 Hofstra L. Rev. 215 (1985)--p. 59

Cochran, Federal Court Certification of Questions of State Law to State Courts: A Theoretical and Empirical Study, 29 J. Legis. 157 (2003)--p. 2

Cohen, The Broken Compass: The Requirement That a Case Arise "Directly" Under Federal Law, 115 U.Pa.L.Rev. 890, 916 (1967)--p. 65

Cotropia, "Arising Under" Jurisdiction and Uniformity in Patent Law, 9 Mich. Telecomm. & Tech. L. Rev. 253 (2003)--p. 60

Dodge, The Constitutionality of the Alien Tort Statute: Some Observations on Text and Context, 42 Va. J. Int'l L. 687, 689 (2002)--p. 7

Entzeroth, Federal Habeas Review of Death Sentences, Where Are We Now?: A Review of *Wiggins v. Smith* and *Miller-El v. Cockrell*, 39 Tulsa L. Rev. 49 (2003)--p. 119

Esler, Michigan v. Long: A Twenty-Year Retrospective, 66 Alb. L. Rev. 835 (2003)--p. 3

Floyd, The Limits of Minimal Diversity, 55 Hastings L.J. 613 (2004)--p. 69

Friedman, Under the Law of Federal Jurisdiction: Allocating Cases Between Federal and State Courts, 104 Colum. L. Rev. 1211, 1264-79 (2004)--pp. 96, 118

Friedman & Gaylord, *Rooker-Feldman*, from the Ground Up, 74 Notre Dame L. Rev. 1129 (1999)--p. 94

Garrett, Innocence, Harmless Error, and Federal Wrongful Conviction Law, 2005 Wis. L. Rev. 35--p. 141

Gerhardt, Rediscovering Nonjusticiability: Judicial Review of Impeachments after *Nixon*, 44 Duke L.J. 231 (1994)--p. 39

Gunther, The Subtle Vices of the "Passive Virtues"—A Comment on Principle and Expediency in Judicial Review, 64 Colum. L. Rev. 1 (1964)--p. 58

Healy, The Rise of Unnecessary Constitutional Rulings, 83 N.C.L. Rev. 847 (2005)--p. 154

Henkin, Is There a "Political Question" Doctrine?, 85 Yale L.J. 597 (1976)--p. 59

Humphrey, The UN Charter and the Universal Declaration of Human Rights, in The International Protection of Human Rights 39, 50 (E. Luard ed. 1967)--p. 14

Ides, Habeas Standards of Review Under 28 U.S.C. § 2254(d)(1): A Commentary on

Statutory Text and Supreme Court Precedent, 60 Wash. & Lee L. Rev. 677 (2003)--p. 119

Issacharoff, Gerrymandering and Political Cartels, 116 Harv. L. Rev. 593, 624 (2002)--p. 50

Issacharoff, Karlan, & Pildes, The Law of Democracy 886 (rev. 2d ed. 2002)--p. 41

Karlan, The Fire Next Time: Reapportionment After the 2000 Census, 50 Stan. L. Rev. 731, 736 (1998)--p. 50

Lee, Section 2254(d) of the Federal Habeas Statute: Is it Beyond Reason?, 56 Hastings L.J. 283 (2004)--p. 118

Lowenstein & Steinberg, Partisan Gerrymandering: A Political Problem Without Judicial Solution, in Political Gerrymandering and the Courts 240, 241 (B. Grofman ed., 1990)--p. 45

Manning, The Eleventh Amendment and the Reading of Precise Constitutional Texts, 113 Yale L.J. 1663 (2004)--p. 149

McCormick, Federalism Re-Constructed: The Eleventh Amendment's Illogical Impact on Congress' Power, 37 Ind. L. Rev. 345 (2004)--p. 152

McCormack, The Justiciability Myth and the Concept of Law, 14 Hastings Const. L.Q. 595 (1987)--p. 59

McCormack, The Political Question Doctrine—Jurisprudentially, 70 U. Det. Mercy L. Rev. 793 (1993)--p. 59

Meltzer, Customary International Law, Foreign Affairs, and Federal Common Law, 42 Va. J. Int'l L. 513, 519 (2002)--p. 18

Meltzer, Jurisdiction and Discretion Revisited, 79 Notre Dame L. Rev. 1891, 1911–15 (2004)--p. 66

Mulhern, In Defense of the Political Question Doctrine, 137 U. Pa. L. Rev. 97 (1988)--p. 59

Nash, Examining the Power of Federal Courts to Certify Questions of State Law, 88 Cornell L. Rev. 1672 (2003)--p. 2

Nash, Resuscitating Deference to Lower Federal Court Judges' Interpretations of State Law, 77 S. Cal. L. Rev. 975 (2004)--p. 2

Nicolas, The Use of Preclusion Doctrine, Antisuit Injunctions, and Forum Non Conveniens Dismissals in Transnational Intellectual Property Litigation, 40 Va. J. Int'l L. 331 (1999)--p. 24

Note, Mr. Smith Goes to Federal Court: Federal Question Jurisdiction over State Law Claims Post-*Merrell Dow*, 115 Harv. L.Rev. 2272, 2280–82 (2002)--p. 64

Parness and Sennott, Expanded Recognition in Written Laws of Ancillary Federal Court Powers: Supplementing the Supplemental Jurisdiction Statute, 64 U. Pitt. L. Rev. 303 (2003)--p. 69

Pfander, Article I Tribunals, Article III Courts, and the Judicial Power of the United States, 118 Harv. L. Rev. 643 (2004)--p. 25

Pfander, Supplemental Jurisdiction and Section 1367: The Case for a Sympathetic Textualism, 148 U. Pa. L.Rev. 109, 114 (1999)--p. 89

Pfander, The Simmering Debate Over Supplemental Jurisdiction, 2002 U. Ill. L. Rev. 1209--p. 69

Pfander, The Tidewater Problem: Article III and Constitutional Change, 79 Notre Dame L. Rev. 1925 (2004)--p. 24

Piar, Using Coram Nobis to Attack Wrongful Convictions: A New Look at an Ancient Writ, 30 N. Ky. L. Rev. 505 (2003)--p. 114

Pildes, Principled Limitations on Racial and Partisan Redistricting, 106 Yale L.J. 2505, 2553–54 (1997)--p. 50

Posner, Report of the Subcommittee on the Role of the Federal Courts and Their Relationship to the States 567–68 (Mar. 12, 1990)--p. 81

Prakash and Yoo, The Origins of Judicial Review, 70 U. Chi. L. Rev. 887 (2003)--p. 175

Purcell, Jr., The Particularly Dubious Case of *Hans v. Louisiana*: An Essay on Law, Race, History, and "Federal Courts," 81 N.C.L. Rev. 1927 (2003)--p. 149

Redish, Federal Jurisdiction: Tensions in the Allocation of Judicial Power 67 (1980)--p. 65

Redish, Judicial Review and the "Political Question," 79 Nw. U.L. Rev. 1031 (1985)--p. 59

Reinstein and Rahdert, Reconstructing *Marbury*, 57 Ark. L. Rev. 729 (2005)--p. 175

Resnick, Constricting Remedies: The Rehnquist Judiciary, Congress, and Federal Power, 78 Ind. L.J. 223 (2003)--p. 4

Risinger, Unsafe Verdicts: The Need for Reformed Standards for the Trial and Review of Factual Innocence Claims, 41 Hous. L. Rev. 1281 (2004)--p. 141

Robel, Sovereignty and Democracy: The States' Obligations to Their Citizens under Federal Statutory Law, 78 Ind. L.J. 543 (2003)--p. 149

Rosenberg, The Ultimate Independence of the Federal Courts: Defying the Supreme Court in the Exercise of Federal Common Law Powers. 36 Conn. L. Rev. 425 (2004)--p. 2

Rowe, Jr., *Rooker-Feldman*: Worth Only the Powder to Blow It Up?, 74 Notre Dame L. Rev. 1081 (1999)--p. 94

Rowe, Burbank, & Mengler, Compounding or Creating Confusion About Supplemental Jurisdiction? A Reply to Professor Freer,

40 Emory L.J. 943, 960 n.90 (1991)--pp. 81, 85
Scharpf, Judicial Review and the Political Question: A Functional Analysis, 75 Yale L.J. 517 (1966)--p. 59
Segall, Article III as a Grant of Power: Protective Jurisdiction, Federalism and the Federal Courts, 54 Fla. L. Rev. 361 (2002)--p. 24
Seidman, The Secret Life of the Political Question Doctrine, 37 John Marshall L. Rev. 441 (2004)--p. 59
Semeraro, A Reasoning–Process Review Model for Federal Habeas Corpus, 94 J. Crim. L. & Criminology 897 (2004)--p. 118
Shannon, The Retroactive and Prospective Application of Judicial Decisions, 26 Harv. J.L. & Pub. Pol'y 811 (2003)--p. 118
Shapiro, Jurisdiction and Discretion, 60 N.Y.U.L.Rev. 543, 568 (1985)--p. 65
Sherry, Judicial Federalism in the Trenches: The *Rooker-Feldman* Doctrine in Action, 74 Notre Dame L. Rev. 1085 (1999)--p. 94
Siegel, Waivers of State Sovereign Immunity and the Ideology of the Eleventh Amendment, 52 Duke L. J. 1167 (2003)--p. 149
Simard, Standing Alone: Do We Still Need the Political Question Doctrine, 100 Dickinson L. Rev. 303 (1996)--p. 59
Sloane, AEDPA's "Adjudication on the Merits" Requirement: Collateral Review, Federalism, and Comity, 78 St. John's L. Rev. 615 (2004)--p. 118
Solimine, Formalism, Pragmatism, and the Conservative Critique of the Eleventh Amendment, 101 Mich. L. Rev. 1463 (2003)--p. 152
Sloss, Constitutional Remedies for Statutory Violations, 89 Iowa L. Rev. 355 (2004)--p. 152
Stith, A Contrast of State and Federal Court Authority to Grant Habeas Relief, 38 Val. U. L. Rev. 421 (2004)--p. 141

Thomas, III, Young, Sharfman, and Briscoe, Is it Ever Too Late for Innocence? Finality, Efficiency, and Claims of Innocence, 64 U. Pitt. L. Rev. 263 (2003)--p. 141
Underwood, Supplemental Serendipity: Congress' Accidental Improvement of Supplemental Jurisdiction, 37 Akron L. Rev. 653 (2004)--p. 69
Wald, Some Observations on the Use of Legislative History in the 1981 Supreme Court Term, 68 Iowa L.Rev. 195, 214 (1983)--p. 80
Wasson, Jr., Resolving Separation of Powers and Federalism Problems Raised by *Erie*, the Rules of Decision Act, and the Rules Enabling Act: A Proposed Solution, 32 Capital U.L. Rev. 519 (2003)--p. 92
Waxman and Morrison, What Kind of Immunity? Federal Officers, State Criminal Law, and the Supremacy Clause. 112 Yale L.J. 2195 (2003)--p. 2
Webster's New International Dictionary 139 (1927)--p. 106
Wechsler, Toward Neutral Principles of Constitutional Law, 73 Harv. L. Rev. 1, 3 (1959)--p. 57
Weinberg, Back to the Future: The New General Common Law, 35 J. Mar. L. & Com. 523 (2004)--p. 1
Winter, The Metaphor of Standing and the Problem of Self–Governance, 40 Stan. L. Rev. 1371, 1381–82 (1988)--p. 26
Woolhandler and Nelson, Does History Defeat Standing Doctrine?, 102 Mich. L. Rev. 689 (2004)--p. 26
Woolley, The Sources of Federal Preclusion Law after *Semtek*, 72 U. Cin. L. Rev. 527 (2003)--p. 92
Wright, Federal Courts 96 (4th ed. 1983)--p. 65
Young, Sorting out the Debate Over Customary International Law, 42 Va. J. Int'l L. 365, 374 (2002)--p. 16

2005 SUPPLEMENT

Federal Courts and the Law of Federal–State Relations

*

CHAPTER I

CHOICE OF LAW IN THE FEDERAL SYSTEM

Page 13, add a footnote after the word "power" in the carryover sentence at the top of the page:

f. Compare the argument in Louise Weinberg, Back to the Future: The New General Common Law, 35 J. Mar. L. & Com. 523 (2004). The constitutional premise of *Erie*, she says, is the positivist view that law must find its source in the authority of a relevant sovereign. The law applied under *Swift* "was not state law, but it was not federal law, either. It was, you might say 'brooding omnipresence' law." She argues that there is no place for such law in our legal system, and that application of a law that is not rooted in the authority, interests, and power of an identifiable sovereign should be regarded under current doctrine as a denial of due process of law.

Compare, she argues, the role of due process in horizontal, state-state choice-of-law situations. Alaska Packers Ass'n v. Industrial Accident Comm'n, 294 U.S. 532 (1935), permits a state court to apply its law only if the state has a "legitimate public interest" in the controversy. Home Insurance Co. v. Dick, 281 U.S. 397 (1930), dealt with "the other side of that coin." It held that a state that did not have an appropriate interest in the controversy cannot apply its law in its courts. A number of states may have sufficient connection to a case to justify application of their law under this standard, but due process is violated if a state that does *not* satisfy this standard seeks to apply its own law. And it would also violate due process, she concludes, if a state was compelled to apply a law derived from the legitimate interests of no identified government.

She argues that the same structure should apply to vertical, federal-state choice-of-law issues. We generally think of these situations in *Erie* terms, but we could just as easily think of them as presenting due process issues. Leaving aside controversies with an international flavor, federal and state courts have two choices when they decide whose law to apply: they may apply the law of a state that satisfies the *Alaska Packers* limitation; or they may apply federal law if the controversy lies within federal delegated powers. Either of these choices implicates a methodology for selecting a rule that serves the interests and policies of the chosen sovereign. But Weinberg concludes that the courts do not have a third option. They may not apply "brooding omnipresence" law, that is, they may not, as *Swift* did, apply abstract principles of law that are not rooted in the authority, interests, and power of an identified sovereign.

Page 15, add at end of footnote g:

State courts will often confront situations in the exercise of their general jurisdiction where principles of federal common law control the outcome. For consideration of how they should proceed in such cases, see Anthony J. Bellia, Jr., State Courts and the Making of Federal Common Law, 153 U. Pa. L. Rev. 825 (2005).

Page 16, add to footnote h:

For a modern application of this doctrine, see Virginia v. Maryland, 540 U.S. 5 (2003). In footnote 9, the Court said: "Federal common law governs interstate bodies of water, ensuring that the water is equitably apportioned between the States and that neither State harms the other's interest in the river."

For an example of the application of federal common law in an admiralty context, see Norfolk Southern Railway Co. v. Kirby, 543 U.S. ___ (2004):

> The courts below appear to have decided this case on an assumption, shared by the parties, that federal rather than state law governs the interpretation of . . . two bills of lading. Respondents now object. They emphasize that, at bottom, this is a diversity case involving tort and contract claims arising out of a rail accident somewhere between Savannah and Huntsville. We think, however, borrowing from Justice Harlan, that "the situation presented here has a more genuinely salty flavor than that." When a contract is a maritime one, and the dispute is not inherently local, federal law controls the contract interpretation.
>
> Our authority to make decisional law for the interpretation of maritime contracts stems from the Constitution's grant of admiralty jurisdiction to federal courts. This suit was properly brought in diversity, but it could also be sustained under the admiralty jurisdiction by virtue of the maritime contracts involved. Indeed, for federal common law to apply in these circumstances, this suit must also be sustainable under the admiralty jurisdiction. Because the grant of admiralty jurisdiction and the power to make admiralty law are mutually dependent, the two are often intertwined in our cases.

Page 19, add at the end of footnote k:

Ronald H. Rosenberg, The Ultimate Independence of the Federal Courts: Defying the Supreme Court in the Exercise of Federal Common Law Powers. 36 Conn. L. Rev. 425 (2004), addresses similar issues in the context of the Comprehensive Environmental Response, Compensation and Liability Act (CERCLA).

Page 22, add at the end of footnote a:

A related question is explored in Jonathan Remy Nash, Resuscitating Deference to Lower Federal Court Judges' Interpretations of State Law, 77 S. Cal. L. Rev. 975 (2004).

Page 23, add to the "see also" citation at the end of footnote b:

Rebecca A Cochran, Federal Court Certification of Questions of State Law to State Courts: A Theoretical and Empirical Study, 29 J. Legis. 157 (2003); Jonathan Remy Nash, Examining the Power of Federal Courts to Certify Questions of State Law, 88 Cornell L. Rev. 1672 (2003).

Page 69, add at the end of footnote d:

The question whether federal officials can be prosecuted *criminally* in state courts is extensively discussed in Seth P. Waxman and Trevor W. Morrison, What Kind of Immunity? Federal Officers, State Criminal Law, and the Supremacy Clause. 112 Yale L.J. 2195 (2003). They take as their point of departure the prosecution of an FBI agent for involuntary manslaughter arising out of the Ruby Ridge incident. The case was removed to federal court under 28 U.S.C. § 1442(a)(1), and ultimately dismissed because the state dropped the charges. The authors conclude that "federal officers acting within the scope of their employment should be immune from state prosecution for taking any action they reasonably believe is necessary and proper to the performance of their federal functions. Properly applied, this standard is effectively coextensive with qualified immunity."

Page 102, add to the citations in Note 2:

Michael Esler, *Michigan v. Long*: A Twenty–Year Retrospective, 66 Alb. L. Rev. 835 (2003);

CHAPTER II

THE POWER OF THE FEDERAL COURTS TO CREATE FEDERAL LAW

Page 176, add at the end of Note 8:

Finally, see Judith Resnick, Constricting Remedies: The Rehnquist Judiciary, Congress, and Federal Power, 78 Ind. L.J. 223 (2003). Resnick argues, among other things, that the Court's approach to implied remedies under federal statutes is being extended to remedies in more ordinary litigation: "[E]ven when litigants are properly before the federal courts because of diversity jurisdiction or by virtue of a federal cause of action expressly provided by Congress, the 5–4 majority deploys the same analytic approach, presuming prohibitions on judicial remediation to defeat plaintiffs' claims."

Page 234, add the following case at the end of Chapter II:

Sosa v. Alvarez–Machain
Supreme Court of the United States, 2004.
542 U.S. 692.

■ JUSTICE SOUTER delivered the opinion of the Court.

The two issues are whether respondent Alvarez–Machain's allegation that the Drug Enforcement Administration instigated his abduction from Mexico for criminal trial in the United States supports a claim against the Government under the Federal Tort Claims Act (FTCA or Act), 28 U.S.C. § 1346(b)(1), §§ 2671–2680, and whether he may recover under the Alien Tort Statute (ATS), 28 U.S.C. § 1350. We hold that he is not entitled to a remedy under either statute.

I

We have considered the underlying facts before, United States v. Alvarez–Machain, 504 U.S. 655 (1992). In 1985, an agent of the Drug Enforcement Administration (DEA), Enrique Camarena–Salazar, was captured on assignment in Mexico and taken to a house in Guadalajara, where he was tortured over the course of a two-day interrogation, then murdered. Based in part on eyewitness testimony, DEA officials in the United States came to believe that respondent Humberto Alvarez–Machain (Alvarez), a Mexican physician, was present at the house and acted to prolong the agent's life in order to extend the interrogation and torture.

In 1990, a federal grand jury indicted Alvarez for the torture and murder of Camarena–Salazar, and the United States District Court for the Central District of California issued a warrant for his arrest. The DEA asked the Mexican Government for help in getting Alvarez into the United States, but when the requests and negotiations proved fruitless, the DEA approved a plan to hire Mexican nationals to seize Alvarez and bring him to the United States for trial. As so planned, a group of Mexicans, including petitioner Jose Francisco Sosa, abducted Alvarez from his house, held him overnight in a motel, and brought him by private plane to El Paso, Texas, where he was arrested by federal officers.

Once in American custody, Alvarez moved to dismiss the indictment on the ground that his seizure was "outrageous governmental conduct," *Alvarez-Machain,* 504 U.S., at 658, and violated the extradition treaty between the United States and Mexico. The District Court agreed, the Ninth Circuit affirmed, and we reversed, holding that the fact of Alvarez's forcible seizure did not affect the jurisdiction of a federal court. The case was tried in 1992, and ended at the close of the Government's case, when the District Court granted Alvarez's motion for a judgment of acquittal.

In 1993, after returning to Mexico, Alvarez began the civil action before us here. He sued Sosa, Mexican citizen and DEA operative Antonio Garate–Bustamante, five unnamed Mexican civilians, the United States, and four DEA agents. So far as it matters here, Alvarez sought damages from the United States under the FTCA, alleging false arrest, and from Sosa under the ATS, for a violation of the law of nations. The former statute authorizes suit "for . . . personal injury . . . caused by the negligent or wrongful act or omission of any employee of the Government while acting within the scope of his office or employment." 28 U.S.C. § 1346(b)(1). The latter provides in its entirety that "the district courts shall have original jurisdiction of any civil action by an alien for a tort only, committed in violation of the law of nations or a treaty of the United States." § 1350.

The District Court granted the Government's motion to dismiss the FTCA claim, but awarded summary judgment and $25,000 in damages to Alvarez on the ATS claim. A three-judge panel of the Ninth Circuit then affirmed the ATS judgment, but reversed the dismissal of the FTCA claim.

A divided en banc court came to the same conclusion. As for the ATS claim, the court called on its own precedent, "that [the ATS] not only provides federal courts with subject matter jurisdiction, but also creates a cause of action for an alleged violation of the law of nations." The Circuit then relied upon what it called the "clear and universally recognized norm prohibiting arbitrary arrest and detention," to support the conclusion that Alvarez's arrest amounted to a tort in violation of international law. On the FTCA claim, the Ninth Circuit held that, because "the DEA had no authority to effect Alvarez's arrest and detention in Mexico," the United States was liable to him under California law for the tort of false arrest.

We granted certiorari ... and ... now reverse....

II

[The Court reversed the judgment of liability under the FTCA on the ground that the statute excepts from its waiver of sovereign immunity claims "arising in a foreign country." 28 U.S.C. § 2680(k). The Court found that exception applicable to this case. Though the Justices were unanimous in this conclusion, Justice Ginsburg, joined by Justice Breyer, concurred in the result as to Part II to offer a somewhat different analysis of the FTCA issue.]

III

Alvarez has also brought an action under the ATS against petitioner, Sosa, who argues (as does the United States supporting him) that there is no relief under the ATS because the statute does no more than vest federal courts with jurisdiction, neither creating nor authorizing the courts to recognize any particular right of action without further congressional action. Although we agree the statute is in terms only jurisdictional, we think that at the time of enactment the jurisdiction enabled federal courts to hear claims in a very limited category defined by the law of nations and recognized at common law. We do not believe, however, that the limited, implicit sanction to entertain the handful of international law cum common law claims understood in 1789 should be taken as authority to recognize the right of action asserted by Alvarez here. . . .

Judge Friendly called the ATS a "legal Lohengrin," IIT v. Vencap, Ltd., 519 F.2d 1001, 1015 (2d Cir. 1975); "no one seems to know whence it came," and for over 170 years after its enactment it provided jurisdiction in only one case. The first Congress passed it as part of the Judiciary Act of 1789, in providing that the new federal district courts "shall also have cognizance, concurrent with the courts of the several States, or the circuit courts, as the case may be, of all causes where an alien sues for a tort only in violation of the law of nations or a treaty of the United States." Act of Sept. 24, 1789, ch. 20, § 9(b).[10]

The parties and amici here advance radically different historical interpretations of this terse provision. Alvarez says that the ATS was intended not simply as a jurisdictional grant, but as authority for the creation of a new cause of action for torts in violation of international law. We think that reading is implausible. As enacted in 1789, the ATS gave the district courts "cognizance" of certain causes of action, and the term bespoke a grant of jurisdiction, not power to mold substantive law. The fact that the ATS was placed in § 9 of the Judiciary Act, a statute otherwise exclusively

---

10. The statute has been slightly modified on a number of occasions since its original enactment. It now reads in its entirety: "The district courts shall have original jurisdiction of any civil action by an alien for a tort only, committed in violation of the law of nations or a treaty of the United States." 28 U.S.C. § 1350.

concerned with federal-court jurisdiction, is itself support for its strictly jurisdictional nature. ... It is unsurprising, then, that an authority on the historical origins of the ATS has written that "section 1350 clearly does not create a statutory cause of action," and that the contrary suggestion is "simply frivolous." William Casto, The Federal Courts' Protective Jurisdiction Over Torts Committed in Violation of the Law of Nations, 18 Conn. L. Rev. 467, 479, 480 (1986) (hereinafter Casto, Law of Nations); cf. William S. Dodge, The Constitutionality of the Alien Tort Statute: Some Observations on Text and Context, 42 Va. J. Int'l L. 687, 689 (2002). In sum, we think the statute was intended as jurisdictional in the sense of addressing the power of the courts to entertain cases concerned with a certain subject.

But holding the ATS jurisdictional raises a new question, this one about the interaction between the ATS at the time of its enactment and the ambient law of the era. Sosa would have it that the ATS was stillborn because there could be no claim for relief without a further statute expressly authorizing adoption of causes of action. Amici professors of federal jurisdiction and legal history take a different tack, that federal courts could entertain claims once the jurisdictional grant was on the books, because torts in violation of the law of nations would have been recognized within the common law of the time. Brief for Vikram Amar et al. as Amici Curiae. We think history and practice give the edge to this latter position.

"When the *United States* declared their independence, they were bound to receive the law of nations, in its modern state of purity and refinement." Ware v. Hylton, 3 U.S. (3 Dall.) 199, 281 (1796) (Wilson, J.). In the years of the early Republic, this law of nations comprised two principal elements, the first covering the general norms governing the behavior of national states with each other .. .. This aspect of the law of nations thus occupied the executive and legislative domains, not the judicial. See 4 W. Blackstone, Commentaries on the Laws of England 68 (1769) (hereinafter Commentaries) ("Offenses against" the law of nations are "principally incident to whole states or nations").

The law of nations included a second, more pedestrian element, however, that did fall within the judicial sphere, as a body of judge-made law regulating the conduct of individuals situated outside domestic boundaries and consequently carrying an international savor. To Blackstone, the law of nations in this sense was implicated "in mercantile questions, such as bills of exchange and the like; in all marine causes, relating to freight, average, demurrage, insurances, bottomry ...; [and] in all disputes relating to prizes, to shipwrecks, to hostages, and ransom bills." Id., at 67. The law merchant [that] emerged from the customary practices of international traders and admiralty required its own transnational regulation. ...

There was, finally, a sphere in which these rules binding individuals for the benefit of other individuals overlapped with the norms of state relationships. Blackstone referred to it when he mentioned three specific offenses against the law of nations addressed by the criminal law of England: violation of safe conducts, infringement of the rights of ambassadors, and piracy. 4 Commentaries 68. An assault against an ambassador, for example, impinged upon the sovereignty of the foreign nation and if not adequately redressed could rise to an issue of war. It was this narrow set of violations of the law of nations, admitting of a judicial remedy and at the same time threatening serious consequences in international affairs, that was probably on minds of the men who drafted the ATS with its reference to tort.

Before there was any ATS, a distinctly American preoccupation with these hybrid international norms had taken shape owing to the distribution of political power from independence through the period of confederation. The Continental Congress was hamstrung by its inability to "cause infractions of treaties, or of the law of nations to be punished," J. Madison, Journal of the Constitutional Convention 60 (E. Scott ed. 1893) .... The Framers responded by vesting the Supreme Court with original jurisdiction over "all Cases affecting Ambassadors, other public ministers and Consuls," U.S. Const., Art. III, § 2, and the First Congress followed through. The Judiciary Act reinforced this Court's original jurisdiction over suits brought by diplomats, see § 13, created alienage jurisdiction, § 11 and, of course, included the ATS, § 9.

Although Congress modified the draft of what became the Judiciary Act, it made hardly any changes to the provisions on aliens, including what became the ATS, see Casto, Law of Nations 498. There is no record of congressional discussion about private actions that might be subject to the jurisdictional provision, or about any need for further legislation to create private remedies; there is no record even of debate on the section. ... [D]espite considerable scholarly attention, it is fair to say that a consensus understanding of what Congress intended has proven elusive.

Still, the history does tend to support two propositions. First, there is every reason to suppose that the First Congress did not pass the ATS as a jurisdictional convenience to be placed on the shelf for use by a future Congress or state legislature that might, some day, authorize the creation of causes of action or itself decide to make some element of the law of nations actionable for the benefit of foreigners. The anxieties of the preconstitutional period cannot be ignored easily enough to think that the statute was not meant to have a practical effect. ...

The second inference to be drawn from the history is that Congress intended the ATS to furnish jurisdiction for a relatively modest set of actions alleging violations of the law of nations. Uppermost in the legislative mind appears to have been offenses against ambassadors, violations of safe conduct were probably understood to be actionable, and individual actions arising out of prize captures and piracy may well have also been contemplated. But the common law appears to have understood only those three of the hybrid variety as definite and actionable, or at any rate, to have assumed only a very limited set of claims. As Blackstone had put it, "offences against this law [of nations] are principally incident to whole states or nations," and not individuals seeking relief in court. 4 Commentaries 68. . . .

In sum, although the ATS is a jurisdictional statute creating no new causes of action, the reasonable inference from the historical materials is that the statute was intended to have practical effect the moment it became law. The jurisdictional grant is best read as having been enacted on the understanding that the common law would provide a cause of action for the modest number of international law violations with a potential for personal liability at the time.

IV

We think it is correct, then, to assume that the First Congress understood that the district courts would recognize private causes of action for certain torts in violation of the law of nations, though we have found no basis to suspect Congress had any examples in mind beyond those torts corresponding to Blackstone's three primary offenses: violation of safe conducts, infringement of the rights of ambassadors, and piracy. We assume, too, that no development in the two centuries from the enactment of § 1350 to the birth of the modern line of cases beginning with Filartiga v. Pena–Irala, 630 F.2d 876 (2d Cir. 1980), has categorically precluded federal courts from recognizing a claim under the law of nations as an element of common law; Congress has not in any relevant way amended § 1350 or limited civil common law power by another statute. Still, there are good reasons for a restrained conception of the discretion a federal court should exercise in considering a new cause of action of this kind. Accordingly, we think courts should require any claim based on the present-day law of nations to rest on a norm of international character accepted by the civilized world and defined with a specificity comparable to the features of the 18th-century paradigms we have recognized. This requirement is fatal to Alvarez's claim.

A

A series of reasons argue for judicial caution when considering the kinds of individual claims that might implement the jurisdiction conferred by the early statute. First, the prevailing conception of the common law has changed since 1789 in a way that counsels restraint in judicially applying internationally generated norms. When § 1350 was enacted, the accepted conception was of the common law as "a transcendental body of law outside of any particular State but obligatory within it unless and until changed by statute." Black and White Taxicab & Transfer Co. v. Brown and Yellow Taxicab & Transfer Co., 276 U.S. 518, 533 (1928) (Holmes, J., dissenting). Now, however, in most cases where a court is asked to state or formulate a common law principle in a new context, there is a general understanding that the law is not so much found or discovered as it is either made or created. ... [A] judge deciding in reliance on an international norm will find a substantial element of discretionary judgment in the decision.

Second, along with, and in part driven by, that conceptual development in understanding common law has come an equally significant rethinking of the role of the federal courts in making it. Erie R. Co. v. Tompkins, 304 U.S. 64 (1938), was the watershed in which we denied the existence of any federal "general" common law, which largely withdrew to havens of specialty, some of them defined by express congressional authorization to devise a body of law directly, e.g., Textile Workers v. Lincoln Mills of Ala., 353 U.S. 448 (1957) (interpretation of collective-bargaining agreements). Elsewhere, this Court has thought it was in order to create federal common law rules in interstitial areas of particular federal interest. And although we have even assumed competence to make judicial rules of decision of particular importance to foreign relations, such as the act of state doctrine, see Banco Nacional de Cuba v. Sabbatino, 376 U.S. 398, 427 (1964), the general practice has been to look for legislative guidance before exercising innovative authority over substantive law. It would be remarkable to take a more aggressive role in exercising a jurisdiction that remained largely in shadow for much of the prior two centuries.

Third, this Court has recently and repeatedly said that a decision to create a private right of action is one better left to legislative judgment in the great majority of cases. Correctional Services Corp. v. Malesko, 534 U.S. 61, 68 (2001); Alexander v. Sandoval, 532 U.S. 275, 286–87 (2001). The creation of a private right of action raises issues beyond the mere consideration whether underlying primary conduct should be allowed or not, entailing, for example, a decision to permit enforcement without the check imposed by prosecutorial discretion. Accordingly, even when Congress has made it clear by statute that a rule applies to purely domestic conduct, we are reluctant to infer intent to provide a private cause of action where the statute does not supply one expressly. While the absence of congressional action addressing private rights of action under an international norm is more equivocal than its failure to provide such a right when it creates a statute, the possible collateral consequences of making international rules privately actionable argue for judicial caution.

Fourth, the subject of those collateral consequences is itself a reason for a high bar to new private causes of action for violating international law, for the potential implications for the foreign relations of the United States of recognizing such causes should make courts particularly wary of impinging on the discretion of the Legislative and Executive Branches in managing foreign affairs. It is one thing for American courts to enforce constitutional limits on our own State and Federal Governments' power, but quite another to consider suits under rules that would go so far as to claim a limit on the power of foreign governments over their own citizens, and to hold that a foreign government or its agent has transgressed those limits. Yet modern international law is very much concerned with just such questions, and apt to stimulate calls for vindicating private interests in § 1350 cases. Since many attempts by federal courts to craft remedies for the violation of new norms of international law would raise risks of adverse foreign policy consequences, they should be undertaken, if at all, with great caution.

The fifth reason is particularly important in light of the first four. We have no congressional mandate to seek out and define new and debatable violations of the law of nations, and modern indications of congressional understanding of the judicial role in the field have not affirmatively encouraged greater judicial creativity. It is true that a clear mandate appears in the Torture Victim Protection Act of 1991, providing authority that "establishes an unambiguous and modern basis for" federal claims of torture and extrajudicial killing, H. R. Rep. No. 102–367, pt. 1, p. 3 (1991). But that affirmative authority is confined to specific subject matter, and although the legislative history includes the remark that § 1350 should "remain intact to permit suits based on other norms that already exist or may ripen in the future into rules of customary international law," Congress as a body has done nothing to promote such suits. Several times, indeed, the Senate has expressly declined to give the federal courts the task of interpreting and applying international human rights law, as when its ratification of the International Covenant on Civil and Political Rights declared that the substantive provisions of the document were not self-executing. 138 Cong. Rec. 8071 (1992).

B

These reasons argue for great caution in adapting the law of nations to private rights. Justice Scalia concludes that caution is too hospitable, and a word is in order to summarize where we have come so far and to focus our difference with him on whether some norms of today's law of nations may ever be recognized legitimately by federal courts in the absence of congressional action beyond § 1350. All Members of the Court agree that § 1350 is only jurisdictional. We also agree, or at least Justice Scalia does not dispute, that the jurisdiction was originally understood to be available to enforce a small number of international norms that a federal court could properly recognize as within the common law enforceable without further statutory authority. Justice Scalia concludes, however, that two subsequent developments should be understood to preclude federal courts from recognizing any further international norms as judicially enforceable today, absent further congressional action. As described before, we now tend to understand common law not as a discoverable reflection of universal reason but, in a positivistic way, as a product of human choice. And we now adhere to a conception of limited judicial power first expressed in reorienting federal diversity jurisdiction, see *Erie R. Co. v. Tompkins*, that federal courts have no authority to derive "general" common law.

Whereas Justice Scalia sees these developments as sufficient to close the door to further independent judicial recognition of actionable international norms, other considerations persuade us that the judicial power should be exercised on the understanding that the door is still ajar subject to vigilant doorkeeping, and thus open to a narrow class of international norms today. *Erie* did not in terms bar any judicial recognition of new substantive rules, no matter what the circumstances, and post-*Erie* understanding has identified limited enclaves in which federal courts may derive some substantive law in a common law way. For two centuries we have affirmed that the domestic law of the United States recognizes the law of nations. See, e.g., *Sabbatino*, 376 U.S., at 423 ("It is, of course, true that United States courts apply international law as a part of our own in appropriate circumstances"); The Paquete Habana, 175 U.S. 677, 700 (1900) ("International law is part of our law, and must be ascertained and administered by the courts of justice of appropriate jurisdiction, as often as questions of right depending upon it are duly presented for their determination"). It would take some explaining to say now that federal courts must avert their gaze entirely from any international norm intended to protect individuals.

We think an attempt to justify such a position would be particularly unconvincing in light of what we know about congressional understanding bearing on this issue lying at the intersection of the judicial and legislative powers. The First Congress, which reflected the understanding of the framing generation and included some of the Framers, assumed that federal courts could properly identify some international norms as enforceable in the exercise of § 1350 jurisdiction. We think it would be unreasonable to assume that the First Congress would have expected federal courts to lose all capacity to recognize enforceable international norms simply because the common law might lose some metaphysical cachet on the road to modern realism. Later Congresses seem to have shared our view. The position we take today has been assumed by some federal courts for 24 years, ever since the Second Circuit decided *Filartiga*, supra.... Congress, however, has not only expressed no disagreement with our view of the proper exercise of the judicial power, but has responded to its most notable instance by enacting legislation supplementing the judicial determination in some detail [referring to the Torture Victim Protection Act].

While we agree with Justice Scalia to the point that we would welcome any congressional guidance in exercising jurisdiction with such obvious potential to affect foreign relations, nothing Congress has done is a reason for us to shut the door to the law of nations entirely. It is enough to say that Congress may do that at any time (explicitly, or implicitly by treaties or statutes that occupy the field) just as it may modify or cancel any judicial decision so far as it rests on recognizing an international norm as such.

C

We must still, however, derive a standard or set of standards for assessing the particular claim Alvarez raises, and for this case it suffices to look to the historical antecedents. Whatever the ultimate criteria for accepting a cause of action subject to jurisdiction under § 1350, we are persuaded that federal courts should not recognize private claims under federal common law for violations of any international law norm with less definite content and acceptance among civilized nations than the historical paradigms familiar when § 1350 was enacted. This limit upon judicial recognition is generally consistent with the reasoning of many of the courts and judges who faced the issue before it reached this Court. See *Filartiga*, 630 F.2d, at 890 ("For purposes of civil liability, the torturer has become—like the pirate and slave trader before him—hostis humani generis, an enemy of all mankind"). And the determination whether a norm is sufficiently definite to support a cause of action should (and, indeed, inevitably must) involve an element of judgment about the practical consequences of making that cause available to litigants in the federal courts.[21]

Thus, Alvarez's detention claim must be gauged against the current state of international law, looking to those sources we have long, albeit cautiously, recognized.

> Where there is no treaty, and no controlling executive or legislative act or judicial decision, resort must be had to the customs and usages of civilized nations; and, as evidence of these, to the works of jurists and commentators, who by years of labor, research and experience, have made themselves peculiarly well acquainted with the subjects of which they treat. Such works are resorted to by judicial tribunals, not for the

---

21. This requirement of clear definition is not meant to be the only principle limiting the availability of relief in the federal courts for violations of customary international law, though it disposes of this case. For example, the European Commission argues as amicus curiae that basic principles of international law require that before asserting a claim in a foreign forum, the claimant must have exhausted any remedies available in the domestic legal system, and perhaps in other fora such as international claims tribunals. Cf. Torture Victim Protection Act of 1991, § 2(b) (exhaustion requirement). We would certainly consider this requirement in an appropriate case.

Another possible limitation that we need not apply here is a policy of case-specific deference to the political branches. For example, there are now pending in federal district court several class actions seeking damages from various corporations alleged to have participated in, or abetted, the regime of apartheid that formerly controlled South Africa. See In re South African Apartheid Litigation, 238 F. Supp. 2d 1379 (JPML 2002) (granting a motion to transfer the cases to the Southern District of New York). The Government of South Africa has said that these cases interfere with the policy embodied by its Truth and Reconciliation Commission, which "deliberately avoided a 'victors' justice' approach to the crimes of apartheid and chose instead one based on confession and absolution, informed by the principles of reconciliation, reconstruction, reparation and goodwill." Declaration of Penuell Mpapa Maduna, Minister of Justice and Constitutional Development, Republic of South Africa (reprinted in App. to Brief for Government of Commonwealth of Australia et al. as Amici Curiae 7a). The United States has agreed. See Letter of William H. Taft IV, Legal Adviser, Dept. of State, to Shannen W. Coffin, Deputy Asst. Atty. Gen., Oct. 27, 2003, reprinted in id., at 2a. In such cases, there is a strong argument that federal courts should give serious weight to the Executive Branch's view of the case's impact on foreign policy.

speculations of their authors concerning what the law ought to be, but for trustworthy evidence of what the law really is.

The Paquete Habana, 175 U.S., at 700.

To begin with, Alvarez cites two well-known international agreements that, despite their moral authority, have little utility under the standard set out in this opinion. He says that his abduction by Sosa was an "arbitrary arrest" within the meaning of the Universal Declaration of Human Rights (Declaration), G. A. Res. 217A (III), U. N. Doc. A/810 (1948). And he traces the rule against arbitrary arrest not only to the Declaration, but also to article nine of the International Covenant on Civil and Political Rights (Covenant), Dec. 19, 1996, 999 U. N. T. S. 171,[22] to which the United States is a party, and to various other conventions to which it is not. But the Declaration does not of its own force impose obligations as a matter of international law. See Humphrey, The UN Charter and the Universal Declaration of Human Rights, in The International Protection of Human Rights 39, 50 (E. Luard ed. 1967) (quoting Eleanor Roosevelt calling the Declaration " 'a statement of principles . . . setting up a common standard of achievement for all peoples and all nations' " and " 'not a treaty or international agreement . . . imposing legal obligations' "). And, although the Covenant does bind the United States as a matter of international law, the United States ratified the Covenant on the express understanding that it was not self-executing and so did not itself create obligations enforceable in the federal courts. Id., at 33. Accordingly, Alvarez cannot say that the Declaration and Covenant themselves establish the relevant and applicable rule of international law. He instead attempts to show that prohibition of arbitrary arrest has attained the status of binding customary international law.

Here, it is useful to examine Alvarez's complaint in greater detail. As he presently argues it, the claim does not rest on the cross-border feature of his abduction. Although the District Court granted relief in part on finding a violation of international law in taking Alvarez across the border from Mexico to the United States, the Court of Appeals rejected that ground of liability for failure to identify a norm of requisite force prohibiting a forcible abduction across a border. Instead, it relied on the conclusion that the law of the United States did not authorize Alvarez's arrest, because the DEA lacked extraterritorial authority under 21 U.S.C. § 878, and because Federal Rule of Criminal Procedure 4(d)(2) limited the warrant for Alvarez's arrest to "the jurisdiction of the United States."[25] It is this position

---

22. Article nine provides that "no one shall be subjected to arbitrary arrest or detention," that "no one shall be deprived of his liberty except on such grounds and in accordance with such procedure as are established by law," and that "anyone who has been the victim of unlawful arrest or detention shall have an enforceable right to compensation." 999 U. N. T. S., at 175–76.

25. The Rule has since been moved and amended and now provides that a warrant may also be executed "anywhere else a federal statute authorizes an arrest." Fed. Rule Crim. Proc. 4(c)(2).

that Alvarez takes now: that his arrest was arbitrary and as such forbidden by international law not because it infringed the prerogatives of Mexico, but because no applicable law authorized it.

Alvarez thus invokes a general prohibition of "arbitrary" detention defined as officially sanctioned action exceeding positive authorization to detain under the domestic law of some government, regardless of the circumstances. Whether or not this is an accurate reading of the Covenant, Alvarez cites little authority that a rule so broad has the status of a binding customary norm today. He certainly cites nothing to justify the federal courts in taking his broad rule as the predicate for a federal lawsuit, for its implications would be breathtaking. His rule would support a cause of action in federal court for any arrest, anywhere in the world, unauthorized by the law of the jurisdiction in which it took place, and would create a cause of action for any seizure of an alien in violation of the Fourth Amendment, supplanting the actions under 42 U.S.C. § 1983 and Bivens v. Six Unknown Fed. Narcotics Agents, 403 U.S. 388 (1971), that now provide damages remedies for such violations. It would create an action in federal court for arrests by state officers who simply exceed their authority; and for the violation of any limit that the law of any country might place on the authority of its own officers to arrest. And all of this assumes that Alvarez could establish that Sosa was acting on behalf of a government when he made the arrest, for otherwise he would need a rule broader still.

Alvarez's failure to marshal support for his proposed rule is underscored by the Restatement (Third) of Foreign Relations Law of the United States § 702 (1987), which says in its discussion of customary international human rights law that a "state violates international law if, as a matter of state policy, it practices, encourages, or condones ... prolonged arbitrary detention." Although the Restatement does not explain its requirements of a "state policy" and of "prolonged" detention, the implication is clear. Any credible invocation of a principle against arbitrary detention that the civilized world accepts as binding customary international law requires a factual basis beyond relatively brief detention in excess of positive authority. ...

Whatever may be said for the broad principle Alvarez advances, in the present, imperfect world, it expresses an aspiration that exceeds any binding customary rule having the specificity we require. Creating a private cause of action to further that aspiration would go beyond any residual common law discretion we think it appropriate to exercise. It is enough to hold that a single illegal detention of less than a day, followed by the transfer of custody to lawful authorities and a prompt arraignment, violates no norm of customary international law so well defined as to support the creation of a federal remedy.

The judgment of the Court of Appeals is reversed.

■ JUSTICE SCALIA, with whom THE CHIEF JUSTICE and JUSTICE THOMAS join, concurring in part and concurring in the judgment.

There is not much that I would add to the Court's detailed opinion, and only one thing that I would subtract: its reservation of a discretionary power in the Federal Judiciary to create causes of action for the enforcement of international-law-based norms. . . .

I

. . . At the time of its enactment, the ATS provided a federal forum in which aliens could bring suit to recover for torts committed in "violation of the law of nations." The law of nations that would have been applied in this federal forum was at the time part of the so-called general common law. See Ernest A. Young, Sorting out the Debate Over Customary International Law, 42 Va. J. Int'l L. 365, 374 (2002); Curtis A. Bradley & Jack L. Goldsmith, Customary International Law as Federal Common Law: A Critique of the Modern Position, 110 Harv. L. Rev. 815, 824 (1997); Brief for Vikram Amar et al. as Amici Curiae 12–13.

General common law was not federal law under the Supremacy Clause, which gave that effect only to the Constitution, the laws of the United States, and treaties. Federal and state courts adjudicating questions of general common law were not adjudicating questions of federal or state law, respectively—the general common law was neither. . . .

This Court's decision in Erie R. Co. v. Tompkins, 304 U.S. 64 (1938), signaled the end of federal-court elaboration and application of the general common law. *Erie* repudiated the holding of Swift v. Tyson, 41 U.S. 1 (1842), that federal courts were free to "express our own opinion" upon "the principles established in the general commercial law." After canvassing the many problems resulting from "the broad province accorded to the so-called 'general law' as to which federal courts exercised an independent judgment," the *Erie* Court extirpated that law with its famous declaration that "there is no federal general common law." *Erie* affected the status of the law of nations in federal courts not merely by the implication of its holding but quite directly, since the question decided in *Swift* turned on the "law merchant," then a subset of the law of nations.

After the death of the old general common law in *Erie* came the birth of a new and different common law pronounced by federal courts. . . . Unlike the general common law that preceded it, however, federal common law was self-consciously "made" rather than "discovered," by judges. . . . Because post-*Erie* federal common law is made, not discovered, federal courts must possess some federal-common-law-making authority before undertaking to craft it. . . . The general rule as formulated in Texas Industries, Inc. v. Radcliff Materials, Inc., 451 U.S. 630, 640–41 (1981), is that "the vesting of jurisdiction in the federal courts does not in and of itself give rise to authority to formulate federal common law." This rule applies not only to applications of federal common law that would displace a state rule, but also to applications that simply create a private cause of action under a federal statute. Indeed, *Texas Industries* itself involved the petitioner's unsuccessful request for an application of the latter sort—creation of a right of contribution to damages assessed under the antitrust laws.

The rule against finding a delegation of substantive lawmaking power in a grant of jurisdiction is subject to exceptions, some better established than others. The most firmly entrenched is admiralty law, derived from the grant of admiralty jurisdiction in Article III, § 2, cl. 3, of the Constitution. In the exercise of that jurisdiction federal courts develop and apply a body of general maritime law, "the well-known and well-developed venerable law of the sea which arose from the custom among seafaring men." R. M. S. Titanic, Inc. v. Haver, 171 F.3d 943, 960 (4th Cir. 1999) (Niemeyer, J.) (internal quotation marks omitted). At the other extreme is Bivens v. Six Unknown Fed. Narcotics Agents, 403 U.S. 388 (1971), which created a private damages cause of action against federal officials for violation of the Fourth Amendment. We have said that the authority to create this cause of action was derived from "our general jurisdiction to decide all cases 'arising under the Constitution, laws, or treaties of the United States.'" Correctional Services Corp. v. Malesko, 534 U.S. 61, 66 (2001) (quoting 28 U.S.C. § 1331). While *Bivens* stands, the ground supporting it has eroded. For the past 25 years, "we have consistently refused to extend *Bivens* liability to any new context." *Correctional Services Corp.*, supra, at 68. *Bivens* is "a relic of the heady days in which this Court assumed common-law powers to create causes of action." 534 U.S., at 75 (SCALIA, J., concurring).

II

With these general principles in mind, I turn to the question presented. The Court's detailed exegesis of the ATS conclusively establishes that it is "a jurisdictional statute creating no new causes of action." The Court provides a persuasive explanation of why respondent's contrary interpretation, that "the ATS was intended not simply as a jurisdictional grant, but as authority for the creation of a new cause of action for torts in violation of international law," is wrong. Indeed, the Court properly endorses the views of one scholar that this interpretation is "'simply frivolous'" (quoting William Casto, The Federal Courts' Protective Jurisdiction Over Torts Committed in Violation of the Law of Nations, 18 Conn. L. Rev. 467, 479, 480 (1986)).

These conclusions are alone enough to dispose of the present case in favor of petitioner Sosa. None of the exceptions to the general rule against finding substantive lawmaking power in a jurisdictional grant apply. *Bivens* provides perhaps the closest analogy. That is shaky authority at best, but at least it can be said that *Bivens* sought to enforce a command of our *own* law—the *United States* Constitution. In modern international human rights litigation of the sort that has proliferated since Filartiga v. Pena–Irala, 630 F.2d 876 (2d Cir. 1980), a federal court must first *create* the underlying federal command. But "the fact that a rule has been recognized as [customary international law], by itself, is not an adequate basis for viewing that rule as part of federal common law." Daniel J. Meltzer, Customary International Law, Foreign Affairs, and Federal Common Law, 42 Va. J. Int'l L. 513, 519 (2002). In Benthamite terms, creating a federal command (federal common law) out of "international norms," and then constructing a cause of action to enforce that command through the purely jurisdictional grant of the ATS, is nonsense upon stilts.

III

The analysis in the Court's opinion departs from my own in this respect: After concluding in Part III that "the ATS is a jurisdictional statute creating no new causes of action," the Court addresses at length in Part IV the "good reasons for a restrained conception of the *discretion* a federal court should exercise in considering a new cause of action" under the ATS (emphasis added). By framing the issue as one of "discretion," the Court skips over the antecedent question of authority. This neglects the "lesson of *Erie*," that "grants of jurisdiction alone" (which the Court has acknowledged the ATS to be) "are not themselves grants of law-making authority." Meltzer, supra, at 541. On this point, the Court observes only that no development between the enactment of the ATS (in 1789) and the birth of modern international human rights litigation under that statute (in 1980) "has categorically *precluded* federal courts from recognizing a claim under the law of nations as an element of common law" (emphasis added). This turns our jurisprudence regarding federal common law on its head. The question is not what case or congressional action *prevents* federal courts from applying the law of nations as part of the general common law; it is what *authorizes* that peculiar exception from *Erie*'s fundamental holding that a general common law *does not exist*.

The Court would apparently find authorization in the understanding of the Congress that enacted the ATS, that "district courts would recognize private causes of action for certain torts in violation of the law of nations." But as discussed above, that understanding rested upon a notion of general common law that has been repudiated by *Erie*.

The Court recognizes that *Erie* was a "watershed" decision heralding an avulsive change, wrought by "conceptual development in understanding common law ... [and accompanied by an] equally significant rethinking of the role of the federal courts in making it." The Court's analysis, however, does not follow through on this insight, interchangeably using the unadorned phrase "common law" in Parts III and IV to refer to pre-*Erie* general common law and post-*Erie* federal common law. This lapse is crucial, because the creation of post-*Erie* federal common law is rooted in a positivist mindset utterly foreign to the American common-law tradition of the late 18th century. Post-*Erie* federal common lawmaking (all that is left to the federal courts) is so far removed from that general-common-law adjudication which applied the "law of nations" that it would be anachronistic to find authorization to do the former in a statutory grant of jurisdiction that was thought to enable the latter. Yet that is precisely what the discretion-only analysis in Part IV suggests.

Because today's federal common law is not our Framers' general common law, the question presented by the suggestion of discretionary authority to enforce the law of nations is not whether to extend old-school general-common-law adjudication. Rather, it is whether to create new federal common law. The Court masks the novelty of its approach when it suggests that the difference between us is that we would "close the door to further independent judicial recognition of actionable international norms," whereas the Court would permit the exercise of judicial power "on the understanding that the door is still ajar subject to vigilant doorkeeping." The general common law was the old door. We do not close that door today, for the deed was done in *Erie*. Federal common law is a *new* door. The question is not whether that door will be left ajar, but whether this Court will open it.

Although I fundamentally disagree with the discretion-based framework employed by the Court, we seem to be in accord that creating a new federal common law of international human rights is a questionable enterprise. We agree that:

- "The general practice has been to look for legislative guidance before exercising innovative authority over substantive law [in the area of foreign relations]. It would be remarkable to take a more aggressive role in exercising a jurisdiction that remained largely in shadow for much of the prior two centuries."

- "The possible collateral consequences of making international rules privately actionable argue for judicial caution."

- "It is one thing for American courts to enforce constitutional limits on our own State and Federal Governments' power, but quite another to consider suits under rules that would go so far as to claim a limit on the power of foreign governments over their own citizens, and to hold that a foreign government or its agent has transgressed those limits."

- "Many attempts by federal courts to craft remedies for the violation of new norms of international law would raise risks of adverse foreign policy consequences."

- "Several times, indeed, the Senate has expressly declined to give the federal courts the task of interpreting and applying international human rights law."

These considerations are not, as the Court thinks them, reasons why courts must be circumspect in use of their extant general-common-law-making powers. They are reasons why courts cannot possibly be thought to have been given, and should not be thought to possess, federal-common-law-making powers with regard to the creation of private federal causes of action for violations of customary international law.

To be sure, today's opinion does not itself precipitate a direct confrontation with Congress by creating a cause of action that Congress has not. But it invites precisely that action by the lower courts.... In holding open the possibility that judges may create rights where Congress has not authorized them to do so, the Court countenances judicial occupation of a domain that belongs to the people's representatives. One does not need a crystal ball to predict that this occupation will not be long in coming, since the Court endorses the reasoning of "many of the courts and judges who faced the issue before it reached this Court," including the Second and Ninth Circuits.

The Ninth Circuit brought us the judgment that the Court reverses today. Perhaps its decision in this particular case, like the decisions of other lower federal courts that receive passing attention in the Court's opinion, "reflects a more assertive view of federal judicial discretion over claims based on customary international law than the position we take today." But the verbal formula it applied is the same verbal formula that the Court explicitly endorses. Endorsing the very formula that led the Ninth Circuit to its result in this case hardly seems to be a recipe for restraint in the future.

The Second Circuit, which started the Judiciary down the path the Court today tries to hedge in, is a good indicator of where that path leads us: directly into confrontation with the political branches. Kadic v. Karadzic, 70 F.3d 232 (2d Cir. 1995), provides a case in point. One of the norms at issue in that case was a norm against genocide set forth in the Convention on the Prevention and Punishment of the Crime of Genocide, Dec. 9, 1948, 78 U. N. T. S. 278. The Second Circuit held that the norm was actionable under the ATS after applying Circuit case law that the Court today endorses. 70 F.3d at 238–39, 241–42. The Court of Appeals then did something that is perfectly logical and yet truly remarkable: It dismissed the determination by Congress and the Executive that this norm should *not* give rise to a private cause of action. We *know* that Congress and the Executive made this determination, because Congress inscribed it into the Genocide Convention Implementation Act of 1987, 18 U.S.C. § 1091 et seq., a law signed by the President attaching criminal penalties to the norm against genocide. The Act, Congress said, shall not "be construed as creating any substantive or procedural right enforceable by law by any party in any proceeding." § 1092. Undeterred, the Second Circuit reasoned that this "decision not to create a *new* private remedy" could hardly be construed as *repealing* by implication the cause of action supplied by the ATS. 70 F.3d at 242 (emphasis added). Does this Court truly wish to encourage the use of a jurisdiction-granting statute with respect to which there is "no record of congressional discussion about private actions that might be subject to the jurisdictional provision, or about any need for further legislation to create private remedies; [and] no record even of debate on the section," to override a clear indication from the political branches that a "specific, universal, and obligatory" norm against genocide is *not* to be enforced through a private damages action? Today's opinion leads the lower courts right down that perilous path.

Though it is not necessary to resolution of the present case, one further consideration deserves mention: Despite the avulsive change of *Erie*, the Framers who included reference to "the Law of Nations" in Article I, § 8, cl. 10, of the Constitution would be entirely content with the post-*Erie* system I have described, and quite terrified by the "discretion" endorsed by the Court. That portion of the general common law known as the law of nations was understood to refer to the accepted practices of nations in their dealings with one another (treatment of ambassadors, immunity of foreign sovereigns from suit, etc.) and with actors on the high seas hostile to all nations and beyond all their territorial jurisdictions (pirates). Those accepted practices have for the most part, if not in their entirety, been enacted into United States statutory law, so that insofar as they are concerned the demise of the general common law is inconsequential. The notion that a law of nations, redefined to mean the consensus of states on *any* subject, can be used by a private citizen to control a sovereign's treatment of *its own citizens* within *its own territory* is a 20th-century invention of internationalist law professors and human-rights advocates. See generally Bradley & Goldsmith, Critique of the Modern Position, 110 Harv. L. Rev., at 831–37. The Framers would, I am confident, be appalled by the proposition that, for example, the American peoples' democratic adoption of the death penalty, see, e.g., Tex. Penal Code Ann. § 12.31 (2003), could be judicially nullified because of the disapproving views of foreigners.

We Americans have a method for making the laws that are over us. We elect representatives to two Houses of Congress, each of which must enact the new law and present it for the approval of a President, whom we also elect. For over two decades now, unelected federal judges have been usurping this lawmaking power by converting what they regard as norms of international law into American law. Today's opinion approves that process in principle, though urging the lower courts to be more restrained.

This Court seems incapable of admitting that some matters—*any* matters—are none of its business. In today's latest victory for its Never Say Never Jurisprudence, the Court ignores its own conclusion that the ATS provides only jurisdiction, wags a finger at the lower courts for going too far, and then—repeating the same formula the ambitious lower courts *themselves* have used—invites them to try again.

It would be bad enough if there were some assurance that future conversions of perceived international norms into American law would be approved by this Court itself. (Though we know ourselves to be eminently reasonable, self-awareness of eminent reasonableness is not really a substitute for democratic election.) But in this illegitimate lawmaking endeavor, the lower federal courts will be the principal actors; we review but a tiny fraction of their decisions. And no one thinks that all of them are eminently reasonable.

American law—the law made by the people's democratically elected representatives—does not recognize a category of activity that is so universally disapproved by other nations that it is automatically unlawful here, and automatically gives rise to a private action for money damages in federal court. That simple principle is what today's decision should have announced.

[The separate opinion of Justice Ginsburg, joined by Justice Breyer, on the FTCA is omitted.]

■ JUSTICE BREYER, concurring in part and concurring in the judgment.

I join ... the Court's opinion in respect to the Alien Tort Statute (ATS) claim. The Court says that to qualify for recognition under the ATS a norm of international law must have a content as definite as, and an acceptance as widespread as, those that characterized 18th-century international norms prohibiting piracy. The norm must extend liability to the type of perpetrator (e.g., a private actor) the plaintiff seeks to sue. And Congress can make clear that courts should not recognize any such norm, through a direct or indirect command or by occupying the field. The Court also suggests that principles of exhaustion might apply, and that courts should give "serious weight" to the Executive Branch's view of the impact on foreign policy that permitting an ATS suit will likely have in a given case or type of case. I believe all of these conditions are important.

I would add one further consideration. Since enforcement of an international norm by one nation's courts implies that other nations' courts may do the same, I would ask whether the exercise of jurisdiction under the ATS is consistent with those notions of comity that lead each nation to respect the sovereign rights of other nations by limiting the reach of its laws and their enforcement. In applying those principles, courts help assure that "the potentially conflicting laws of different nations" will "work together in harmony," a matter of increasing importance in an ever more interdependent world. F. Hoffmann–La Roche Ltd. v. Empagran S. A., 542 U.S. 155 (2004); cf. Murray v. The Schooner Charming Betsy, 6 U.S. (2 Cranch) 64 (1804). Such consideration is necessary to ensure that ATS litigation does not undermine the very harmony that it was intended to promote.

These comity concerns normally do not arise (or at least are mitigated) if the conduct in question takes place in the country that provides the cause of action or if that conduct involves that country's own national—where, say, an American assaults a foreign diplomat and the diplomat brings suit in an American court. See Restatement (Third) of Foreign Relations Law of the United States §§ 402(1), (2) (1986) (hereinafter Restatement) (describing traditional bases of territorial and nationality jurisdiction). They do arise, however, when foreign persons injured abroad bring suit in the United States under the ATS, asking the courts to recognize a claim that a certain kind of foreign conduct violates an international norm.

Since different courts in different nations will not necessarily apply even similar substantive laws similarly, workable harmony, in practice, depends upon more than substantive uniformity among the laws of those nations. That is to say, substantive uniformity does not *automatically* mean that universal jurisdiction is appropriate. Thus, in the 18th century, nations reached consensus not only on the substantive principle that acts of piracy were universally wrong but also on the jurisdictional principle that any nation that found a pirate could prosecute him.

Today international law will sometimes similarly reflect not only substantive agreement as to certain universally condemned behavior but also procedural agreement that universal jurisdiction exists to prosecute a subset of that behavior. See Restatement § 404, and Comment *a;* International Law Association, Final Report on the Exercise of Universal Jurisdiction in Respect of Gross Human Rights Offences 2 (2000). That subset includes torture, genocide, crimes against humanity, and war crimes.

The fact that this procedural consensus exists suggests that recognition of universal jurisdiction in respect to a limited set of norms is consistent with principles of international comity. That is, allowing every nation's courts to adjudicate foreign conduct involving foreign parties in such cases will not significantly threaten the practical harmony that comity principles seek to protect. That consensus concerns criminal jurisdiction, but consensus as to universal criminal jurisdiction itself suggests that universal tort jurisdiction would be no more threatening. Cf. Restatement § 404, Comment *b.* That is because the criminal courts of many nations combine civil and criminal proceedings, allowing those injured by criminal conduct to be represented, and to recover damages, in the criminal proceeding itself. Thus, universal criminal jurisdiction necessarily contemplates a significant degree of civil tort recovery as well.

Taking these matters into account, as I believe courts should, I can find no similar procedural consensus supporting the exercise of jurisdiction in this case. That lack of consensus provides additional support for the Court's conclusion that the ATS does not recognize the claim at issue here—where the underlying substantive claim concerns arbitrary arrest, outside the United States, of a citizen of one foreign country by another.

CHAPTER III

CONGRESSIONAL CONTROL OF THE FEDERAL COURTS

Page 277, add at the end of footnote c:

Cf. Peter Nicolas, The Use of Preclusion Doctrine, Antisuit Injunctions, and Forum Non Conveniens Dismissals in Transnational Intellectual Property Litigation, 40 Va. J. Int'l L. 331 (1999) (arguing that federal subject matter jurisdiction should be used to resolve claims arising under foreign international property laws, thereby reducing opportunities for litigation gamesmanship in transnational intellectual property disputes).

Page 277, add to the end of Note 3:

Congress enacted the Air Transportation Safety and System Stabilization Act, Pub. Law No. 107–42, 115 Stat. 230, on September 22, 2001. Section 408(b) provides:

> (b) Federal Cause of Action.—
>
> (1) Availability of Action.—There shall exist a Federal cause of action for damages arising out of the hijacking and subsequent crashes of American Airlines flights 11 and 77, and United Airlines flights 93 and 175, on September 11, 2001. [T]his cause of action shall be the exclusive remedy for damages arising out of the hijacking and subsequent crashes of such flights.
>
> (2) Substantive Law.—The substantive law for decision in any such suit shall be derived from the law, including choice of law principles, of the State in which the crash occurred unless such law is inconsistent with or preempted by Federal law.
>
> (3) Jurisdiction.—The United States District Court for the Southern District of New York shall have original and exclusive jurisdiction over all actions brought for any claim (including any claim for loss of property, personal injury, or death) resulting from or relating to the terrorist-related aircraft crashes of September 11, 2001.

Is this statute constitutional? It is argued in Eric J. Segall, Article III as a Grant of Power: Protective Jurisdiction, Federalism and the Federal Courts, 54 Fla. L. Rev. 361 (2002), that it is. Segall concludes that a "pure jurisdictional statute that furthers a legitimate Article I concern is properly a 'law' under which a claim may arise."

Page 286, add at the end of footnote a:

For an exploration of an alternative solution to the *Tidewater* problem, see James E. Pfander, The Tidewater Problem: Article III and Constitutional Change, 79 Notre Dame L. Rev. 1925 (2004).

Page 320, add at the end of Note 3:

A major recent article on this subject is James E. Pfander, Article I Tribunals, Article III Courts, and the Judicial Power of the United States, 118 Harv. L. Rev. 643 (2004). Pfander builds on the textual distinction between Article I's reference to "inferior tribunals" and Article III's reference to "inferior courts." He argues that Congress "may give Article I tribunals power over matters that it has structured to fall outside the scope of the judicial power under Article III." Examples include public-rights claims, military courts-martial, and litigation in the territories. For such matters, non-Article III adjudication is permitted, so long as the Article I tribunals remain "inferior" to the Supreme Court.

The obvious way of maintaining such inferiority is some avenue of review or supervision by the Supreme Court. Pfander's theory is therefore similar to those emphasizing appellate review (see Fallon, Saphire and Solimine, and Bator), but he claims a better fit with the decided cases. In particular, Pfander claims that his "inferior tribunals" approach explains why some schemes with Article III appellate review have been struck down (e.g., *Northern Pipeline*), while others without "strict" appellate review have been upheld (e.g., courts-martial).

CHAPTER IV

JUSTICIABILITY

Page 381, add the following at the end of Note 6:

Finally, an important recent article examines the history antecedents of modern standing doctrine. Ann Woolhandler and Caleb Nelson, Does History Defeat Standing Doctrine?, 102 Mich. L. Rev. 689 (2004). Woolhandler and Nelson respond to attacks by Steven L. Winter and others on the historical foundation of the modern law of standing. According to Winter, history demonstrates the lack of any constitutional objection to "the adjudication of group rights at the behest of any member of the public, without regard to the necessity of personal interest, injury, or standing." Steven L. Winter, The Metaphor of Standing and the Problem of Self-Governance, 40 Stan. L. Rev. 1371, 1381–82 (1988). Woolhandler and Nelson contend that standing doctrine does indeed have a long history and that the history places the requirement of standing "in a far more sympathetic light than most modern-day discussions suggest."

Page 414, add the following case at the end of Section 1:

Elk Grove Unified School District v. Newdow
Supreme Court of the United States, 2004.
542 U.S. 1.

■ JUSTICE STEVENS delivered the opinion of the Court.

Each day elementary school teachers in the Elk Grove Unified School District (School District) lead their classes in a group recitation of the Pledge of Allegiance. Respondent, Michael A. Newdow, is an atheist whose daughter participates in that daily exercise. Because the Pledge contains the words "under God," he views the School District's policy as a religious indoctrination of his child that violates the First Amendment. A divided panel of the Court of Appeals for the Ninth Circuit agreed with Newdow. In light of the obvious importance of that decision, we granted certiorari to review the First Amendment issue and, preliminarily, the question whether Newdow has standing to invoke the jurisdiction of the federal courts. We conclude that Newdow lacks standing and therefore reverse the Court of Appeals' decision. . . .

Under California law, "every public elementary school" must begin each day with "appropriate patriotic exercises." Cal. Educ. Code Ann. § 52720 (West 1989). The statute provides that "[t]he giving of the Pledge of Allegiance to the Flag of the United States of America shall satisfy" this requirement. Ibid. The Elk Grove Unified School District has implemented the state law by requiring that "[e]ach elementary school class recite the pledge of allegiance to the flag once each day." Consistent with our case law, the School District permits students who object on religious grounds to abstain from the recitation. See West Virginia Bd. of Ed. v. Barnette, 319 U.S. 624 (1943).

In March 2000, Newdow filed suit in the United States District Court for the Eastern District of California against the United States Congress, the President of the United States, the State of California, and the Elk Grove Unified School District and its superintendent. At the time of filing, Newdow's daughter was enrolled in kindergarten in the Elk Grove Unified School District and participated in the daily recitation of the Pledge. Styled as a mandamus action, the complaint explains that Newdow is an atheist who was ordained more than 20 years ago in a ministry that "espouses the religious philosophy that the true and eternal bonds of righteousness and virtue stem from reason rather than mythology." The complaint seeks a declaration that the 1954 Act's addition of the words "under God" violated the Establishment and Free Exercise Clauses of the United States Constitution, as well as an injunction against the School District's policy requiring daily recitation of the Pledge. It alleges that Newdow has standing to sue on his own behalf and on behalf of his daughter as "next friend."

The case was referred to a Magistrate Judge, whose brief findings and recommendation concluded, "the Pledge does not violate the Establishment Clause." The District Court adopted that recommendation and dismissed the complaint on July 21, 2000. The Court of Appeals reversed and issued three separate decisions discussing the merits and Newdow's standing.

In its first opinion the appeals court unanimously held that Newdow has standing "as a parent to challenge a practice that interferes with his right to direct the religious education of his daughter." Newdow v. U.S. Congress, 292 F.3d 597, 602 (9th Cir. 2002) *(Newdow I)*. That holding sustained Newdow's standing to challenge not only the policy of the School District, where his daughter still is enrolled, but also the 1954 Act of Congress that had amended the Pledge, because his " 'injury in fact' " was " 'fairly traceable' " to its enactment. On the merits, over the dissent of one judge, the court held that both the 1954 Act and the School District's policy violate the Establishment Clause of the First Amendment.

After the Court of Appeals' initial opinion was announced, Sandra Banning, the mother of Newdow's daughter, filed a motion for leave to intervene, or alternatively to dismiss the complaint. She declared that although she and Newdow shared "physical custody" of their daughter, a state-court order granted her "exclusive legal custody" of the child, "including the sole right to represent [the daughter's] legal interests and make all decision[s] about her education" and welfare. Banning further stated that her daughter is a Christian who believes in God and has no objection either to reciting or hearing others recite the Pledge of Allegiance, or to its reference to God. Banning expressed the belief that her daughter would be harmed if the litigation were permitted to proceed, because others might incorrectly perceive the child as sharing her father's atheist views. Banning accordingly concluded, as her daughter's sole legal custodian, that it was not in the child's interest to be a party to Newdow's lawsuit. On September 25, 2002, the California Superior Court entered an order enjoining Newdow from including his daughter as an unnamed party or suing as her "next friend." That order did not purport to answer the question of Newdow's Article III standing. See Newdow v. U.S. Congress, 313 F.3d 500, 502 (9th Cir. 2002) *(Newdow II)*.

In a second published opinion, the Court of Appeals reconsidered Newdow's standing in light of Banning's motion. The court noted that Newdow no longer claimed to represent his daughter, but unanimously concluded that "the grant of sole legal custody to Banning" did not deprive Newdow, "as a noncustodial parent, of Article III standing to object to unconstitutional government action affecting his child." Id., at 502–03. The court held that under California law Newdow retains the right to expose his child to his particular religious views even if those views contradict the mother's, and that Banning's objections as sole legal custodian do not defeat Newdow's right to seek redress for an alleged injury to his own parental interests.

On February 28, 2003, the Court of Appeals issued an order amending its first opinion and denying rehearing en banc. Newdow v. U.S. Congress, 328 F.3d 466, 468 (9th Cir. 2003) *(Newdow III)*. The amended opinion omitted the initial opinion's discussion of Newdow's standing to challenge the 1954 Act and declined to determine whether Newdow was entitled to declaratory relief regarding the constitutionality of that Act. Nine judges dissented from the denial of en banc review. We granted the School District's petition for a writ of certiorari to consider two questions: (1) whether Newdow has standing as a noncustodial parent to challenge the School District's policy, and (2) if so, whether the policy offends the First Amendment.

In every federal case, the party bringing the suit must establish standing to prosecute the action. . . . Even in cases concededly within our jurisdiction under Article III, we abide by "a series of rules under which [we have] avoided passing upon a large part of all the constitutional questions pressed upon [us] for decision." Ashwander v. TVA, 297 U.S. 288, 346 (1936) (Brandeis, J., concurring). . . .

Consistent with these principles, our standing jurisprudence contains two strands: Article III standing, which enforces the Constitution's case or controversy requirement, see Lujan v. Defenders of Wildlife, 504 U.S. 555, 559–62 (1992); and prudential standing, which embodies "judicially self-imposed limits on the exercise of federal jurisdiction," Allen v. Wright, 468 U.S. 737, 751 (1984). The Article III limitations are familiar: The plaintiff must show that the conduct of which he complains has caused him to suffer an "injury in fact" that a favorable judgment will redress. See *Lujan*, 504 U.S., at 560–61. Although we have not exhaustively defined the prudential dimensions of the standing doctrine, we have explained that prudential standing encompasses "the general prohibition on a litigant's raising another person's legal rights, the rule barring adjudication of generalized grievances more appropriately addressed in the representative branches, and the requirement that a plaintiff's complaint fall within the zone of interests protected by the law invoked." *Allen*, 468 U.S., at 751. "Without such limitations—closely related to Art. III concerns but essentially matters of judicial self-governance—the courts would be called upon to decide abstract questions of wide public significance even though other governmental institutions may be more competent to address the questions and even though judicial intervention may be unnecessary to protect individual rights." *Warth*, 422 U.S., at 500.

One of the principal areas in which this Court has customarily declined to intervene is the realm of domestic relations. Long ago we observed that "[t]he whole subject of the domestic relations of husband and wife, parent and child, belongs to the laws of the States and not to the laws of the United States." . . . So strong is our deference to state law in this area that we have recognized a "domestic relations exception" that "divests the federal courts of power to issue divorce, alimony, and child custody decrees." Ankenbrandt v. Richards, 504 U.S. 689, 703 (1992). We have also acknowledged that it might be appropriate for the federal courts to decline to hear a case involving "elements of the domestic relationship," id., at 705, even when divorce, alimony, or child custody is not strict at issue:

> This would be so when a case presents "difficult questions of state law bearing on policy problems of substantial public import whose importance transcends the result in the case at bar." Such might well be the case if a federal suit were filed prior to effectuation of a divorce, alimony, or child custody decree, and the suit depended on a determination of the status of the parties.

Id., at 705–06 (quoting Colorado River Water Conservation Dist. v. United States, 424 U.S. 800 (1976)). Thus, while rare instances arise in which it is necessary to answer a substantial federal question that transcends or exists apart from the family law issue, see, e.g., Palmore v. Sidoti, 466 U.S. 429, 432–34 (1984), in general it is appropriate for the federal courts to leave delicate issues of domestic relations to the state courts.[5]

---

5. Our holding does not rest, as The Chief Justice suggests, on either the domestic relations exception or the abstention doctrine. Rather, our prudential standing analysis is informed by the variety of contexts in which federal courts decline to intervene because as Ankenbrandt v. Richards, 504 U.S. 689 (1992), contemplated, the suit "depend[s] on a determination of the status of the parties," id., at 706. . . . The Chief Justice, in this respect, misses our point: The *merits* question undoubtedly transcends the domestic relations issue, but the *standing* question surely does not.

As explained briefly above, the extent of the standing problem raised by the domestic relations issues in this case was not apparent until August 5, 2002, when Banning filed her motion for leave to intervene or dismiss the complaint following the Court of Appeals' initial decision. At that time, the child's custody was governed by a February 6, 2002, order of the California Superior Court. That order provided that Banning had " '*sole* legal custody as to the rights and responsibilities to make decisions relating to the health, education and welfare of' " her daughter. *Newdow II*, 313 F.3d, at 502. The order stated that the two parents should " 'consult with one another on substantial decisions relating to' " the child's " 'psychological and educational needs,' " but it authorized Banning to " 'exercise legal control' " if the parents could not reach " 'mutual agreement.' "

That family court order was the controlling document at the time of the Court of Appeals' standing decision. After the Court of Appeals ruled, however, the Superior Court held another conference regarding the child's custody. At a hearing on September 11, 2003, the Superior Court announced that the parents have "joint legal custody," but that Banning "makes the final decisions if the two . . . disagree."

Newdow contends that despite Banning's final authority, he retains "an unrestricted right to inculcate in his daughter—free from governmental interference—the atheistic beliefs he finds persuasive." The difficulty with that argument is that Newdow's rights, as in many cases touching upon family relations, cannot be viewed in isolation. This case concerns not merely Newdow's interest in inculcating his child with his views on religion, but also the rights of the child's mother as a parent generally and under the Superior Court orders specifically. And most important, it implicates the interests of a young child who finds herself at the center of a highly public debate over her custody, the propriety of a widespread national ritual, and the meaning of our Constitution.

The interests of the affected persons in this case are in many respects antagonistic. Of course, legal disharmony in family relations is not uncommon, and in many instances that disharmony poses no bar to federal-court adjudication of proper federal questions. What makes this case different is that Newdow's standing derives entirely from his relationship with his daughter, but he lacks the right to litigate as her next friend. In marked contrast to our case law on jus tertii, see, e.g., Singleton v. Wulff, 428 U.S. 106, 113–18 (1976) (plurality opinion), the interests of this parent and this child are not parallel and, indeed, are potentially in conflict.

Newdow's parental status is defined by California's domestic relations law. Our custom on questions of state law ordinarily is to defer to the interpretation of the Court of Appeals for the Circuit in which the State is located. In this case, the Court of Appeals, which possesses greater familiarity with California law, concluded that state law vests in Newdow a cognizable right to influence his daughter's religious upbringing. *Newdow II*, 313 F.3d, at 504–05. The court based its ruling on two intermediate state appellate cases holding that "while the custodial parent undoubtedly has the right to make ultimate decisions concerning the child's religious upbringing, a court will not enjoin the noncustodial parent from discussing religion with the child or involving the child in his or her religious activities in the absence of a showing that the child will be thereby harmed." In re Marriage of Murga, 103 Cal. App. 3d 498, 505, 163 Cal. Rptr. 79, 82 (1980). See also In re Marriage of Mentry, 142 Cal. App. 3d 260, 268–70, 190 Cal. Rptr. 843, 849–50 (1983) (relying on Murga to invalidate portion of restraining order barring noncustodial father from engaging children in religious activity or discussion without custodial parent's consent). Animated by a conception of "family privacy" that includes "not simply a policy of minimum state intervention but also a presumption of parental autonomy," 142 Cal. App. 3d, at 267–68, 190 Cal. Rptr., at 848, the state cases create a zone of private authority within which each parent, whether custodial or noncustodial, remains free to impart to the child his or her religious perspective.

Nothing that either Banning or the School Board has done, however, impairs Newdow's right to instruct his daughter in his religious views. Instead, Newdow requests relief that is more ambitious than that sought in *Mentry* and *Murga*. He wishes to forestall his daughter's exposure to religious ideas that her mother, who wields a form of veto power, endorses, and to use his parental status to challenge the influences to which his daughter may be exposed in school when he and Banning disagree. The California cases simply do not stand for the proposition that Newdow has a right to dictate to others what they may and may not say to his child respecting religion. . . .

In our view, it is improper for the federal courts to entertain a claim by a plaintiff whose standing to sue is founded on family law rights that are in dispute when prosecution of the lawsuit may have an adverse effect on the person who is the source of the plaintiff's claimed standing. When hard questions of domestic relations are sure to affect the outcome, the prudent course is for the federal court to stay its hand rather than reach out to resolve a weighty question of federal constitutional law. There is a vast difference between Newdow's right to communicate with his child—which both California law and the First Amendment recognize—and his claimed right to shield his daughter from influences to which she is exposed in school despite the terms of the custody order. We conclude that, having been deprived under California law of the right to sue as next friend, Newdow lacks prudential standing to bring this suit in federal court.[8]

---

8. Newdow's complaint and brief cite several additional bases for standing: that Newdow "at times has himself attended—and will in the future attend—class with his daughter"; that he "has considered teaching elementary school students in [the district]"; that he "has attended and will continue to attend" school board meetings at which the Pledge is "routinely recited"; and that the School District uses his tax dollars to implement its Pledge policy. Even if these arguments suffice to establish Article III stand-

The judgment of the Court of Appeals is reversed.

■ CHIEF JUSTICE REHNQUIST, with whom JUSTICE O'CONNOR joins, and with whom JUSTICE THOMAS joins [in relevant part], concurring in the judgment.

The Court today erects a novel prudential standing principle in order to avoid reaching the merits of the constitutional claim. I dissent from that ruling. On the merits, I conclude that the Elk Grove Unified School District (School District) policy that requires teachers to lead willing students in reciting the Pledge of Allegiance, which includes the words "under God," does not violate the Establishment Clause of the First Amendment.

The Court correctly notes that "our standing jurisprudence contains two strands: Article III standing, which enforces the Constitution's case or controversy requirement, see Lujan v. Defenders of Wildlife, 504 U.S. 555, 559–62 (1992); and prudential standing, which embodies 'judicially self-imposed limits on the exercise of federal jurisdiction, [Allen v. Wright, 468 U.S. 737, 751 (1984)].'" To be clear, the Court does not dispute that respondent Newdow (hereinafter respondent) satisfies the requisites of Article III standing. But curiously the Court incorporates criticism of the Court of Appeals' Article III standing decision into its justification for its novel prudential standing principle. The Court concludes that respondent lacks prudential standing, under its new standing principle, to bring his suit in federal court.

[H]ere is the Court's new prudential standing principle: "[I]t is improper for the federal courts to entertain a claim by a plaintiff whose standing to sue is founded on family law rights that are in dispute when prosecution of the lawsuit may have an adverse effect on the person who is the source of the plaintiff's claimed standing." The Court loosely bases this novel prudential standing limitation on the domestic relations exception to diversity-of-citizenship jurisdiction pursuant to 28 U.S.C. § 1332, the abstention doctrine, and criticisms of the Court of Appeals' construction of California state law, coupled with the prudential standing prohibition on a litigant's raising another person's legal rights.

First, the Court relies heavily on Ankenbrandt v. Richards, 504 U.S. 689 (1992), in which we discussed both the domestic relations exception and the abstention doctrine. In *Ankenbrandt*, the mother of two children sued her former spouse and his female companion on behalf of the children, alleging physical and sexual abuse of the children. The lower courts declined jurisdiction based on the domestic relations exception to diversity jurisdiction and abstention under Younger v. Harris, 401 U.S. 37 (1971). We reversed, concluding that the domestic relations exception only applies

ing, they do not respond to our prudential concerns. As for taxpayer standing, Newdow does not reside in or pay taxes to the School District; he alleges that he pays taxes to the District only "indirectly" through his child support payments to Banning. That allegation does not amount to the "direct dollars-and-cents injury" that our strict taxpayer-standing doctrine requires. Doremus v. Bd. of Ed. of Hawthorne, 342 U.S. 429, 434 (1952).

when a party seeks to have a district court issue a "divorce, alimony, and child custody decree," *Ankenbrandt*, 504 U.S., at 704. We further held that abstention was inappropriate because "the status of the domestic relationship ha[d] been determined as a matter of state law, and in any event ha[d] no bearing on the underlying torts alleged," id., at 706. . . .

The domestic relations exception is not a prudential limitation on our federal jurisdiction. It is a limiting construction of the statute defining federal diversity jurisdiction, 28 U.S.C. § 1332, which "divests the federal courts of power to issue divorce, alimony, and child custody decrees," *Ankenbrandt*, 504 U.S., at 703. This case does not involve diversity jurisdiction, and respondent does not ask this Court to issue a divorce, alimony, or child custody decree. Instead it involves a substantial federal question about the constitutionality of the School District's conducting the pledge ceremony, which is the source of our jurisdiction. Therefore, the domestic relations exception to diversity jurisdiction forms no basis for denying standing to respondent.

When we discussed abstention in *Ankenbrandt*, we first noted that "[a]bstention rarely should be invoked, because the federal courts have a 'virtually unflagging obligation . . . to exercise the jurisdiction given them.'" Id., at 705 (quoting Colorado River Water Conservation Dist. v. United States, 424 U.S. 800, 817 (1976)). *Ankenbrandt*'s discussion of abstention by no means supports the proposition that only in the rare instances where "a substantial federal question . . . transcends or exists apart from the family law issue," should federal courts decide the federal issue. As in *Ankenbrandt*, "the status of the domestic relationship has been determined as a matter of state law, and in any event has no bearing on the underlying [constitutional violation] alleged." 504 U.S., at 706. Sandra Banning and respondent now share joint custody of their daughter, respondent retains the right to expose his daughter to his religious views, and the state of their domestic affairs has nothing to do with the underlying constitutional claim. Abstention forms no basis for denying respondent standing. . . .

Finally, it seems the Court bases its new prudential standing principle, in part, on criticisms of the Court of Appeals' construction of state law, coupled with the prudential principle prohibiting third-party standing. In the Court of Appeals' original opinion, it held unanimously that respondent satisfied the Article III standing requirements, stating respondent "has standing as a parent to challenge a practice that interferes with his right to direct the education of his daughter." Newdow v. United States Congress, 292 F.3d 597, 602 (9th Cir. 2002). After Banning moved for leave to intervene, the Court of Appeals reexamined respondent's standing to determine whether the parents' court-ordered custodial arrangement altered respondent's standing. Newdow v. United States Congress, 313 F.3d 500 (9th Cir. 2002). The court examined whether respondent could assert an injury in fact by asking whether, under California law, "noncustodial parents maintain the right to expose and educate their children to their individual religious views, even if those religious views contradict those of the custodial parent." Id., at 504. The Court of Appeals again unanimously concluded that the respondent satisfied Article III standing, despite the custody order, because he retained sufficient parental rights under California law. Id., at 504–05 (citing In re Marriage of Murga v. Peterson, 103 Cal. App. 3d 498, 163 Cal. Rptr. 79 (1980); In re Marriage of Mentry, 142 Cal. App. 3d 260, 190 Cal. Rptr. 843 (1983)).

The Court, contrary to the Court of Appeals' interpretation of California case law, concludes that respondent "requests relief that is more ambitious than that sought in *Mentry* and *Murga*" because he seeks to restrain the act of a third party outside the parent-child sphere. The Court then mischaracterizes respondent's alleged interest based on the Court's de novo construction of California law.

The correct characterization of respondent's interest rests on the interpretation of state law. As the Court recognizes, we have a "settled and firm policy of deferring to regional courts of appeals in matters that involve the construction of state law." Bowen v. Massachusetts, 487 U.S. 879, 908 (1988). We do so "not only to render unnecessary review of their decisions in this respect, but also to reflect our belief that district courts and courts of appeals are better schooled in and more able to interpret the laws of their respective States." Brockett v. Spokane Arcades, Inc., 472 U.S. 491, 500 (1985) (internal quotation marks and citation omitted). In contrast to the Court, I would defer to the Court of Appeals' interpretation of California law because it is our settled policy to do so, and because I think that the Court of Appeals has the better reading of *Murga*, supra, and *Mentry*, supra.

The Court does not take issue with the fact that, under California law, respondent retains a right to influence his daughter's religious upbringing and to expose her to his views. But it relies on Banning's view of the merits of this case to diminish respondent's interest, stating that the respondent "wishes to forestall his daughter's exposure to religious ideas that her mother, who wields a form of veto power, endorses, and to use his parental status to challenge the influences to which his daughter may be exposed in school when he and Banning disagree." As alleged by respondent and as recognized by the Court of Appeals, respondent wishes to enjoin the School District from endorsing a form of religion inconsistent with his own views because he has a right to expose his daughter to those views without the State's placing its imprimatur on a particular religion. Under the Court of Appeals' construction of California law, Banning's "veto power" does not override respondent's right to challenge the pledge ceremony.

The Court concludes that the California cases "do not stand for the proposition that [respondent] has a right to dictate to others what they may or may not say to his child respecting religion." Surely, under California case law and the current custody order, respondent may not tell

Banning what she may say to their child respecting religion, and respondent does not seek to. Just as surely, respondent cannot name his daughter as a party to a lawsuit against Banning's wishes. But his claim is different: Respondent does not seek to tell just anyone what he or she may say to his daughter, and he does not seek to vindicate solely her rights.

Respondent asserts that the School District's pledge ceremony infringes his right under California law to expose his daughter to his religious views. While she is intimately associated with the source of respondent's standing (the father-daughter relationship and respondent's rights thereunder), the daughter is not the source of respondent's standing; instead it is their relationship that provides respondent his standing, which is clear once respondent's interest is properly described. The Court's criticisms of the Court of Appeals' Article III standing decision and the prudential prohibition on third-party standing provide no basis for denying respondent standing.

Although the Court may have succeeded in confining this novel principle almost narrowly enough to be, like the proverbial excursion ticket—good for this day only—our doctrine of prudential standing should be governed by general principles, rather than ad hoc improvisations.

[In their separate opinions concurring in the judgment, Justices O'Connor and Thomas addressed the merits of the Establishment Clause claim, which they both rejected. They did not write separately on standing.]

Page 459, delete Section 3: The Political Question, pages 459–75, and substitute the following:

SECTION 3: THE POLITICAL QUESTION

INTRODUCTORY NOTES ON THE HISTORY OF THE DOCTRINE

1. *Luther v. Borden.* The political question doctrine asserts that some issues are in some sense too "political" for judicial resolution. Cases presenting such issues are said to be nonjusticiable.

This idea has a long history. The leading early case arose out of the Dorr Rebellion against the "charter" government of Rhode Island. Dorr was elected governor under a new state constitution in 1842, but the pre-existing charter government refused to admit the validity of these proceedings. Dorr tried to take power by force, but was repulsed. The charter government then called a constitutional convention, and a peaceful transition to the new government was made in May 1843.

In 1842 Borden and other state officers, acting under the authority of martial law, broke into Luther's house. Luther sued for trespass, claiming that the charter government had been displaced in 1842 and therefore could not authorize the defendants' acts. In this way, Luther sought to litigate the existence and authority of the charter government in the interval between the purported approval of a new constitution in May 1842 and the actual transfer of authority to the new government in May 1843. The lower court, however, declined to consider this issue and entered a verdict for defendants. In Luther v. Borden, 48 U.S. (7 How.) 1 (1849), the Supreme Court affirmed.

Speaking through Chief Justice Taney, the Court offered several reasons for refusing to inquire into the continued validity of the charter government. Grave practical difficulties would follow if all acts of the established government could be called into question. Moreover, the state courts had approved the charter government's authority during that period and accepted its acts as valid. Finally, as to Art. IV, § 4, which provides that the "United States shall guarantee to every State a Republican Form of Government," Taney disclaimed judicial authority:

> Congress must necessarily decide what government is established in the state before it can determine whether it is republican or not. And when the senators and representatives of a state are admitted into the councils of the Union, the authority of the government under which they are appointed, as well as its republican character, is recognized by the proper constitutional authority. And its decision is binding on every other department of the government, and could not be questioned in a judicial tribunal.

2. Baker v. Carr. After *Luther v. Borden,* guarantee clause questions were usually held nonjusticiable.[a] This position eventually assumed great importance, for it blocked attempts to litigate the constitutionality of legislative malapportionment. In Colegrove v. Green, 328 U.S. 549 (1946), for example, the Court refused to reach the merits of a constitutional attack on Illinois' congressional districting. Speaking for a plurality, Justice Frankfurter described the issue as one "of a peculiarly political nature and therefore not meet for judicial determination." The controversy concerned "matters that bring courts into immediate and active relations with party contests," an involvement from which the courts have "traditionally remained aloof." In subsequent cases, the Court followed *Colegrove* in turning aside constitutional attacks on legislative districting. See, e.g., South v. Peters, 339 U.S. 276 (1950).

---

a. See, e.g., Taylor & Marshall v. Beckham, 178 U.S. 548 (1900) (refusing to adjudicate the claim that state resolution of a disputed gubernatorial election deprived the voters of a republican form of government); Pacific States Tel. & Tel. Co. v. Oregon, 223 U.S. 118 (1912) (refusing to adjudicate company's claim that a special tax imposed by initiative and referendum rather than by the usual legislative process violated the guarantee clause). See generally Arthur Earl Bonfield, The Guarantee Clause of Article IV, Section 4: A Study in Constitutional Desuetude, 46 Minn.L.Rev. 513 (1962).

All this was changed by Baker v. Carr, 369 U.S. 186 (1962). Plaintiffs claimed that the malapportionment of the Tennessee legislature denied equal protection to voters in the more populous districts. The trial court dismissed the suit on the authority of *Colegrove*, but the Supreme Court reversed. Speaking for the Court, Justice Brennan said that "the mere fact that the suit seeks protection of a political right does not mean it presents a political question." Brennan found the guarantee-clause cases irrelevant. The nonjusticiability of such claims had "nothing to do with their touching upon matters of state governmental organization." Their only significance was in holding that the particular constitutional provision was "not a repository of judicially manageable standards." The equal protection clause was different.

Brennan recast the political question doctrine as exclusively concerned with separation of powers: "[I]t is the relationship between the judiciary and the coordinate branches of the federal government, and not the federal judiciary's relationship to the states, which gives rise to the 'political question.'"

Finally, in a famous passage Brennan identified the ingredients of a "political question":

> Prominent on the surface of any case held to involve a political question is found a textually demonstrable constitutional commitment of the issue to a coordinate political department; or a lack of judicially discoverable and manageable standards for resolving it; or the impossibility of deciding without an initial policy determination of a kind clearly for nonjudicial discretion; or the impossibility of a court's undertaking independent resolution without expressing lack of the respect due coordinate branches of government; or an unusual need for unquestioning adherence to a political decision already made; or the potentiality of embarrassment from multifarious pronouncements by various departments on one question.

Unless one of these factors is "inextricable from the case at bar," said the Court, there should be no dismissal for nonjusticiability on the ground of a political question. Accordingly, the case was remanded for trial on the merits.[b]

3. ***Powell v. McCormack.*** *Baker v. Carr* listed six factors. Powell v. McCormack, 395 U.S. 486 (1969), isolated one of those factors—the "textually demonstrable constitutional commitment"—and construed it in a way that threatened to end the political question exception to justiciability.

The question was whether the House of Representatives could refuse to seat Representative Adam Clayton Powell, Jr., on the grounds that he

---

b. Two years later, in Reynolds v. Sims, 377 U.S. 533 (1964), the Court ruled that both houses of a state legislature must be elected from districts "as nearly of equal population as is practicable."

had misused House funds. Powell sued Speaker John W. McCormack and other officials, claiming that he could not be excluded from the House for dishonesty but only for failure to meet the three requirements of Art. I, § 2, cl. 2: "No Person shall be a Representative who shall not have attained to the Age of twenty five Years, and been several Years a Citizen of the United States, and who shall not, when elected, be an Inhabitant of that State in which he shall be chosen." The defendants claimed that the issue was a political question and therefore nonjusticiable.

Speaking for the Court, Chief Justice Warren focused on *Baker*'s first criterion—"a textually demonstrable constitutional commitment of the issue to a coordinate political department." The House had a good candidate. Art. I, § 5, cl. 1 provides that "Each House shall be the Judge of the Elections, Returns and Qualifications of its own Members...." The Chief Justice responded, however, that "[i]n order to determine the scope of any 'textual commitment' under Art. I, § 5, we necessarily must determine the meaning" of that provision. After examining the history of the question, the Court concluded that "the Constitution leaves the House without authority to *exclude* any person, duly elected by his constituents, who meets all the requirements for membership expressly prescribed in the Constitution."[c]

Under this approach, the political question doctrine is self-liquidating. The Constitution will never contain a textual commitment to act contrary to the Constitution. If the Court construes the Constitution on the merits in order to determine the authority of another branch, there is no room left for an independent doctrine of nonjusticiability. So construed, the political question doctrine shields from judicial scrutiny only those actions that the judges have interpreted the Constitution to permit. In other words, the doctrine applies only where it does not matter.

Nevertheless, *Powell v. McCormack* purported to apply the political question doctrine, not to kill it. Thus, the door was left ajar for revival in future cases of the idea that political concerns might render a case nonjusticiable.[d]

---

c. A different question would have been presented had the House *expelled* Representative Powell after he had been seated. Art. I, § 5, cl. 2 explicitly provides for the authority to expel a Member but requires "the Concurrence of two thirds." Representative Powell was *excluded* on a simple majority vote.

d. The first post-*Powell* application of the doctrine came in Gilligan v. Morgan, 413 U.S. 1 (1973), which arose in the aftermath of the shootings at Kent State University in May 1970. Members of the student government sued to enjoin the governor from premature use of the National Guard and to enjoin the Guard from violating students' rights. Most aspects of the suit were dismissed, but the Court of Appeals ordered a trial on the claim that the training and leadership of the Ohio National Guard made the unnecessary use of deadly force "inevitable." The Supreme Court reversed. Characterizing the complaint as a "broad call on judicial power to assume continuing regulatory jurisdiction over the activities of the Ohio National Guard" and commenting that it is "difficult to conceive of an area of governmental activity in which the courts have less competence," Chief Justice Burger found a political

4. *Nixon v. United States*. Walter Nixon was a federal judge who was convicted of making false statements before a grand jury investigating a bribery scandal. Although sentenced to prison, Judge Nixon refused to resign his office. The House of Representatives therefore impeached him, and the case moved to the Senate for trial. The Senate proceeded under a rule allowing the presiding officer to appoint a committee of Senators to "receive evidence and take testimony." The committee did so and reported back to the full Senate, which, after briefing and argument, voted to remove Nixon from office. Nixon then sued, claiming that the Senate's use of a committee violated its constitutional obligation under Art. I, § 3, cl. 6, which provides that, "The Senate shall have the sole Power to *try* all Impeachments" [emphasis added]. Nixon claimed that the use of a committee to hear evidence was so unlike a judicial trial that it violated the Constitution. The Supreme Court had no trouble rejecting this claim, but divided over whether the suit was nonjusticiable.

Writing for the Court, Chief Justice Rehnquist first examined the meaning of the word "try" and concluded that it "lack[ed] sufficient precision to afford any judicially manageable standard of review of the Senate's actions." This conclusion was reinforced by the Constitution's reference to the Senate's "sole" power and by considerations of history and separation of powers. Although suffused with consideration of the merits, the Court's opinion purported to conclude that the controversy was nonjusticiable.

In an opinion concurring in the judgment, Justice White, joined by Justice Blackmun, insisted that Nixon's claim was justiciable, albeit without merit. Justice White admitted, however, that "it will likely make little difference whether the Court's or my view controls this case."[e]

Vieth v. Jubelirer
Supreme Court of the United States, 2004.
541 U.S. 267.

■ JUSTICE SCALIA announced the judgment of the Court and delivered an opinion, in which THE CHIEF JUSTICE, JUSTICE O'CONNOR, and JUSTICE THOMAS join.

Plaintiff-appellants ... challenge a map drawn by the Pennsylvania General Assembly establishing districts for the election of congressional

---

question within the meaning of *Baker v. Carr*.

e. For divergent reactions to this decision, see Rebecca L. Brown, When Political Questions Affects Individual Rights: The Other *Nixon v. United States*, 1993 Sup. Ct. Rev. 125 (criticizing the curtailment of judicial review); Michael J. Gerhardt, Rediscovering Nonjusticiability: Judicial Review of Impeachments after *Nixon*, 44 Duke L.J. 231 (1994) (defending the political question doctrine as peculiarly appropriate for impeachments).

Representatives, on the ground that the district constitutes an unconstitutional political gerrymander. . . .

I

[Plaintiffs were registered Democrats, who claimed that the redistricting following the 2000 census by the Republican-controlled state legislature constituted an unconstitutional political gerrymander. A three-judge court convened pursuant to 28 U.S.C. § 2284 dismissed the gerrymander claim, and plaintiffs appealed directly to the Supreme Court.]

II

Political gerrymanders are not new to the American scene. . . . [In 1812], there occurred the notoriously outrageous political districting in Massachusetts that gave the gerrymander its name—an amalgam of Massachusetts Governor Elbridge Gerry and the creature ("salamander") which the outline of an election district he was credited with forming was thought to resemble. . . .

It is significant that the Framers provided a remedy for such practices in the Constitution. Art. I, § 4, while leaving in state legislatures the initial power to draw districts for federal elections, permitted Congress to "make or alter" those districts if it wished.[3] . . . The power bestowed on Congress to regulate elections, and in particular to restrain the practice of political gerrymandering, has not lain dormant. In the Apportionment Act of 1842, Congress provided that Representatives must be elected from single-member districts "composed of contiguous territory." Congress again imposed these requirements in the Apportionment Act of 1862, and in 1872 further required that districts "contai[n] as nearly as practicable an equal number of inhabitants." In the Apportionment Act of 1901, Congress imposed a compactness requirement. The requirements of contiguity, compactness, and equality of population were repeated in the 1911 apportionment legislation, but were not thereafter continued. Today, only the single-member-district-requirement remains. Recent history, however, attests to Congress's awareness of the sort of districting practices appellants protest, and of its power under Art. I, § 4 to control them. Since 1980, no fewer than five bills have been introduced to regulate gerrymandering in congressional districting.

Eighteen years ago, we held that the Equal Protection Clause grants judges the power—and duty—to control political gerrymandering. Davis v. Bandemer, 478 U.S. 109 (1986). It is to consideration of this precedent that we now turn.

---

3. Art. I, § 4 provides as follows: "The Times, Places and Manner of holding Elections for Senators and Representatives, shall be prescribed in each State by the Legislature thereof; but the Congress may at any time by Law make or alter such Regulations, except as to the Places of chusing Senators."

III

As Chief Justice Marshall proclaimed two centuries ago, "[I]t is emphatically the province and duty of the judicial department to say what the law is." Marbury v. Madison, 5 U.S. (1 Cranch) 137, 177 (1803). Sometimes, however, the law is that the judicial department has no business entertaining the claim of unlawfulness—because the question is entrusted to one of the political branches or involves no judicially enforceable rights. Such questions are said to be "nonjusticiable," or "political questions."

In Baker v. Carr, 369 U.S. 186, 217 (1962), we set forth six independent tests for the existence of a political question:

> [1] a textually demonstrable constitutional commitment of the issue to a coordinate political department; or [2] a lack of judicially discoverable and manageable standards for resolving it; or [3] the impossibility or deciding without an initial policy determination of a kind clearly for nonjudicial discretion; or [4] the impossibility of a court's undertaking independent resolution without expressing lack of the respect due coordinate branches of government; or [5] an unusual need for unquestioning adherence to a political decision already made; or [6] the potentiality of embarrassment from multifarious pronouncements by various departments on one question.

These tests are probably listed in descending order of both importance and certainty. The second is at issue here....

Over the dissent of three Justices, the Court held in *Davis v. Bandemer* that, since it was "not persuaded that there are no judicially discernible and manageable standards by which political gerrymander cases are to be decided," such cases *were* justiciable. The clumsy shifting of the burden of proof for the premise (the Court was "not persuaded" that standards do not exist, rather than "persuaded" that they do) was necessitated by the uncomfortable fact that the six-Justice majority could not discern what the judicially discernable standards might be. There was no majority on that point. ...

Nor can it be said that the lower courts have, over 18 years, succeeded in shaping the standard that this Court was initially unable to enunciate. They have simply applied the standard set forth in *Bandemer*'s four-Justice plurality opinion. This might be thought to prove that the four-Justice plurality standard has met the test of time—but for the fact that its application has almost invariably produced the same result (except for the incurring of attorney's fees) as would have obtained if the question were nonjusticiable: judicial intervention has been refused. As one commentary has put it, "[t]hroughout its subsequent history, *Bandemer* has served almost exclusively as an invitation to litigation without much prospect of redress." S. Issacharoff, P. Karlan, & R. Pildes, The Law of Democracy 886 (rev. 2d ed. 2002). The one case in which relief was provided (and merely preliminary relief, at that) did *not* involve the drawing of district lines;[5] in *all* of the cases we are aware of involving that most common form of political gerrymandering, relief was denied.

Eighteen years of judicial effort with virtually nothing to show for it justify us in revisiting the question whether the standard promised by *Bandemer* exists. As the following discussion reveals, no judicially discernible and manageable standards for adjudicating political gerrymandering claims have emerged. Lacking them, we must conclude that political gerrymandering claims are nonjusticiable and that *Bandemer* was wrongly decided.

A

We begin our review of possible standards with that proposed by Justice White's plurality opinion in *Bandemer*.... The plurality concluded that a political gerrymandering claim could succeed only where plaintiffs showed "both intentional discrimination against an identifiable political group and an actual discriminatory effect on that group." As to the intent element, the plurality acknowledged that "[a]s long as redistricting is done by a legislature, it should not be very difficult to prove that the likely political consequences of the reapportionment were intended." However, the effects prong was significantly harder to satisfy. Relief could not be based merely upon the fact that a group of persons banded together for political purposes had failed to achieve representation commensurate with its numbers, or that the apportionment scheme made its winning of elections more difficult. Rather, it would have to be shown that, taking into account a variety of historical factors and projected election results, the group had been "denied its chance to effectively influence the political process" as a whole, which could be achieved even without electing a candidate. It would not be enough to establish, for example, that Democrats had been "placed in a district with a supermajority of other Democratic voters" or that the district "departs from pre-existing political boundaries." Rather, in a challenge to an individual district the inquiry would focus "on the opportunity of members of the group to participate in party deliberations in the slating and nomination of candidates, their opportunity

---

5. See Republican Party of North Carolina v. Martin, 980 F.2d 943 (4th Cir. 1992) (upholding denial of Federal Rule of Civil Procedure 12(b)(6) judgment for the defendants); Republic Party of North Carolina v. North Carolina State Board of Elections, 27 F.3d 563 (4th Cir. 1994) (unpublished opinion) (upholding, as modified, a preliminary injunction). *Martin* dealt with North Carolina's system of electing superior court judges statewide, a system that had resulted in the election of only a single Republican judge since 1900.

[In a later footnote, the plurality noted that in 1994 the district court found a violation of *Bandemer*, and five days later, the Republicans won *every* contested superior court judge election statewide. That result caused the Fourth Circuit to remand the case for reconsideration. Republican Party of North Carolina v. Hunt, 77 F.3d 470 (4th Cir.1996) (per curiam) (unpublished).—Addition to footnote by eds.]

to register and vote, and hence their chance to directly influence the election returns and to secure the attention of the winning candidate." A statewide challenge, by contrast, would involve an analysis of the "the voters' direct *or indirect* influence on the elections of the state legislature as a whole." (Emphasis added). With what has proved to be a gross understatement, the plurality acknowledged this was "of necessity a difficult inquiry." . . .

In the lower courts, the legacy of the plurality's test is one long record of puzzlement and consternation. . . . Because this standard was misguided when proposed, has not been improved in subsequent application, and is not even defended before us today by the appellants, we decline to affirm it as a constitutional requirement.

B

Appellants take a run at enunciating their own workable standard based on Art. I, § 2, and the Equal Protection Clause. . . . Appellants' proposed standard retains the two-pronged framework of the *Bandemer* plurality—intent plus effect—but modifies the type of showing sufficient to establish each.

To satisfy appellants' intent standard, a plaintiff must "show that the mapmakers acted with a *predominant intent* to achieve partisan advantage," which can be shown "by direct evidence or by circumstantial evidence that other neutral and legitimate redistricting criteria were subordinated to the goal of achieving partisan advantage." (Emphasis added). As compared with the *Bandemer* plurality's test of mere intent to disadvantage the plaintiff's group, this proposal seemingly makes the standard more difficult to meet—but only at the expense of making the standard more indeterminate.

"Predominant intent" to disadvantage the plaintiff political group refers to the relative importance of that goal as compared with all the other goals that the map seeks to pursue—contiguity of district, compactness of districts, observance of the lines of political subdivision, protection of incumbents of all parties, cohesion of natural racial and ethnic neighborhoods, compliance with requirements of the Voting Rights Act of 1965 regarding racial distribution, etc. Appellants contend that their intent test *must* be discernible and manageable because it has been borrowed from our racial gerrymandering cases. See Miller v. Johnson, 515 U.S. 900 (1995); Shaw v. Reno, 509 U.S. 630 (1993). To begin with, in a very important respect that is not so. In the racial gerrymandering context, the predominant intent test has been applied to the challenged district in which the plaintiffs voted. Here, however, appellants do not assert that an apportionment fails their intent test if any single district does so. Since "it would be quixotic to attempt to bar state legislatures from considering politics as they redraw district lines," appellants propose a test that is satisfied only when "partisan advantage was the predominant motivation *behind the entire statewide plan.*" (Emphasis added.) Vague as the "predominant motivation" test might be when used to evaluate single districts, it all but evaporates when applied statewide. Does it mean, for example, that partisan intent must outweigh all other goals—contiguity, compactness, preservation of neighborhoods, etc.—*statewide*? And how is the statewide "outweighing" to be determined? If three-fifths of the map's districts forgo the pursuit of partisan ends in favor of strictly observing political-subdivision lines, and only two-fifths ignore those lines to disadvantage the plaintiffs, is the observance of political subdivisions the "predominant" goal between those two? We are sure appellants do not think so.

Even within the narrower compass of challenges to a single district, applying a "predominant intent" test to *racial* gerrymandering is easier and less disruptive. The Constitution clearly contemplates districting by political entities, see Art. I, § 4, and unsurprisingly that turns out to be root-and-branch a matter of politics. By contrast, the purpose of segregating voters on the basis of race is not a lawful one, and is much more rarely encountered. Determining whether the shape of a particular district is so substantially affected by the presence of a rare and constitutionally suspect motive as to invalidate it is quite different from determining whether it is so substantially affected by the excess of an ordinary and lawful motive as to invalidate it. Moreover, the fact that partisan districting is a lawful and common practice means that there is almost *always* room for an election-impeding lawsuit contending that partisan advantage was the predominant motivation; not so for claims of racial gerrymandering. Finally, courts might be justified in accepting a modest degree of unmanageability to enforce constitutional command which (like the 14th Amendment obligation to refrain from racial discrimination) is clear; whereas they are not justified in inferring a judicially enforceable constitutional obligation (the obligation not to apply *too much* partisanship in districting) which is both dubious and severely unmanageable. For these reasons, to the extent that our racial gerrymandering cases represent a model of discernible and manageable standards, they provide no comfort here.

The effects prong of appellants' proposal replaces the *Bandemer* plurality's vague test of "denied its chance to effectively influence the political process," with criteria that are seemingly more specific. The requisite effect is established when "(1) the plaintiffs show that the districts systematically 'pack' and 'crack' the rival party's voters,[7] *and* the (2) the court's examination of the 'totality of the circumstances' confirms that the map can thwart the plaintiffs' ability to translate a majority of votes into a majority of seats." Brief for Appellants 20 (emphasis and footnote added). This test is based loosely on our cases applying § 2 of the Voting Rights Act, 42 U.S.C. § 1973, to discrimination by race, see e.g., Johnson v. De Grandy, 512 U.S.

---

7. "Packing" refers to the practice of filling a district with a supermajority of a given group or party. "Cracking" involving the splitting of a group or party among several districts to deny that group or party a majority in any of those districts.

997 (1994). But a person's politics is rarely as readily discernible—and *never* as permanently discernible—as a person's race. Political affiliation is not an immutable characteristic, but may shift from one election to the next; and even within a given election, not all voters follow the party line. We dare say (and hope) that the political party which puts forward an utterly incompetent candidate will lose even in its registration stronghold. These facts make it impossible to assess the effects of partisan gerrymandering, to fashion a standard for evaluating a violation, and finally to craft a remedy.

Assuming, however, that the effects of partisan gerrymandering can be determined, appellants' test would invalidate the districting only when it prevents a majority of the electorate from electing a majority of representatives. Before considering whether this particular standard is judicially manageable we question whether it is judicially discernible in the sense of being relevant to some constitutional violation. Deny it as appellants may (and do), this standard rests upon the principle that groups (or at least political-action groups) have a right to proportional representation. But the Constitution contains no such principle. It guarantees equal protection of the law to persons, not equal representation in government to equivalently sized groups. It nowhere says that farmers or urban dwellers, Christian fundamentalists or Jews, Republicans or Democrats, must be accorded political strength in proportion to their total numbers.

Even if the standard were relevant, however, it is not judicially manageable. To begin with, how is a party's majority status to be determined? Appellants propose using the results of statewide races as the benchmark of party support. But as their own complaint describes, in the 2000 Pennsylvania statewide elections some Republicans won and some Democrats won. Morever, to think that majority status in statewide races establishes majority status for district contests, one would have to believe that the only factor determining voting behavior at all levels is political affiliation. That is assuredly not true. As one law review comment has put it:

> There is no statewide vote in this country for the House of Representatives or the state legislature. Rather, there are separate elections between separate candidates in separate districts, and that is all there is. If the districts change, the candidates change, their strengths and weaknesses change, their campaigns change, their ability to raise money changes, the issues change—everything changes. Political parties do not compete for the highest statewide vote totals or the highest mean district vote percentages: They compete for specific seats.

Lowenstein & Steinberg, Partisan Gerrymandering: A Political Problem Without Judicial Solution, in Political Gerrymandering and the Courts 240, 241 (B. Grofman ed., 1990).

But if we could identify a majority party, we would find it impossible to assure that that party wins a majority of seats—unless we radically revise the States' traditional structure for elections. In any winner-take-all district system, there can be no guarantee, no matter how the district lines are drawn that a majority of party votes statewide will produce a majority of seats for that party. . . . Consider, for example, a legislature that draws district lines with no objectives in mind except compactness and respect for the lines of political subdivisions. Under that system, political groups that tend to cluster (as is the case with Democratic voters in cities) would be systematically affected by what might be called a "natural" packing effect.

Our one-person, one-vote cases, see Reynolds v. Sims, 377 U.S. 533 (1964); Wesberry v. Sanders, 376 U.S. 1 (1964), have no bearing upon this question. . . . [T]he easily administrable standard of population equality adopted by *Wesberry* and *Reynolds* enables judges to decide whether a violation has occurred (and to remedy it) essentially on the basis of three readily determined factors—where the plaintiff lives, how many voters are in his district, and how many voters are in other districts; whereas requiring judges to decide whether a district system will produce a statewide majority for a majority party casts them forth upon a sea of imponderables, and asks them to make determinations that not even election experts can agree upon.

For these reasons, we find appellants' proposed standards neither discernible nor manageable.

C

For many of the same reasons, we also reject the standard suggested by Justice Powell in *Bandemer*. He agreed with the plurality that a plaintiff should show intent and effect, but believed that the ultimate inquiry ought to focus on whether district boundaries had been drawn solely for partisan ends to the exclusion of "all other neutral factors relevant to the fairness of districting." Under that inquiry, the courts should consider numerous factors. . . . The most important would be "the shapes of voting districts and adherence to established political subdivision boundaries." "Other relevant considerations include the nature of the legislative procedures by which the apportionment law was adopted and legislative history reflecting contemporaneous legislative goals." These factors, which "bear directly on the fairness of a redistricting plan," combined with "evidence concerning population disparities and statistics tending to show vote dilution," make out a claim of unconstitutional partisan gerrymandering. Ibid.

[This] is essentially a totality-of-the-circumstances analysis, where all conceivable factors, none of which is dispositive, are weighed with an eye to ascertaining whether the particular gerrymander has gone too far—or, in Justice Powell's terminology, whether it is not "fair." "Fairness" does not seem to us a judicially manageable standard. . . . Some criterion more solid and more demonstrably met than that seems to us necessary to enable the state legislatures to discern the limits of their districting discretion, to meaningfully constrain the discretion of the courts, and to win public acceptance for the courts' intrusion into a process that is at the very founding of democratic decisionmaking. . . .

[The remainder of the lengthy plurality opinion addressed defects in the various solutions proposed in the dissenting opinions of Justices Stevens, Souter (joined by Ginsburg), and Breyer and in the position adopted by Justice Kennedy.]

Eighteen years of essentially pointless litigation have persuaded us that *Bandemer* is incapable of principled application. We would therefore overrule that case, and decline to adjudicate these political gerrymandering claims.

■ JUSTICE KENNEDY, concurring in the judgment.

A decision ordering the correction of all election district lines drawn for partisan reasons would commit federal and state courts to unprecedented intervention in the American political process. The Court is correct to refrain from directing this substantial intrusion into the Nation's political life. . . .

There are . . . weighty arguments for holding cases like these to be nonjusticiable; and those arguments may prevail in the long run. In my view, however, the arguments are not so compelling that they require us now to bar all future claims of injury from a partisan gerrymander. . . .

The failings of the many proposed standards for measuring the burden a gerrymander imposes on representational rights make our intervention improper. If workable standards do emerge to measure these burdens, however, courts should be prepared to order relief. With these observations, I join the judgment of the plurality.

■ JUSTICE STEVENS, dissenting.

The central question presented by this case is whether political gerrymandering claims are justiciable. Although our reasons for coming to this conclusion differ, five Members of the Court are convinced that the plurality's answer to that question is erroneous. Moreover, as is apparent from our separate writings today, we share the view that, even if these appellants are not entitled to prevail, it would be contrary to precedent and profoundly unwise to foreclose all judicial review of similar claims that might be advanced in the future. . . .

Although we reaffirm the central holding of the Court in Davis v. Bandemer, 478 U.S. 109 (1986), we have not reached agreement on the standard that should govern partisan gerrymandering claims. I would decide this case on a narrow ground. Plaintiff-appellants urge us to craft new rules that in effect would authorize judicial review of statewide election results to protect the democratic process from a transient majority's abuse of its power to define voting districts. I agree with the Court's refusal to undertake that ambitious project. I am persuaded, however, that the District Court failed to apply well-settled propositions of law when it granted the defendants' motion to dismiss plaintiff-appellant Susan Furey's gerrymandering claim.

According to the complaint, Furey is a registered Democrat who resides at an address in Montgomery County, Pennsylvania, that was located under the 1992 districting plan in Congressional District 13. Under the new plan, adopted by the General Assembly in 2002, Furey's address now places her in the "non-compact" District 6. Furey alleges that the new districting plan was created "solely" to effectuate the interests of Republicans, and that the General Assembly relied "exclusively" on a principle of "maximum partisan advantage" when drawing the plan. In my judgment, Furey's allegations are plainly sufficient to establish: (1) that she has standing to challenge the constitutionality of District 6; (2) that her district-specific claim is not foreclosed by the *Bandemer* plurality's rejection of a statewide claim of political gerrymandering; and (3) that she has stated a claim that, at least with respect to District 6, Pennsylvania's redistricting plan violates the equal protection principles enunciated in our voting rights cases both before and after *Bandemer*. . . .

The plurality opinion in *Bandemer* dealt with a claim that the Indiana apportionment scheme for state legislative districts discriminated against Democratic voters on a statewide basis. In my judgment, the *Bandemer* Court was correct to entertain the statewide challenge, because the plaintiffs in that case alleged a group harm that affected members of their party throughout the State. In the subsequent line of racial gerrymandering cases, however, the Court shifted its focus from statewide challenges and required, as a matter of standing, that plaintiffs stating race-based equal protection claims actually reside in the districts they are challenging. See United States v. Hays, 515 U.S. 737, 745 (1995). Because *Hays* has altered the standing rules for gerrymandering claims—and because, in my view, racial and political gerrymanders are species of the same constitutional concern—the *Hays* standing rule requires dismissal of the statewide claim. . . .

A challenge to a specific district or districts, on the other hand, alleges a different type of injury entirely—one that our recent racial gerrymandering cases have recognized as cognizable. In Shaw v. Reno, 509 U.S. 630 (1993) (*Shaw I*), we [upheld a claim of racial gerrymandering.] After describing the pernicious consequences of race-conscious districting—even when designed to enhance the representation of the minority—and after explaining why dramatically irregular shapes " 'have sufficient probative force to call for an explanation,' " we described the message a misshapen district sends to elected officials:

> When a district obviously is created solely to effectuate the perceived common interests of one racial group, elected officials are more likely to believe that their primary obligation is to represent

only the members of that group, rather than their constituency as a whole. This is altogether antithetical to our system of representative democracy.

Undergirding the *Shaw* cases is the premise that racial gerrymanders effect a constitutional wrong when they disrupt the representational norms that ordinarily tether elected officials to their constituencies as a whole. ...

The risk of representational harms identified in the *Shaw* cases is equally great, if not greater, in the context of partisan gerrymanders. *Shaw I* was born of the concern that an official elected from a racially gerrymandered district will feel beholden only to a portion of her constituents, and that those constituents will be defined by race. The parallel danger of a partisan gerrymander is that the representative will perceive that the people who put her in power are those who drew the map rather than those who cast ballots. ...

In evaluating a claim that a governmental decision violates the Equal Protection Clause, we have long required a showing of discriminatory purpose. See Washington v. Davis, 426 U.S. 229 (1976). That requirement applies with full force to districting decisions. ... Consistent with that principle, our recent racial gerrymandering cases have examined the shape of the district and the purpose of the districting body to determine whether race, above all other criteria, predominated in the line-drawing process. We began by holding in *Shaw I* that a districting scheme could be "so irrational on its face that it [could] be understood only as an effort to segregate voters into separate voting districts because of their race." ... Just as irrational shape can serve as an objective indicator of an impermissible legislative purpose, other objective features of a districting map can save the plan from invalidation. We have explained that "traditional districting principles," which include "compactness, contiguity, and respect for political subdivisions," are "important not because they are constitutionally required ... but because they are objective factors that may serve to defeat a claim that a district has been gerrymandered on racial lines." *Shaw I*, 509 U.S., at 647. ...

In my view, the same standards should apply to claims of political gerrymandering.... The racial gerrymandering cases therefore supply a judicially manageable standard for determining when partisanship, like race, has played too great a role in the districting process. Just as race can be a factor in, but cannot dictate the outcome of, the districting process, so too can partisanship be a permissible consideration in drawing lines, so long as it does not predominate. If, as plaintiff-appellant Furey has alleged, the predominant motive of the legislators who designed District 6, and the sole justification for its bizarre shape, was a purpose to discriminate against a political minority, that invidious purpose should invalidate the district. ...

In sum, in evaluating a challenge to a specific district, I would apply the standard set forth in the *Shaw* cases and ask whether the legislature allowed partisan considerations to dominate and control the lines drawn, forsaking all neutral principles. Under my analysis, if no neutral criterion can be identified to justify the lines drawn, and if the only possible explanation for a district's bizarre shape is a naked desire to increase partisan strength, then no rational basis exists to save the district from an equal protection challenge. Such a narrow test would cover only a few meritorious claims, but it would preclude extreme abuses . . . and would perhaps shorten the time period in which the pernicious effects of such a gerrymander are felt. This test would mitigate the current trend under which partisan considerations are becoming the be-all and end-all in apportioning representatives. . . .

■ JUSTICE SOUTER, with whom JUSTICE GINSBURG joins, dissenting. . . .

The plurality says, in effect, that courts have been trying to devise practical criteria for political gerrymandering for nearly 20 years, without being any closer to something workable than we were when Davis v. Bandemer, 478 U.S. 109 (1986), was decided. While this is true enough, I do not accept it as sound counsel of despair. For I take it that the principal reason we have not gone from theoretical justiciability to practical administrability in political gerrymandering cases is that the *Davis* plurality's specification that any criterion of forbidden gerrymandering must require a showing that members of the plaintiff's group had "essentially been shut out of the political process." That is, in order to avoid a threshold for relief so low that almost any electoral defeat (let along failure to achieve proportionate results) would support a gerrymandering claim, the *Davis* plurality required a demonstration of such pervasive devaluation over such a period of time as to raise real doubt that a case could ever be made out. . . .

Since this Court has created the problem no one else has been able to solve, it is up to us to make a fresh start. There are a good many voices saying it is high time that we did, for in the years since *Davis*, the increasing efficiency of partisan redistricting has damaged the democratic process to a degree that our predecessors only began to imagine. E.g., Issacharoff, Gerrymandering and Political Cartels, 116 Harv. L. Rev. 593, 624 (2002)(The "pattern of incumbent entrenchment has gotten worse as the computer technology for more exquisite gerrymandering has improved"); Karlan, The Fire Next Time: Reapportionment After the 2000 Census, 50 Stan. L. Rev. 731, 736 (1998) ("Finer-grained census data, better predictive methods, and more powerful computers allow for increasingly sophisticated equipopulous gerrymanders"); Pildes, Principled Limitations on Racial and Partisan Redistricting, 106 Yale L.J. 2505, 2553–54 (1997) ("Recent cases now document in microscopic detail the astonishing precision with which redistricters can carve up individual precincts and distribute them between districts with confidence concerning the racial and partisan consequences"). . . .

I would therefore preserve *Davis*'s holding that political gerrymandering is a justiciable issue, but otherwise start anew. I would adopt a political gerrymandering test analogous to the summary judgment standard crafted in McDonnell Douglas Corp. v. Green, 411 U.S. 792 (1973), calling for a plaintiff to satisfy elements of a prima facie cause of action, at which point the State would have the opportunity not only to rebut the evidence supporting the plaintiff's case, but to offer an affirmative justification for the districting choices, even assuming the proof of the plaintiff's allegations. My own judgment is that we would have better luck at devising a workable prima facie case if we concentrated as much as possible on suspect characteristics of individual districts instead of statewide patterns. . . . [F]or now, I would conceive of a statewide challenge as itself a function of claims that individual districts are illegitimately drawn. . . .

For a claim based on a specific single-member district, I would require the plaintiff to make out a prima facie case with five elements. First, the resident plaintiff would identify a cohesive political group to which he belonged, which would normally be a major party. . . .

Second, a plaintiff would need to show that the district of his residence paid little or no heed to those traditional districting principles whose disregard can be shown straightforwardly: contiguity, compactness, respect for political subdivisions, and conformity with geographic features like rivers and mountains. Because such considerations are already relevant to justifying small deviations from absolute population equality, Karcher v. Daggett, 462 U.S. 725, 740 (1983), and because compactness in particular is relevant to demonstrating possible majority-minority district under the Voting Rights Act of 1965, Johnson v. De Grandy, 512 U.S. 997, 1008 (1994), there is no doubt that a test relying on these standards would fall within judicial competence. . . .

Third, the plaintiff would need to establish specific correlations between the district's deviations from traditional districting principles and the distribution of the population of his group. For example, one of the districts to which appellants object most strongly in this case is District 6, which they say "looms like a dragon descending on Philadelphia from the west, splitting up towns and communities throughout Montgomery and Berks Counties." To make their claim stick, they would need to point to specific protuberances on the draconian shape that reach out to include Democrats, or fissures in it that squirm away from Republicans. . . .

Fourth a plaintiff would need to present the court with a hypothetical district including his residence, one in which the proportion of the plaintiff's was lower (in a packing claim) or higher (in a cracking one) and which at the same time deviated less from traditional districting principles than the actual district. Drawing the hypothetical district would, of course, necessarily involve redrawing at least one contiguous district,[4] and a

---

[4]. It would not necessarily involve redrawing other noncontiguous districts, and I would not permit a plaintiff to ask for such a remedy unless he first made out a prima facie case as to multiple districts.

plaintiff would have to show that this could be done subject to traditional districting principles without packing or cracking his group (or another) worse than in the district being challenged.

Fifth, and finally, the plaintiff would have to show that the defendants acted intentionally to manipulate the shape of the district in order to pack or crack his group. See Washington v. Davis, 426 U.S. 229 (1976). In substantiating claims of political gerrymandering under a plan devised by a single major party, proving intent should not be hard, once the third and fourth (correlation and cause) elements are established, politicians not being politically disinterested or characteristically naive. I would, however, treat any showing of intent in a major-party case too equivocal to count unless the entire legislature were controlled by the governor's party (or the dominant legislative party were vetoproof). . . .

A plaintiff who got this far would have shown that his State intentionally acted to dilute his vote, having ignored reasonable alternatives consistent with traditional districting principles. I would then shift the burden to the defendants to justify their decision by reference to objectives other than naked partisan advantage. . . . The State might, for example, posit the need to avoid racial vote dilution. It might plead one person, one vote, a standard compatible with gerrymandering but in some places perhaps unattainable without some lopsided proportions. The State might adopt the object of proportional representation among its political parties through its districting process.

This is not, however, the time or place for a comprehensive list of legitimate objectives a State might present. The point here is simply that the Constitution should not petrify traditional districting objectives as exclusive, and it is enough to say that the State would be required to explain itself, to demonstrate whatever reasons it gave were more than a pretext for an old-fashioned gerrymander. . . .

■ JUSTICE BREYER, dissenting.

The use of purely political considerations in drawing district boundaries is not a "necessary evil" that, for lack of judicially manageable standards, the Constitution inevitably must tolerate. Rather, pure politics often helps to secure constitutionally important democratic objectives. But sometimes it does not. Sometimes purely political "gerrymandering" will fail to advance any plausible democratic objective while simultaneously threatening serious democratic harm. And sometimes when that is so, courts can identify an equal protection violation and provide a remedy. . . .

I

[O]ne should begin by asking why single-member electoral districts are the norm, why the Constitution does not insist that the membership of legislatures better reflect different political views held by different groups of voters. History, of course, is part of the answer, but it does not tell the entire story. The answer also lies in the fact that a single-member-district system helps to assure certain democratic objectives better than many "more representative" (i.e., proportional) electoral systems. Of course, single-member districts mean that only parties with candidates who finish "first past the post" will elect legislators. That fact means in turn that a party with a bare majority of votes or even a plurality of votes will often obtain a large legislative majority, perhaps freezing out smaller parties. But single-member districts thereby diminish the need for coalition governments. And that fact makes it easier for voters to identify which party is responsible for government decisionmaking (and which rascals to throw out), while simultaneously providing greater legislative stability. . . .

If single-member districts are the norm, however, the political considerations will likely play an important, and proper, role in the drawing of district boundaries. . . . Given a fairly large state population with a fairly large congressional delegation, districts assigned so as to be perfectly random in respect to politics would translate a small shift in political sentiment, say a shift from 51% Republican to 40% Republican, into a seismic shift in the makeup of the legislative delegation, say from 100% Republican to 100% Democrat. Any such exaggeration of tiny electoral changes—virtually wiping out legislative representation of the minority party—would itself seem highly undemocratic.

Given the resulting need for single-member districts with nonrandom boundaries, it is not surprising that "traditional" districting principles have rarely, if ever, been politically neutral. . . . [T]raditional or historically-based boundaries are not, and should not be, "politics free." Rather, those boundaries represent a series of compromises of principle—among the virtues of, for example, close representation of voter views, ease of identifying "government" and "opposition" parties, and stability in government. They also represent an uneasy truce, sanctioned by tradition, among different parties seeking political advantage.

As I have said, reference back to these underlying considerations helps explain why the legislature's use of political boundary drawing considerations ordinarily does *not* violate the Constitution's Equal Protection Clause. The reason lies not simply in the difficulty of identifying abuse or finding an appropriate judicial remedy. The reason is more fundamental: Ordinarily, there simply is no abuse. The use of purely political boundary-drawing factors, even where harmful to the members of one party, will often nonetheless find justification in other desirable democratic ends, such as maintaining relatively stable legislatures in which a minority party retains significant representation.

II

At the same time, these considerations can help identify at least once circumstance where use of purely political boundary-drawing factors can amount to a serious, and remediable, abuse, namely the *unjustified* use of political factors to entrench a minority in power. By entrenchment I mean a situation in which a party that enjoys only minority support among the populace has nonetheless contrived to take, and hold, legislative power. By *unjustified* entrenchment I mean that the minority's hold on power is purely the result of partisan manipulation and not other factors. . . . Unless some other justification can be found in particular circumstances, political gerrymandering that entrenches a minority party in power violates basic democratic norms and lacks countervailing justification. For this reason, whether political gerrymandering does, or does not, violate the Constitution in other instances, gerrymandering that leads to entrenchment amounts to an abuse that violates the Constitution's Equal Protection Clause.

III

Courts need not intervene often to prevent the kind of abuse I have described, because those harmed constitute a political majority, and a majority normally can work its political will. . . . But we cannot always count on a severely gerrymandered legislature itself to find and implement a remedy. The party that controls the process has no incentive to change it. . . .

When it is necessary, a court should prove capable of finding an appropriate remedy. Courts have developed districting remedies in other cases [citing Voting Rights Act and one-person, one-vote decisions]. The bottom line is that courts should be able to identify the presence of one important gerrymandering evil, the unjustified entrenching in power of a political party that the voters have rejected. They should be able to separate the unjustified abuse of partisan boundary-drawing considerations to achieve that end from their more ordinary and justified use. And they should be able to design a remedy for extreme cases.

IV

I do not claim that the problem of identification and separation is easily resolved, even in extreme instances. But courts can identify a number of strong indicia of abuse. The presence of actual entrenchment . . . is such a sign, particularly when accompanied by the use of partisan boundary drawing criteria in the way that Justice Stevens describes, i.e., a use that both departs from traditional criteria and cannot be explained other than by efforts to achieve partisan advantage. Below, I set forth several sets of circumstances that lay out the indicia of abuse I have in mind. The scenarios fall along a continuum: The more permanently entrenched the minority's hold on power becomes, the less evidence courts will need that the minority engaged in gerrymandering to achieve the desired result.

Consider, for example, the following sets of circumstances. First, suppose that the legislature has proceeded to redraw boundaries in what seem to be ordinary ways, but the entrenchment harm has become obvious. E.g., (a) the legislature has not redrawn district boundaries more than once within the traditional 10-year period; and (b) no radical departure from traditional districting criteria is alleged; but (c) a majority party (as measured by the votes actually cast for all candidates who identify themselves as members of that party in the relevant set of elections; i.e., in congressional elections if a congressional map is being challenged) has *twice* failed to obtain a majority of the relevant legislative seats in elections; and (d) the failure cannot be explained by the existence of multiple parties or in other neutral ways. In my view, these circumstances would be sufficient to support a claim of unconstitutional entrenchment.

Second, suppose that plaintiffs could point to more serious departures from redistricting norms. E.g., (a) the legislature has not redrawn district boundaries more than once within the traditional 10-year period; but the boundary-drawing criteria depart radically from previous or traditional criteria; (c) the departure cannot be justified or explained other than by reference to an effort to obtain partisan advantage; and (d) a majority party (as defined above) has once failed to obtain a majority of the relevant seats in [an] election using the challenged map (which fact cannot be explained by the existence of multiple parties or in other neutral ways). These circumstances could also add up to unconstitutional gerrymandering.

Third, suppose that the legislature clearly departs from ordinary districting norms, but the entrenchment harm, while seriously threatened, has not yet occurred. E.g., (a) the legislature has redrawn district boundaries more than once within the traditional 10-year census-related period—either, as here, at the behest of a court that struck down an initial plan as unlawful, see Vieth v. Pennsylvania, 195 F. Supp. 2d 672 (M.D. Pa. 2002) (finding that Pennsylvania's first redistricting plan violated the one person, one-vote mandate), or of its own accord; (b) the boundary-drawing criteria depart radically from previous traditional boundary-drawing criteria; (c) strong, objective, unrefuted statistical evidence demonstrates that a party with a minority of the popular vote within the State in all likelihood will obtain a majority of the seats in the relevant representative delegation; and (d) the jettisoning of traditional districting criteria cannot be justified or explained other than by reference to an effort to obtain partisan political advantage. To my mind, such circumstances could also support a claim, because the presence of midcycle redistricting, for any reason, raises a fair inference that partisan machinations played a major role in the map-drawing process. . . .

In the case before us, there is a strong likelihood that the plaintiffs' complaint could be amended readily to assert circumstances consistent with those I have set forth as appropriate for judicial intervention. For that reason, I would authorize the plaintiffs to proceed; and I dissent from the majority's contrary determination.

ADDITIONAL NOTES ON THE POLITICAL QUESTION

1. Questions and Comments on *Vieth v. Jubelirer*. Unlike some political-question cases, *Vieth v. Jubelirer* presents an issue of broad application and great importance. Political gerrymandering is widespread, consequential, and, from a judicial point of view, apparently intractable. Almost everyone agrees that unrestrained partisanship in drawing district lines is a bad thing, but it is hard to know what to do about it. In particular, it is hard to know whether courts should get deeply involved and, if so, on what criteria. The various opinions in *Vieth* introduce that problem and the arguments on both sides.

For present purposes, perhaps the most important analytical question is whether the various concerns debated in *Vieth* are properly conceptualized as relating to justiciability. One might think of them as related to the merits: Does the Constitution forbid *all* consideration of partisan advantage in districting (a position embraced by none of the Justices), or does it forbid only *too much* consideration of partisan advantage, or does it forbid nothing at all unless race or some other independently invalid factor is involved? Is there conceptual advantage in formulating the problem one way or the other? Are there useful analogies to the law of racial gerrymandering? What, if anything, turns on the terms of the analysis?

2. The Political Question Doctrine in Foreign Affairs: *Goldwater v. Carter*. Though successful resort to the political question doctrine in purely domestic disputes is unusual, the doctrine may have greater vitality in foreign affairs. Courts often invoke the political question doctrine to defeat attempts to litigate the legality of U.S. foreign policy. The chief example is the Vietnam War. See, e.g., Atlee v. Richardson, 411 U.S. 911 (1973). Subsequent efforts to challenge American military actions abroad have usually met the same fate. See, e.g., Crockett v. Reagan, 720 F.2d 1355 (D.C.Cir.1983) (dismissing a legal challenge to U.S. military involvement in El Salvador); Sanchez–Espinoza v. Reagan, 770 F.2d 202 (D.C.Cir. 1985) (dismissing a legal challenge to U.S. aid to the Nicaraguan "Contras").[a]

A noteworthy application of the political question doctrine occurred when members of Congress sued President Carter to challenge the Presi-

---

a. Even in foreign affairs cases, the political question doctrine does not always prevail. In Ramirez de Arellano v. Weinberger, 745 F.2d 1500 (D.C.Cir.1984), a U.S. citizen who owned a cattle ranch in Honduras challenged the use of his land to establish a U.S.-sponsored regional training center for the army of El Salvador. Despite the obvious foreign policy implications, the D.C. Circuit found this suit justiciable. Speaking for the majority, Judge Wilkey noted that the complaint did not purport to challenge the conduct of foreign policy but merely asserted the right of a U.S. citizen to be free from illegal occupation and seizure of his property. To dismiss this suit as a political question, said Wilkey, "would mean that virtually *anything* done by the United States officials to United States citizens on foreign soil is nonjusticiable.... That is not the law." The Supreme Court granted certiorari, vacated the judgment below, and remanded for reconsideration in light of later developments. Weinberger v. Ramirez de Arellano, 471 U.S. 1113 (1985).

dent's power to terminate a mutual defense treaty with Taiwan. The treaty included a power of termination but did not specify how that power could be exercised. The District Court held that the President could not act unilaterally. The Court of Appeals reversed. In Goldwater v. Carter, 444 U.S. 996 (1979), the Supreme Court ordered the complaint dismissed.

Speaking for himself and three others, Justice Rehnquist found a political question. Since the Constitution did not speak to the question of congressional participation in the termination of treaties, the issue should "be controlled by political standards." This was especially so because the question involved foreign relations, an area in which the courts have traditionally been reluctant to intervene. Justice Marshall concurred in the result without opinion.

Other Justices were, to one or another degree, willing to address the merits. Justice Powell disagreed that the case presented a political question but nevertheless concluded that the dispute would not be ripe for adjudication "unless and until each branch has taken action asserting its constitutional authority" and the conflict has reached "constitutional impasse." Justices Blackmun and White voted to set the case for argument. Finally, Justice Brennan voted to affirm the judgment of the Court of Appeals on the ground that the President's action was supported by the established presidential authority to recognize foreign governments.

3. The Political Question Doctrine and Judicial Review. To the extent that the political question doctrine actually affects results, there are fundamental questions concerning its relation to judicial review. Is the doctrine a sensible restraint on judicial activism or an unprincipled evasion of judicial responsibility? This question has drawn the attention of leading scholars.

Herbert Wechsler argued, partly in rebuttal to Learned Hand, that the power of judicial review is no mere invention of necessity but is "grounded in the language of the Constitution." Herbert Wechsler, Toward Neutral Principles of Constitutional Law, 73 Harv. L. Rev. 1, 3 (1959). This premise led to a narrow view of the doctrine of the political question:

> [A]ll the doctrine can defensibly imply is that the courts are called upon to judge whether the Constitution has committed to another agency of government the autonomous determination of the issue raised, a finding that itself requires interpretation. [T]he only proper judgment that may lead to an abstention from decision is that the Constitution has committed the determination of the issue to another agency of government than the courts. Difficult as it may be to make that judgment wisely, whatever factors may be rightly weighed in situations where the answer is not clear, what is involved is itself an act of constitutional interpretation, to be made and judged by standards that should govern the interpretive process generally. This, I submit, is toto caelo different from a broad discretion to abstain or intervene.

This pronouncement produced a response from Alexander Bickel:

> [O]nly by means of a play on words can the broad discretion that the courts have in fact exercised be turned into an act of constitutional interpretation. The political-question doctrine simply resists being domesticated in this fashion. There is something different about it, in kind, not in degree, from the general "interpretive process"; something greatly more flexible, something of prudence, not construction and not principle. And it is something that cannot exist within the four corners of *Marbury v. Madison*.

Alexander Bickel, The Supreme Court, 1960 Term—Foreword: The Passive Virtues, 75 Harv. L. Rev. 40, 46 (1961). (Bickel later expanded these views in his book, The Least Dangerous Branch (1962).)

For Bickel, as for Wechsler, the scope of the political question doctrine was intimately related to the rationale for judicial review. For Bickel, however, judicial review was not so much a *duty,* imposed by the Constitution on an obedient Court, as a *power,* to be used or withheld on the basis of discerning judgment. In Bickel's view, the task of the Court was to safeguard principle in a world of political expediency. "[T]he role of the Court and its raison d'etre are to evolve, to defend, and to protect principle." In some circumstances, it would be appropriate for the Court to attempt to coerce adherence to principle by the political branches. In others, "there ought to be discretion free of principled rules." After all, "no society, certainly not a large and heterogeneous one, can fail in time to explode if it is deprived of the arts of compromise, if it knows no way to muddle through." In such situations, the Court may have to tolerate unprincipled actions, but it should at least avoid "legitimating" them by pronouncements of constitutionality.

It is in this frame of reference that Bickel placed his view of a political question:

> Such is the basis of the political question doctrine: the Court's sense of lack of capacity, compounded in unequal part of the strangeness of the issue and the suspicion that it will have to yield more often and more substantially to expediency than to principle; the sheer momentousness of it, which unbalances judgment and prevents one from subsuming the normal calculations of probabilities; the anxiety not so much that judicial judgment will be ignored, as that perhaps it should be, but won't; finally and in sum ("in a mature democracy"), the inner vulnerability of an institution which is electorally irresponsible and has no earth to draw strength from.

These views drew the a riposte accusing Bickel of a "100 percent insistence on principle, 20 percent of the time." Gerald Gunther, The Subtle Vices of the "Passive Virtues"—A Comment on Principle and Expediency in Judicial Review, 64 Colum. L. Rev. 1 (1964). In Gunther's view, Bickel's reliance on prudential considerations was "ultimately law-debasing."

Which is the better view of the legitimacy of nonjusticiability determinations for politically sensitive issues? Does the answer depend on how the doctrine is interpreted and applied?

4. Bibliography. In addition to the works already cited, see Theodore Y. Blumoff, Judicial Review, Foreign Affairs and Legislative Standing, 25 Ga. L. Rev. 227 (1991) (analyzing legislative standing in foreign affairs cases); Linda Champlin and Alan Schwarz, Political Question Doctrine and Allocation of the Foreign Affairs Power, 13 Hofstra L. Rev. 215 (1985) (arguing that the political question doctrine involves an *assumption* of constitutionality that is only proper, if at all, in some foreign affairs controversies); Louis Henkin, Is There a "Political Question" Doctrine?, 85 Yale L.J. 597 (1976) (arguing that the political question doctrine is "an unnecessary, deceptive packaging" of several established limitations on the judicial role, none of which depends on any extraordinary notion of nonjusticiability); Wayne McCormack, The Justiciability Myth and the Concept of Law, 14 Hastings Const. L.Q. 595 (1987)(arguing that there is—or should be—"no such thing" as a political question doctrine); Wayne McCormack, The Political Question Doctrine—Jurisprudentially, 70 U. Det. Mercy L. Rev. 793 (1993) (reiterating that the political question doctrine is "nothing more than a subterfuge for making explicit review on the merits of particular claims"); J. Peter Mulhern, In Defense of the Political Question Doctrine, 137 U. Pa. L. Rev. 97 (1988) (endorsing the political question doctrine as a useful device allowing courts "to remove themselves from areas in which they do not belong"); Martin H. Redish, Judicial Review and the "Political Question," 79 Nw. U.L. Rev. 1031 (1985) (arguing, in response to Henkin, that there is, but that there should not be, a political question doctrine); Fritz W. Scharpf, Judicial Review and the Political Question: A Functional Analysis, 75 Yale L.J. 517 (1966) (analyzing both the "classical," i.e. Wechsler, and "prudential," i.e., Bickel, versions of the doctrine); Linda Sandstrom Simard, Standing Alone: Do We Still Need the Political Question Doctrine, 100 Dickinson L. Rev. 303 (1996) (arguing that the evolution of standing doctrine and the increasing restrictions it places on federal court adjudication have obviated the need for an independent doctrine of the political question). For comments on *Powell v. McCormack,* see the Symposium in 17 U.C.L.A. L. Rev. 1 (1969).

For a more recent major article, see Rachel E. Barkow, More Supreme Than Court? The Fall of the Political Question Doctrine and the Rise of Judicial Supremacy, 102 Colum. L. Rev. 237 (2002). Barkow documents and criticizes the demise of the political question doctrine and relates that development to a "disconcerting" rise in "judicial immodesty" that has left the Supreme Court "blind to its own aggrandizement at the expense of the other branches."

Finally, for a wide-ranging essay discussing when the political question doctrine matters and why, see Louis Michael Seidman, The Secret Life of the Political Question Doctrine, 37 John Marshall L. Rev. 441 (2004).

CHAPTER V

SUBJECT MATTER JURISDICTION

Page 479, add at the end of footnote d:

For exploration of the implications of *Holmes* in the context of patent litigation, see Christopher A. Cotropia, "Arising Under" Jurisdiction and Uniformity in Patent Law, 9 Mich. Telecomm. & Tech. L. Rev. 253 (2003). Cotropia concludes that "uniformity in patent law created by the Federal Circuit could potentially be undone" by *Holmes.*

Page 487, read with the Note on *Merrill Dow Pharmaceuticals, Inc. v. Thompson*:

Grable & Sons Metal Products, Inc. v. Darue Engineering & Manufacturing

Supreme Court of the United States, 2005.
545 U.S. ___.

■ JUSTICE SOUTER delivered the opinion of the Court.

The question is whether want of a federal cause of action to try claims of title to land obtained at a federal tax sale precludes removal to federal court of a state action with non-diverse parties raising a disputed issue of federal title law. We answer no, and hold that the national interest in providing a federal forum for federal tax litigation is sufficiently substantial to support the exercise of federal question jurisdiction over the disputed issue on removal, which would not distort any division of labor between the state and federal courts, provided or assumed by Congress.

I

In 1994, the Internal Revenue Service seized Michigan real property belonging to petitioner Grable & Sons Metal Products, Inc., to satisfy Grable's federal tax delinquency. Title 26 U.S.C. § 6335 required the IRS to give notice of the seizure, and there is no dispute that Grable received actual notice by certified mail before the IRS sold the property to respondent Darue Engineering & Manufacturing. Although Grable also received notice of the sale itself, it did not exercise its statutory right to redeem the property within 180 days of the sale, § 6337(b)(1), and after that period had passed, the Government gave Darue a quitclaim deed. § 6339.

Five years later, Grable brought a quiet title action in state court, claiming that Darue's record title was invalid because the IRS had failed to notify Grable of its seizure of the property in the exact manner required by

§ 6335(a), which provides that written notice must be "given by the Secretary to the owner of the property [or] left at his usual place of abode or business." Grable said that the statute required personal service, not service by certified mail.

Darue removed the case to Federal District Court as presenting a federal question, because the claim of title depended on the interpretation of the notice statute in the federal tax law. The District Court declined to remand the case at Grable's behest after finding that the "claim does pose a significant question of federal law," and ruling that Grable's lack of a federal right of action to enforce its claim against Darue did not bar the exercise of federal jurisdiction. On the merits, the court granted summary judgment to Darue, holding that although § 6335 by its terms required personal service, substantial compliance with the statute was enough.

The Court of Appeals for the Sixth Circuit affirmed. On the jurisdictional question, the panel thought it sufficed that the title claim raised an issue of federal law that had to be resolved, and implicated a substantial federal interest (in construing federal tax law). The court went on to affirm the District Court's judgment on the merits. We granted certiorari on the jurisdictional question alone, to resolve a split within the Courts of Appeals on whether Merrell Dow Pharmaceuticals Inc. v. Thompson, 478 U.S. 804 (1986), always requires a federal cause of action as a condition for exercising federal-question jurisdiction. We now affirm.

II

Darue was entitled to remove the quiet title action if Grable could have brought it in federal district court originally, 28 U.S.C. § 1441(a), as a civil action "arising under the Constitution, laws, or treaties of the United States," § 1331. This provision for federal-question jurisdiction is invoked by and large by plaintiffs pleading a cause of action created by federal law (e.g., claims under 42 U.S.C. § 1983). There is, however, another long-standing, if less frequently encountered, variety of federal "arising under" jurisdiction, this Court having recognized for nearly 100 years that in certain cases federal question jurisdiction will lie over state-law claims that implicate significant federal issues. E.g., Hopkins v. Walker, 244 U.S. 486, 490–91 (1917). The doctrine captures the commonsense notion that a federal court ought to be able to hear claims recognized under state law that nonetheless turn on substantial questions of federal law, and thus justify resort to the experience, solicitude, and hope of uniformity that a federal forum offers on federal issues, see ALI, Study of the Division of Jurisdiction Between State and Federal Courts 164–66 (1968).

The classic example is Smith v. Kansas City Title & Trust Co., 255 U.S. 180 (1921), a suit by a shareholder claiming that the defendant corporation could not lawfully buy certain bonds of the National Government because their issuance was unconstitutional. Although Missouri law provided the cause of action, the Court recognized federal-question jurisdiction because the principal issue in the case was the federal constitutionality of the bond issue. *Smith* thus held, in a somewhat generous statement of the scope of the doctrine, that a state-law claim could give rise to federal-question jurisdiction so long as it "appears from the [complaint] that the right to relief depends upon the construction or application of [federal law]."

The *Smith* statement has been subject to some trimming to fit earlier and later cases recognizing the vitality of the basic doctrine, but shying away from the expansive view that mere need to apply federal law in a state-law claim will suffice to open the "arising under" door. As early as 1912, this Court had confined federal-question jurisdiction over state-law claims to those that "really and substantially involv[e] a dispute or controversy respecting the validity, construction or effect of [federal] law." Shulthis v. McDougal, 225 U.S. 561, 569 (1912). This limitation was the ancestor of Justice Cardozo's later explanation that a request to exercise federal-question jurisdiction over a state action calls for a "common-sense accommodation of judgment to [the] kaleidoscopic situations" that present a federal issue, in "a selective process which picks the substantial causes out of the web and lays the other ones aside." Gully v. First Nat. Bank in Meridian, 299 U.S. 109, 117–18 (1936). It has in fact become a constant refrain in such cases that federal jurisdiction demands not only a contested federal issue, but a substantial one, indicating a serious federal interest in claiming the advantages thought to be inherent in a federal forum.

But even when the state action discloses a contested and substantial federal question, the exercise of federal jurisdiction is subject to a possible veto. For the federal issue will ultimately qualify for a federal forum only if federal jurisdiction is consistent with congressional judgment about the sound division of labor between state and federal courts governing the application of § 1331. Thus, Franchise Tax Bd. of Cal. v. Construction Laborers Vacation Trust for Southern Cal., 463 U.S. 1, 28 (1983), explained that the appropriateness of a federal forum to hear an embedded issue could be evaluated only after considering the "welter of issues regarding the interrelation of federal and state authority and the proper management of the federal judicial system." Because arising-under jurisdiction to hear a state-law claim always raises the possibility of upsetting the state-federal line drawn (or at least assumed) by Congress, the presence of a disputed federal issue and the ostensible importance of a federal forum are never necessarily dispositive; there must always be an assessment of any disruptive portent in exercising federal jurisdiction.

These considerations have kept us from stating a "single, precise, all-embracing" test for jurisdiction over federal issues embedded in state-law claims between nondiverse parties. Christianson v. Colt Industries Operating Corp., 486 U.S. 800, 821 (1988) (Stevens, J., concurring). We have not kept them out simply because they appeared in state raiment, as Justice Holmes would have done, see *Smith*, supra, at 214, (dissenting opinion), but neither have we treated "federal issue" as a password opening federal courts to any state action embracing a point of federal law. Instead, the question is, does a state-law claim necessarily raise a stated federal issue, actually disputed and substantial, which a federal forum may entertain without disturbing any congressionally approved balance of federal and state judicial responsibilities.

III

A

This case warrants federal jurisdiction. Grable's state complaint must specify "the facts establishing the superiority of [its] claim," Mich. Ct. Rule 3.411(B)(2)(c) (West 2005), and Grable has premised its superior title claim on a failure by the IRS to give it adequate notice, as defined by federal law. Whether Grable was given notice within the meaning of the federal statute is thus an essential element of its quiet title claim, and the meaning of the federal statute is actually in dispute; it appears to be the only legal or factual issue contested in the case. The meaning of the federal tax provision is an important issue of federal law that sensibly belongs in a federal court. The Government has a strong interest in the "prompt and certain collection of delinquent taxes," United States v. Rodgers, 461 U.S. 677, 709 (1983), and the ability of the IRS to satisfy its claims from the property of delinquents requires clear terms of notice to allow buyers like Darue to satisfy themselves that the Service has touched the bases necessary for good title. The Government thus has a direct interest in the availability of a federal forum to vindicate its own administrative action, and buyers (as well as tax delinquents) may find it valuable to come before judges used to federal tax matters. Finally, because it will be the rare state title case that raises a contested matter of federal law, federal jurisdiction to resolve genuine disagreement over federal tax title provisions will portend only a microscopic effect on the federal-state division of labor.

This conclusion puts us in venerable company, quiet title actions having been the subject of some of the earliest exercises of federal-question jurisdiction over state-law claims. In *Hopkins,* 244 U.S., at 490–91, the question was federal jurisdiction over a quiet title action based on the plaintiffs' allegation that federal mining law gave them the superior claim. Just as in this case, "the facts showing the plaintiffs' title and the existence and invalidity of the instrument or record sought to be eliminated as a cloud upon the title are essential parts of the plaintiffs' cause of action."[3]

---

3. The quiet title cases also show the limiting effect of the requirement that the federal issue in a state-law claim must actually be in dispute to justify federal-question jurisdiction. In Shulthis v. McDougal, 225 U.S. 561 (1912), this Court found that there was no federal question jurisdiction to hear a plaintiff's quiet title claim in part because the federal statutes on which title depended were not subject to "any controversy respecting their validity, construction, or effect." As the Court put it, the requirement of an actual dispute about federal law was "especially" important in "suit[s] involving rights to land

As in this case again, "it is plain that a controversy respecting the construction and effect of the [federal] laws is involved and is sufficiently real and substantial." This Court therefore upheld federal jurisdiction in *Hopkins*, as well as in the similar quiet title matters of Northern Pacific R. Co. v. Soderberg, 188 U.S. 526, 528 (1903), and Wilson Cypress Co. v. Del Pozo Y Marcos, 236 U.S. 635, 643–44 (1915). Consistent with those cases, the recognition of federal jurisdiction is in order here.

B

Merrell Dow Pharmaceuticals Inc. v. Thompson, 478 U.S. 804 (1986), on which Grable rests its position, is not to the contrary. *Merrell Dow* considered a state tort claim resting in part on the allegation that the defendant drug company had violated a federal misbranding prohibition, and was thus presumptively negligent under Ohio law. The Court assumed that federal law would have to be applied to resolve the claim, but after closely examining the strength of the federal interest at stake and the implications of opening the federal forum, held federal jurisdiction unavailable. Congress had not provided a private federal cause of action for violation of the federal branding requirement, and the Court found "it would ... flout, or at least undermine, congressional intent to conclude that federal courts might nevertheless exercise federal-question jurisdiction and provide remedies for violations of that federal statute solely because the violation ... is said to be a ... 'proximate cause' under state law."

Because federal law provides for no quiet title action that could be brought against Darue,[4] Grable argues that there can be no federal jurisdiction here, stressing some broad language in *Merrell Dow* (including the passage just quoted) that on its face supports Grable's position, see Note, Mr. Smith Goes to Federal Court: Federal Question Jurisdiction over State Law Claims Post-*Merrell Dow,* 115 Harv. L.Rev. 2272, 2280–82 (2002) (discussing split in Circuit Courts over private right of action requirement after *Merrell Dow*). But an opinion is to be read as a whole, and *Merrell Dow* cannot be read whole as overturning decades of precedent, as it would have done by effectively adopting the Holmes dissent in *Smith,* and converting a federal cause of action from a sufficient condition for federal-question jurisdiction[5] into a necessary one.

In the first place, *Merrell Dow* disclaimed the adoption of any bright-line rule, as when the Court reiterated that "in exploring the outer reaches

acquired under a law of the United States," because otherwise "every suit to establish title to land in the central and western states would so arise [under federal law], as all titles in those States are traceable back to those laws."

4. Federal law does provide a quiet title cause of action against the Federal Government. 28 U.S.C. § 2410. That right of action is not relevant here, however, because the federal government no longer has any interest in the property, having transferred its interest to Darue through the quitclaim deed.

5. For an extremely rare exception to the sufficiency of a federal right of action, see Shoshone Mining Co. v. Rutter, 177 U.S. 505, 507 (1900).

of § 1331, determinations about federal jurisdiction require sensitive judgments about congressional intent, judicial power, and the federal system." The opinion included a lengthy footnote explaining that questions of jurisdiction over state-law claims require "careful judgments," about the "nature of the federal interest at stake."[a] And as a final indication that it

---

[a] Justice Souter was referring to footnote 12, which appeared at the end of the passage from Justice Stevens' *Merrell Dow* opinion quoted in the Casebook at page 488. That footnote read:

> Several commentators have suggested that our § 1331 decisions can best be understood as an evaluation of the nature of the federal interest at stake. See, e.g., Shapiro, Jurisdiction and Discretion, 60 N.Y.U.L.Rev. 543, 568 (1985); C. Wright, Federal Courts 96 (4th ed. 1983); Cohen, The Broken Compass: The Requirement That a Case Arise "Directly" Under Federal Law, 115 U.Pa.L.Rev. 890, 916 (1967). Cf. Kravitz v. Homeowners Warranty Corp., 542 F.Supp. 317, 320 (ED Pa.1982) (Pollak, J.) ("I cannot identify any compelling reasons of federal judicial policy for embracing a case of this kind as a federal question case. The essential Pennsylvania elements of plaintiffs' suit for rescission would be more appropriately dealt with by a Court of Common Pleas than by this court; and, with respect to the lesser-included issue of federal law, Pennsylvania's courts are fully competent to interpret the Magnuson–Moss Warranty Act and the relevant F.T.C. regulations, subject to review by the United States Supreme Court").
>
> Focusing on the nature of the federal interest, moreover, suggests that the widely perceived "irreconcilable" conflict between the finding of federal jurisdiction in Smith v. Kansas City Title & Trust Co., 255 U.S. 180 (1921), and the finding of no jurisdiction in Moore v. Chesapeake & Ohio R. Co., 291 U.S. 205 (1934), see, e.g., M. Redish, Federal Jurisdiction: Tensions in the Allocation of Judicial Power 67 (1980), is far from clear. For the difference in results can be seen as manifestations of the differences in the nature of the federal issues at stake. In *Smith*, as the Court emphasized, the issue was the constitutionality of an important federal statute. See 255 U.S., at 201 ("It is ... apparent that the controversy concerns the constitutional validity of an act of Congress which is directly drawn in question. The decision depends upon the determination of this issue"). In *Moore*, in contrast, the Court emphasized that the violation of the federal standard as an element of state tort recovery did not fundamentally change the state tort nature of the action. See 291 U.S., at 216–17 (" 'The action fell within the familiar category of cases involving the duty of a master to his servant. This duty is defined by the common law, except as it may be modified by legislation. The federal statute, in the present case, touched the duty of the master at a single point and, save as provided in the statute, the right of the plaintiff to recover was left to be determined by the law of the State' ").
>
> The importance of the nature of the federal issue in federal-question jurisdiction is highlighted by the fact that, despite the usual reliability of the Holmes test as an inclusionary principle, this Court has sometimes found that formally federal causes of action were not properly brought under federal-question jurisdiction because of the overwhelming predominance of state-law issues. See Shulthis v. McDougal, 225 U.S. 561, 569–70 (1912) ("A suit to enforce a right which takes its origin in the laws of the United States is not necessarily, or for that reason alone, one arising under those laws, for a suit does not so arise unless it really and substantially involves a dispute or controversy respecting the validity, construction or effect of such a law, upon the determination of which the result depends. This is especially so of a suit involving rights to land acquired under a law of the United States. If it were not, every suit to establish title to land in the central and western States would so arise, as all titles in those States are traceable back to those laws"); Shoshone Mining Co. v. Rutter, 177 U.S. 505, 507 (1900) ("We pointed out in the former opinion that it was well settled that a suit to enforce a right which takes its origin in the laws of the United States is

did not mean to make a federal right of action mandatory, it expressly approved the exercise of jurisdiction sustained in *Smith,* despite the want of any federal cause of action available to *Smith's* shareholder plaintiff. *Merrell Dow* then, did not toss out, but specifically retained the contextual enquiry that had been *Smith's* hallmark for over 60 years. At the end of *Merrell Dow,* Justice Holmes was still dissenting.

Accordingly, *Merrell Dow* should be read in its entirety as treating the absence of a federal private right of action as evidence relevant to, but not dispositive of, the "sensitive judgments about congressional intent" that § 1331 requires. The absence of any federal cause of action affected *Merrell Dow's* result two ways. The Court saw the fact as worth some consideration in the assessment of substantiality. But its primary importance emerged when the Court treated the combination of no federal cause of action and no preemption of state remedies for misbranding as an important clue to Congress's conception of the scope of jurisdiction to be exercised under § 1331. The Court saw the missing cause of action not as a missing federal door key, always required, but as a missing welcome mat, required in the circumstances, when exercising federal jurisdiction over a state misbranding action would have attracted a horde of original filings and removal cases raising other state claims with embedded federal issues. For if the federal labeling standard without a federal cause of action could get a state claim into federal court, so could any other federal standard without a federal cause of action. And that would have meant a tremendous number of cases.

One only needed to consider the treatment of federal violations generally in garden variety state tort law. "The violation of federal statutes and regulations is commonly given negligence per se effect in state tort proceedings."[6] Restatement (Third) of Torts (proposed final draft) § 14, Comment a. ... A general rule of exercising federal jurisdiction over state claims resting on federal mislabeling and other statutory violations would thus have heralded a potentially enormous shift of traditionally state cases into federal courts. Expressing concern over the "increased volume of federal litigation," and noting the importance of adhering to "legislative intent," *Merrell Dow* thought it improbable that the Congress, having made no provision for a federal cause of action, would have meant to welcome any state-law tort case implicating federal law "solely because the violation of

not necessarily one arising under the Constitution or laws of the United States, within the meaning of the jurisdiction clauses, for if it did every action to establish title to real estate (at least in the newer States) would be such a one, as all titles in those States come from the United States or by virtue of its laws").

To the citations in the first paragraph of Justice Stevens' footnote 12, one might add Daniel J. Meltzer, Jurisdiction and Discretion Revisited, 79 Notre Dame L. Rev. 1891, 1911–15 (2004).—[Footnote by eds.]

6. Other jurisdictions treat a violation of a federal statute as evidence of negligence or, like Ohio itself in Merrell Dow Pharmaceuticals Inc. v. Thompson, 478 U.S. 804 (1986), as creating a rebuttable presumption of negligence. Restatement (Third) of Torts (proposed final draft) § 14, Comment c. Either approach could still implicate issues of federal law.

the federal statute is said to [create] a rebuttable presumption [of negligence] ... under state law." In this situation, no welcome mat meant keep out. *Merrell Dow's* analysis thus fits within the framework of examining the importance of having a federal forum for the issue, and the consistency of such a forum with Congress's intended division of labor between state and federal courts.

As already indicated, however, a comparable analysis yields a different jurisdictional conclusion in this case. Although Congress also indicated ambivalence in this case by providing no private right of action to Grable, it is the rare state quiet title action that involves contested issues of federal law, see n. 3, supra. Consequently, jurisdiction over actions like Grable's would not materially affect, or threaten to affect, the normal currents of litigation. Given the absence of threatening structural consequences and the clear interest the Government, its buyers, and its delinquents have in the availability of a federal forum, there is no good reason to shirk from federal jurisdiction over the dispositive and contested federal issue at the heart of the state-law title claim.[7]

IV

The judgment of the Court of Appeals, upholding federal jurisdiction over Grable's quiet title action, is affirmed.

It is so ordered.

■ JUSTICE THOMAS, concurring.

The Court faithfully applies our precedents interpreting 28 U.S.C. § 1331 to authorize federal-court jurisdiction over some cases in which state law creates the cause of action but requires determination of an issue of federal law, e.g., Smith v. Kansas City Title & Trust Co., 255 U.S. 180 (1921); Merrell Dow Pharmaceuticals Inc. v. Thompson, 478 U.S. 804 (1986). In this case, no one has asked us to overrule those precedents and adopt the rule Justice Holmes set forth in American Well Works Co. v. Layne & Bowler Co., 241 U.S. 257 (1916), limiting § 1331 jurisdiction to cases in which federal law creates the cause of action pleaded on the face of the plaintiff's complaint. In an appropriate case, and perhaps with the benefit of better evidence as to the original meaning of § 1331's text, I would be willing to consider that course.*

---

7. At oral argument Grable's counsel espoused the position that after *Merrell Dow*, federal-question jurisdiction over state-law claims absent a federal right of action, could be recognized only where a constitutional issue was at stake. There is, however, no reason in text or otherwise to draw such a rough line. As *Merrell Dow* itself suggested, constitutional questions may be the more likely ones to reach the level of substantiality that can justify federal jurisdiction. But a flat ban on statutory questions would mechanically exclude significant questions of federal law like the one this case presents.

* This Court has long construed the scope of the statutory grant of federal-question jurisdiction more narrowly than the scope of the constitutional grant of such jurisdiction. See Merrell Dow Pharmaceuticals Inc. v. Thompson, 478 U.S. 804, 807–08

Jurisdictional rules should be clear. Whatever the virtues of the *Smith* standard, it is anything but clear. [As the Court states at various points of its opinion,] the standard "calls for a 'common-sense accommodation of judgment to [the] kaleidoscopic situations' that present a federal issue, in 'a selective process which picks the substantial causes out of the web and lays the other ones aside' " (quoting Gully v. First Nat. Bank in Meridian, 299 U.S. 109, 117–18 (1936)); "[T]he question is, does a state-law claim necessarily raise a stated federal issue, actually disputed and substantial, which a federal forum may entertain without disturbing any congressionally approved balance of federal and state judicial responsibilities"; " '[D]eterminations about federal jurisdiction require sensitive judgments about congressional intent, judicial power, and the federal system' "; "the absence of a federal private right of action [is] evidence relevant to, but not dispositive of, the 'sensitive judgments about congressional intent' that § 1331 requires" (quoting *Merrell Dow*, supra, at 810).

Whatever the vices of the *American Well Works* rule, it is clear. Moreover, it accounts for the " 'vast majority' " of cases that come within § 1331 under our current case law, *Merrell Dow*, supra, at 808—further indication that trying to sort out which cases fall within the smaller *Smith* category may not be worth the effort it entails. Accordingly, I would be willing in appropriate circumstances to reconsider our interpretation of § 1331.

Page 493, add at the end of Note 10:

For historically grounded analysis of the concept of "cause of action," with particular attention to "arising under" jurisdiction, standing, and implied rights of action, see Anthony J. Bellia, Jr., Article III and the Cause of Action, 89 Iowa L. Rev. 777 (2004).

Page 511, add a footnote at the end of the first indented quotation at the top of the page:

f. The Court followed *Metropolitan Life Ins. v. Taylor* in Aetna Health Inc. v. Davila, 542 U.S. 200 (2004). *Aetna Health Inc.* also involved ERISA claims.—[Footnote by eds.]

Page 527, add at the end of footnote g:

It is concluded in Debra Lyn Bassett, The Hidden Bias in Diversity Jurisdiction, 81 Wash. U.L.Q. 119 (2003), that "[w]hat has been missed in [the diversity] debate is that, far from being an antidote to local bias, diversity jurisdiction today embodies, and indeed promotes, a form of bias by its very existence—a bias against rural areas so pervasive as to require the abolition of diversity jurisdiction."

(1986). I assume for present purposes that this distinction is proper—that is, that the language of 28 U.S.C. § 1331, "[t]he district courts shall have original jurisdiction of all *civil actions arising under* the Constitution, laws, or treaties of the United States" (emphasis added), is narrower than the language of Art. III, § 2, cl. 1, of the Constitution, "[t]he judicial Power shall extend to all *Cases,* in Law and Equity, *arising under* this Constitution, the Laws of the United States, and Treaties made, or which shall be made, under their Authority . . . " (emphases added).

Page 528, add at the end of footnote h:

For a response to Rowe and Sibley and criticism of an ALI proposal based on their work, see C. Douglas Floyd, The Limits of Minimal Diversity, 55 Hastings L.J. 613 (2004).

Page 528, add at the end of footnote i:

The *Caterpillar* rationale did not prevail, however, in Grupo Dataflux v. Atlas Global Group, L.P., 541 U.S. 567 (2004). In that case the Court held, by a five-to-four vote, that a post-filing change in citizenship that cured a defect in diversity jurisdiction did not save the verdict. At the time of filing, Atlas was a partnership with members in Mexico, Texas, and Delaware. It sued Grupo, a citizen of Mexico. Three years later, a six-day trial resulted in a verdict for Atlas. Because partnerships are citizens of each place in which any of its partners is a citizen, diversity was lacking when the suit was filed. In a transaction unrelated to the suit, the Mexican partners left the partnership a month before the trial. The jurisdictional issue was not identified until after the verdict. Justice Scalia for the majority held that there should be no exception on these facts to the rule that "jurisdiction . . . depends on the state of things at the time of the action brought." For the other dissenters (Stevens, Souter, and Breyer), Justice Ginsburg said that "salvage operations are ordinarily preferable to the wrecking ball."

Page 545, add to the citations in Note 2:

Jeffrey A. Parness and Daniel J. Sennott, Expanded Recognition in Written Laws of Ancillary Federal Court Powers: Supplementing the Supplemental Jurisdiction Statute, 64 U. Pitt. L. Rev. 303 (2003); James E. Pfander, The Simmering Debate Over Supplemental Jurisdiction, 2002 U. Ill. L. Rev. 1209; James M. Underwood, Supplemental Serendipity: Congress' Accidental Improvement of Supplemental Jurisdiction, 37 Akron L. Rev. 653 (2004).

Page 547, add at the end of Section 2:

Exxon Mobil Corporation v. Allapattah Services, Inc.

Supreme Court of the United States, 2005.
545 U.S. ___.

■ JUSTICE KENNEDY delivered the opinion of the Court.

These consolidated cases present the question whether a federal court in a diversity action may exercise supplemental jurisdiction over additional plaintiffs whose claims do not satisfy the minimum amount-in-controversy requirement, provided the claims are part of the same case or controversy as the claims of plaintiffs who do allege a sufficient amount in controversy. Our decision turns on the correct interpretation of 28 U.S.C. § 1367. . . .

We hold that, where the other elements of jurisdiction are present and at least one named plaintiff in the action satisfies the amount-in-controversy requirement, § 1367 does authorize supplemental jurisdiction over the claims of other plaintiffs in the same Article III case or controversy, even if those claims are for less than the jurisdictional amount specified in the statute setting forth the requirements for diversity jurisdiction. . . .

I

In 1991, about 10,000 Exxon dealers filed a class-action suit against the Exxon Corporation in the United States District Court for the Northern District of Florida. The dealers alleged an intentional and systematic scheme by Exxon under which they were overcharged for fuel purchased from Exxon. The plaintiffs invoked the District Court's § 1332(a) diversity jurisdiction. After a unanimous jury verdict in favor of the plaintiffs, the District Court certified the case for interlocutory review, asking whether it had properly exercised § 1367 supplemental jurisdiction over the claims of class members who did not meet the jurisdictional minimum amount in controversy. The Court of Appeals for the Eleventh Circuit upheld the District Court's extension of supplemental jurisdiction to these class members. . . .

In the other case now before us the Court of Appeals for the First Circuit took a different position on the meaning of § 1367(a). In that case, a 9-year-old girl sued Star–Kist in a diversity action in the United States District Court for the District of Puerto Rico, seeking damages for unusually severe injuries she received when she sliced her finger on a tuna can. Her family joined in the suit, seeking damages for emotional distress and certain medical expenses. The District Court granted summary judgment to Star–Kist, finding that none of the plaintiffs met the minimum amount-in-controversy requirement. The Court of Appeals for the First Circuit, however, ruled that the injured girl, but not her family members, had made allegations of damages in the requisite amount. . . . The court held that § 1367 authorizes supplemental jurisdiction only when the district court has original jurisdiction over the action, and that in a diversity case original jurisdiction is lacking if one plaintiff fails to satisfy the amount-in-controversy requirement. . . .

II

A

. . . In order to provide a neutral forum for what have come to be known as diversity cases, Congress . . . has granted district courts original jurisdiction in civil actions between citizens of different States, between U.S. citizens and foreign citizens, or by foreign states against U.S. citizens. To ensure that diversity jurisdiction does not flood the federal courts with minor disputes, § 1332(a) requires that the matter in controversy in a diversity case exceed a specified amount, currently $75,000.

Although the district courts may not exercise jurisdiction absent a statutory basis, it is well established—in certain classes of cases—that, once a court has original jurisdiction over some claims in the action, it may exercise supplemental jurisdiction over additional claims that are part of the same case or controversy. The leading modern case for this principle is Mine Workers v. Gibbs, 383 U.S. 715 (1966). In *Gibbs*, the plaintiff alleged the defendant's conduct violated both federal and state law. The District

Court, *Gibbs* held, had original jurisdiction over the action based on the federal claims. *Gibbs* confirmed that the District Court had the additional power (though not the obligation) to exercise supplemental jurisdiction over related state claims that arose from the same Article III case or controversy.

As we later noted, the decision allowing jurisdiction over pendent state claims in *Gibbs* did not mention, let alone come to grips with, the text of the jurisdictional statutes and the bedrock principle that federal courts have no jurisdiction without statutory authorization. Finley v. United States, 490 U.S. 545, 548 (1989). In *Finley,* we nonetheless reaffirmed and rationalized *Gibbs* and its progeny by inferring from it the interpretive principle that, in cases involving supplemental jurisdiction over additional claims between parties properly in federal court, the jurisdictional statutes should be read broadly, on the assumption that in this context Congress intended to authorize courts to exercise their full Article III power to dispose of an " 'entire action before the court [which] comprises but one constitutional case.' "

We have not, however, applied *Gibbs*' expansive interpretive approach to other aspects of the jurisdictional statutes. For instance, we have consistently interpreted § 1332 as requiring complete diversity: In a case with multiple plaintiffs and multiple defendants, the presence in the action of a single plaintiff from the same State as a single defendant deprives the district court of original diversity jurisdiction over the entire action. Strawbridge v. Curtiss, 7 U.S. (3 Cranch) 267 (1806); Owen Equipment & Erection Co. v. Kroger, 437 U.S. 365, 375 (1978). The complete diversity requirement is not mandated by the Constitution, State Farm Fire & Casualty Co. v. Tashire, 386 U.S. 523, 530–31 (1967), or by the plain text of § 1332(a). The Court, nonetheless, has adhered to the complete diversity rule in light of the purpose of the diversity requirement, which is to provide a federal forum for important disputes where state courts might favor, or be perceived as favoring, home-state litigants. The presence of parties from the same State on both sides of a case dispels this concern, eliminating a principal reason for conferring § 1332 jurisdiction over any of the claims in the action. The specific purpose of the complete diversity rule explains both why we have not adopted *Gibbs*' expansive interpretive approach to this aspect of the jurisdictional statute and why *Gibbs* does not undermine the complete diversity rule. In order for a federal court to invoke supplemental jurisdiction under *Gibbs,* it must first have original jurisdiction over at least one claim in the action. Incomplete diversity destroys original jurisdiction with respect to all claims, so there is nothing to which supplemental jurisdiction can adhere.

In contrast to the diversity requirement, most of the other statutory prerequisites for federal jurisdiction, including the federal-question and amount-in-controversy requirements, can be analyzed claim by claim. True, it does not follow by necessity from this that a district court has authority to exercise supplemental jurisdiction over all claims provided there is original jurisdiction over just one. Before the enactment of § 1367, the Court declined in contexts other than the pendent-claim instance to follow *Gibbs'* expansive approach to interpretation of the jurisdictional statutes. The Court took a more restrictive view of the proper interpretation of these statutes in so-called pendent-party cases involving supplemental jurisdiction over claims involving additional parties—plaintiffs or defendants— where the district courts would lack original jurisdiction over claims by each of the parties standing alone.

Thus, with respect to plaintiff-specific jurisdictional requirements, the Court held in Clark v. Paul Gray, Inc., 306 U.S. 583 (1939), that every plaintiff must separately satisfy the amount-in-controversy requirement. Though *Clark* was a federal-question case, at that time federal-question jurisdiction had an amount-in-controversy requirement analogous to the amount-in-controversy requirement for diversity cases. "Proper practice," *Clark* held, "requires that where each of several plaintiffs is bound to establish the jurisdictional amount with respect to his own claim, the suit should be dismissed as to those who fail to show that the requisite amount is involved." The Court reaffirmed this rule, in the context of a class action brought invoking § 1332(a) diversity jurisdiction, in Zahn v. International Paper Co., 414 U.S. 291 (1973). It follows "inescapably" from *Clark,* the Court held in *Zahn,* that "any plaintiff without the jurisdictional amount must be dismissed from the case, even though others allege jurisdictionally sufficient claims."

The Court took a similar approach with respect to supplemental jurisdiction over claims against additional defendants that fall outside the district courts' original jurisdiction. In Aldinger v. Howard, 427 U.S. 1 (1976), the plaintiff brought a 42 U.S.C. § 1983 action against county officials in district court pursuant to the statutory grant of jurisdiction in 28 U.S.C. § 1343(3). The plaintiff further alleged the court had supplemental jurisdiction over her related state-law claims against the county, even though the county was not suable under § 1983 and so was not subject to § 1343(3)'s original jurisdiction. The Court held that supplemental jurisdiction could not be exercised because Congress, in enacting § 1343(3), had declined (albeit implicitly) to extend federal jurisdiction over any party who could not be sued under the federal civil rights statutes. "Before it can be concluded that [supplemental] jurisdiction [over additional parties] exists," *Aldinger* held, "a federal court must satisfy itself not only that Art[icle] III permits it, but that Congress in the statutes conferring jurisdiction has not expressly or by implication negated its existence."

In Finley v. United States, 490 U.S. 545 (1989), we confronted a similar issue in a different statutory context. The plaintiff in *Finley* brought a Federal Tort Claims Act negligence suit against the Federal Aviation Administration in District Court, which had original jurisdiction under § 1346(b). The plaintiff tried to add related claims against other defendants, invoking the District Court's supplemental jurisdiction over so-called pendent parties. We held that the District Court lacked a sufficient statutory basis for exercising supplemental jurisdiction over these claims. Relying primarily on *Zahn, Aldinger,* and *Kroger,* we held in *Finley* that "a grant of jurisdiction over claims involving particular parties does not itself confer jurisdiction over additional claims by or against different parties." While *Finley* did not "limit or impair" *Gibbs'* liberal approach to interpreting the jurisdictional statutes in the context of supplemental jurisdiction over additional claims involving the same parties, *Finley* nevertheless declined to extend that interpretive assumption to claims involving additional parties. *Finley* held that in the context of parties, in contrast to claims, "we will not assume that the full constitutional power has been congressionally authorized, and will not read jurisdictional statutes broadly."

As the jurisdictional statutes existed in 1989, then, here is how matters stood: First, the diversity requirement in § 1332(a) required complete diversity; absent complete diversity, the district court lacked original jurisdiction over all of the claims in the action. Second, if the district court had original jurisdiction over at least one claim, the jurisdictional statutes implicitly authorized supplemental jurisdiction over all other claims between the same parties arising out of the same Article III case or controversy. Third, even when the district court had original jurisdiction over one or more claims between particular parties, the jurisdictional statutes did not authorize supplemental jurisdiction over additional claims involving other parties.

B

In *Finley* we emphasized that "[w]hatever we say regarding the scope of jurisdiction conferred by a particular statute can of course be changed by Congress." In 1990, Congress accepted the invitation. It passed the Judicial Improvements Act, 104 Stat. 5089, which enacted § 1367, the provision which controls these cases.

Section 1367 provides, in relevant part:

(a) Except as provided in subsections (b) and (c) or as expressly provided otherwise by Federal statute, in any civil action of which the district courts have original jurisdiction, the district courts shall have supplemental jurisdiction over all other claims that are so related to claims in the action within such original jurisdiction that they form part of the same case or controversy under Article III of the United States Constitution. Such supplemental jurisdiction shall include claims that involve the joinder or intervention of additional parties.

(b) In any civil action of which the district courts have original jurisdiction founded solely on section 1332 of this title, the district courts shall not have supplemental jurisdiction under subsection (a) over claims by plaintiffs against persons made parties under Rule 14, 19, 20, or 24 of the Federal Rules of Civil Procedure, or over claims by persons proposed to be joined as plaintiffs under Rule 19 of such rules, or seeking to intervene as plaintiffs under Rule 24 of such rules, when exercising supplemental jurisdiction over such claims would be inconsistent with the jurisdictional requirements of section 1332.

All parties to this litigation and all courts to consider the question agree that § 1367 overturned the result in *Finley*. There is no warrant, however, for assuming that § 1367 did no more than to overrule *Finley* and otherwise to codify the existing state of the law of supplemental jurisdiction. We must not give jurisdictional statutes a more expansive interpretation than their text warrants; but it is just as important not to adopt an artificial construction that is narrower than what the text provides. No sound canon of interpretation requires Congress to speak with extraordinary clarity in order to modify the rules of federal jurisdiction within appropriate constitutional bounds. Ordinary principles of statutory construction apply. In order to determine the scope of supplemental jurisdiction authorized by § 1367, then, we must examine the statute's text in light of context, structure, and related statutory provisions.

Section 1367(a) is a broad grant of supplemental jurisdiction over other claims within the same case or controversy, as long as the action is one in which the district courts would have original jurisdiction. The last sentence of § 1367(a) makes it clear that the grant of supplemental jurisdiction extends to claims involving joinder or intervention of additional parties. The single question before us, therefore, is whether a diversity case in which the claims of some plaintiffs satisfy the amount-in-controversy requirement, but the claims of others plaintiffs do not, presents a "civil action of which the district courts have original jurisdiction." If the answer is yes, § 1367(a) confers supplemental jurisdiction over all claims, including those that do not independently satisfy the amount-in-controversy requirement, if the claims are part of the same Article III case or controversy. If the answer is no, § 1367(a) is inapplicable and, in light of our holdings in *Clark* and *Zahn*, the district court has no statutory basis for exercising supplemental jurisdiction over the additional claims.

We now conclude the answer must be yes. When the well-pleaded complaint contains at least one claim that satisfies the amount-in-controversy requirement, and there are no other relevant jurisdictional defects, the district court, beyond all question, has original jurisdiction over that claim. The presence of other claims in the complaint, over which the district court may lack original jurisdiction, is of no moment. If the court has original jurisdiction over a single claim in the complaint, it has original jurisdiction over a "civil action" within the meaning of § 1367(a), even if the civil action over which it has jurisdiction comprises fewer claims than were included in the complaint. Once the court determines it has original jurisdiction over the civil action, it can turn to the question whether it has a constitutional and statutory basis for exercising supplemental jurisdiction over the other claims in the action.

Section 1367(a) commences with the direction that §§ 1367(b) and (c), or other relevant statutes, may provide specific exceptions, but otherwise § 1367(a) is a broad jurisdictional grant, with no distinction drawn between pendent-claim and pendent-party cases. In fact, the last sentence of § 1367(a) makes clear that the provision grants supplemental jurisdiction over claims involving joinder or intervention of additional parties. The terms of § 1367 do not acknowledge any distinction between pendent jurisdiction and the doctrine of so-called ancillary jurisdiction. Though the doctrines of pendent and ancillary jurisdiction developed separately as a historical matter, the Court has recognized that the doctrines are "two species of the same generic problem," *Kroger,* 437 U.S., at 370. Nothing in § 1367 indicates a congressional intent to recognize, preserve, or create some meaningful, substantive distinction between the jurisdictional categories we have historically labeled pendent and ancillary.

If § 1367(a) were the sum total of the relevant statutory language, our holding would rest on that language alone. The statute, of course, instructs us to examine § 1367(b) to determine if any of its exceptions apply, so we proceed to that section. While § 1367(b) qualifies the broad rule of § 1367(a), it does not withdraw supplemental jurisdiction over the claims of the additional parties at issue here. The specific exceptions to § 1367(a) contained in § 1367(b), moreover, provide additional support for our conclusion that § 1367(a) confers supplemental jurisdiction over these claims. Section 1367(b), which applies only to diversity cases, withholds supplemental jurisdiction over the claims of plaintiffs proposed to be joined as indispensable parties under Federal Rule of Civil Procedure 19, or who seek to intervene pursuant to Rule 24. Nothing in the text of § 1367(b), however, withholds supplemental jurisdiction over the claims of plaintiffs permissively joined under Rule 20 (like the additional plaintiffs in [one of the cases before us]) or certified as class-action members pursuant to Rule 23 (like the [others]). The natural, indeed the necessary, inference is that § 1367 confers supplemental jurisdiction over claims by Rule 20 and Rule 23 plaintiffs. This inference, at least with respect to Rule 20 plaintiffs, is strengthened by the fact that § 1367(b) explicitly excludes supplemental jurisdiction over claims against defendants joined under Rule 20.

We cannot accept the view, urged by some of the parties, commentators, and Courts of Appeals, that a district court lacks original jurisdiction over a civil action unless the court has original jurisdiction over every claim in the complaint. As we understand this position, it requires assuming either that all claims in the complaint must stand or fall as a single, indivisible "civil action" as a matter of definitional necessity—what we will refer to as the "indivisibility theory"—or else that the inclusion of a claim or party falling outside the district court's original jurisdiction somehow contaminates every other claim in the complaint, depriving the court of original jurisdiction over any of these claims—what we will refer to as the "contamination theory."

The indivisibility theory is easily dismissed, as it is inconsistent with the whole notion of supplemental jurisdiction. If a district court must have original jurisdiction over every claim in the complaint in order to have "original jurisdiction" over a "civil action," then in *Gibbs* there was no civil action of which the district court could assume original jurisdiction under § 1331, and so no basis for exercising supplemental jurisdiction over any of the claims. The indivisibility theory is further belied by our practice—in both federal-question and diversity cases—of allowing federal courts to cure jurisdictional defects by dismissing the offending parties rather than dismissing the entire action. . . . If the presence of jurisdictionally problematic claims in the complaint meant the district court was without original jurisdiction over the single, indivisible civil action before it, then the district court would have to dismiss the whole action rather than particular parties.

We also find it unconvincing to say that the definitional indivisibility theory applies in the context of diversity cases but not in the context of federal-question cases. The broad and general language of the statute does not permit this result. The contention is premised on the notion that the phrase "original jurisdiction of all civil actions" means different things in § 1331 and § 1332. It is implausible, however, to say that the identical phrase means one thing (original jurisdiction in all actions where at least one claim in the complaint meets the following requirements) in § 1331 and something else (original jurisdiction in all actions where every claim in the complaint meets the following requirements) in § 1332.

The contamination theory, as we have noted, can make some sense in the special context of the complete diversity requirement because the presence of nondiverse parties on both sides of a lawsuit eliminates the justification for providing a federal forum. The theory, however, makes little sense with respect to the amount-in-controversy requirement, which is meant to ensure that a dispute is sufficiently important to warrant federal-court attention. The presence of a single nondiverse party may eliminate the fear of bias with respect to all claims, but the presence of a claim that falls short of the minimum amount in controversy does nothing to reduce the importance of the claims that do meet this requirement.

It is fallacious to suppose, simply from the proposition that § 1332 imposes both the diversity requirement and the amount-in-controversy requirement, that the contamination theory germane to the former is also relevant to the latter. There is no inherent logical connection between the amount-in-controversy requirement and § 1332 diversity jurisdiction. After all, federal-question jurisdiction once had an amount-in-controversy requirement as well. If such a requirement were revived under § 1331, it is clear beyond peradventure that § 1367(a) provides supplemental jurisdiction over federal-question cases where some, but not all, of the federal-law claims involve a sufficient amount in controversy. In other words, § 1367(a) unambiguously overrules the holding and the result in *Clark*. If that is so, however, it would be quite extraordinary to say that § 1367 did not also overrule *Zahn,* a case that was premised in substantial part on the holding in *Clark*.

In addition to the theoretical difficulties with the argument that a district court has original jurisdiction over a civil action only if it has original jurisdiction over each individual claim in the complaint, we have already considered and rejected a virtually identical argument in the closely analogous context of removal jurisdiction. In Chicago v. International College of Surgeons, 522 U.S. 156 (1997), the plaintiff brought federal-and state-law claims in state court. The defendant removed to federal court. The plaintiff objected to removal, citing the text of the removal statute, § 1441(a). That statutory provision, which bears a striking similarity to the relevant portion of § 1367, authorizes removal of "any civil action ... of which the district courts of the United States have original jurisdiction ... ." The *College of Surgeons* plaintiff urged that, because its state-law claims were not within the District Court's original jurisdiction, § 1441(a) did not authorize removal. We disagreed. The federal law claims, we held, "suffice to make the actions 'civil actions' within the 'original jurisdiction' of the district courts.... Nothing in the jurisdictional statutes suggests that the presence of related state law claims somehow alters the fact that [the plaintiff's] complaints, by virtue of their federal claims, were 'civil actions' within the federal courts' 'original jurisdiction.'" Once the case was removed, the District Court had original jurisdiction over the federal law claims and supplemental jurisdiction under § 1367(a) over the state-law claims.

[Justice Ginsburg's] dissent in *College of Surgeons* argued that because the plaintiff sought on-the-record review of a local administrative agency decision, the review it sought was outside the scope of the District Court's jurisdiction. We rejected both the suggestion that state-law claims involving administrative appeals are beyond the scope of § 1367 supplemental jurisdiction and the claim that the administrative review posture of the case deprived the District Court of original jurisdiction over the federal-law claims in the case. More importantly for present purposes, *College of Surgeons* stressed that a district court has original jurisdiction of a civil action for purposes of § 1441(a) as long as it has original jurisdiction over a subset of the claims constituting the action. Even the *College of Surgeons* dissent, which took issue with the Court's interpretation of § 1367, did not appear to contest this view of § 1441(a).

Although *College of Surgeons* involved additional claims between the same parties, its interpretation of § 1441(a) applies equally to cases involving additional parties whose claims fall short of the jurisdictional amount. If we were to adopt the contrary view that the presence of additional parties means there is no "civil action ... of which the district courts ... have original jurisdiction," those cases simply would not be removable. To our knowledge, no court has issued a reasoned opinion adopting this view of the removal statute. It is settled, of course, that absent complete diversity a case is not removable because the district court would lack original jurisdiction. Caterpillar Inc. v. Lewis, 519 U.S. 61, 73 (1996). This, however, is altogether consistent with our view of § 1441(a). A failure of complete diversity, unlike the failure of some claims to meet the requisite amount in controversy, contaminates every claim in the action.

We also reject the argument, similar to the attempted distinction of *College of Surgeons* discussed above, that while the presence of additional claims over which the district court lacks jurisdiction does not mean the civil action is outside the purview of § 1367(a), the presence of additional parties does. The basis for this distinction is not altogether clear, and it is in considerable tension with statutory text. Section 1367(a) applies by its terms to any civil action of which the district courts have original jurisdiction, and the last sentence of § 1367(a) expressly contemplates that the court may have supplemental jurisdiction over additional parties. So it cannot be the case that the presence of those parties destroys the court's original jurisdiction, within the meaning of § 1367(a), over a civil action otherwise properly before it. Also, § 1367(b) expressly withholds supplemental jurisdiction in diversity cases over claims by plaintiffs joined as indispensable parties under Rule 19. If joinder of such parties were sufficient to deprive the district court of original jurisdiction over the civil action within the meaning of § 1367(a), this specific limitation on supplemental jurisdiction in § 1367(b) would be superfluous. The argument that the presence of additional parties removes the civil action from the scope of § 1367(a) also would mean that § 1367 left the *Finley* result undisturbed. *Finley,* after all, involved a Federal Tort Claims Act suit against a federal defendant and state-law claims against additional defendants not otherwise subject to federal jurisdiction. Yet all concede that one purpose of § 1367 was to change the result reached in *Finley.*

Finally, it is suggested that our interpretation of § 1367(a) creates an anomaly regarding the exceptions listed in § 1367(b): It is not immediately obvious why Congress would withhold supplemental jurisdiction over plaintiffs joined as parties "needed for just adjudication" under Rule 19 but would allow supplemental jurisdiction over plaintiffs permissively joined under Rule 20. The omission of Rule 20 plaintiffs from the list of exceptions in § 1367(b) may have been an "unintentional drafting gap." If that is the case, it is up to Congress rather than the courts to fix it. The omission may seem odd, but it is not absurd. An alternative explanation for the different treatment of Rule 19 and Rule 20 is that Congress was concerned that extending supplemental jurisdiction to Rule 19 plaintiffs would allow circumvention of the complete diversity rule: A nondiverse plaintiff might be omitted intentionally from the original action, but joined later under Rule 19 as a necessary party. The contamination theory described above, if applicable, means this ruse would fail, but Congress may have wanted to make assurance double sure. More generally, Congress may have concluded that federal jurisdiction is only appropriate if the district court would have original jurisdiction over the claims of all those plaintiffs who are so essential to the action that they could be joined under Rule 19.

To the extent that the omission of Rule 20 plaintiffs from the list of § 1367(b) exceptions is anomalous, moreover, it is no more anomalous than the inclusion of Rule 19 plaintiffs in that list would be if the alternative view of § 1367(a) were to prevail. If the district court lacks original jurisdiction over a civil diversity action where any plaintiff's claims fail to comply with all the requirements of § 1332, there is no need for a special § 1367(b) exception for Rule 19 plaintiffs who do not meet these requirements. Though the omission of Rule 20 plaintiffs from § 1367(b) presents something of a puzzle on our view of the statute, the inclusion of Rule 19 plaintiffs in this section is at least as difficult to explain under the alternative view.

And so we circle back to the original question. When the well-pleaded complaint in district court includes multiple claims, all part of the same case or controversy, and some, but not all, of the claims are within the court's original jurisdiction, does the court have before it "any civil action of which the district courts have original jurisdiction"? It does. Under § 1367, the court has original jurisdiction over the civil action comprising the claims for which there is no jurisdictional defect. No other reading of § 1367 is plausible in light of the text and structure of the jurisdictional statute. Though the special nature and purpose of the diversity requirement mean that a single nondiverse party can contaminate every other claim in the lawsuit, the contamination does not occur with respect to jurisdictional defects that go only to the substantive importance of individual claims.

It follows from this conclusion that the threshold requirement of § 1367(a) is satisfied in cases, like those now before us, where some, but not all, of the plaintiffs in a diversity action allege a sufficient amount in controversy. We hold that § 1367 by its plain text overruled *Clark* and *Zahn* and authorized supplemental jurisdiction over all claims by diverse parties arising out of the same Article III case or controversy, subject only to enumerated exceptions not applicable in the cases now before us.

C

The proponents of the alternative view of § 1367 insist that the statute is at least ambiguous and that we should look to other interpretive tools, including the legislative history of § 1367, which supposedly demonstrate Congress did not intend § 1367 to overrule *Zahn*. We can reject this argument at the very outset simply because § 1367 is not ambiguous. For the reasons elaborated above, interpreting § 1367 to foreclose supplemental jurisdiction over plaintiffs in diversity cases who do not meet the minimum amount in controversy is inconsistent with the text, read in light of other statutory provisions and our established jurisprudence. Even if we were to stipulate, however, that the reading these proponents urge upon us is textually plausible, the legislative history cited to support it would not alter our view as to the best interpretation of § 1367.

Those who urge that the legislative history refutes our interpretation rely primarily on the House Judiciary Committee Report on the Judicial Improvements Act. H.R.Rep. No. 101–734 (1990) (House Report or Report). This Report explained that § 1367 would "authorize jurisdiction in a case like *Finley,* as well as essentially restore the pre-*Finley* understandings of the authorization for and limits on other forms of supplemental jurisdiction." The Report stated that § 1367(a) "generally authorizes the district court to exercise jurisdiction over a supplemental claim whenever it forms part of the same constitutional case or controversy as the claim or claims that provide the basis of the district court's original jurisdiction," and in so doing codifies *Gibbs* and fills the statutory gap recognized in *Finley.* The Report then remarked that § 1367(b) "is not intended to affect the jurisdictional requirements of [§ 1332] in diversity-only class actions, as those requirements were interpreted prior to *Finley,*" citing, without further elaboration, *Zahn* and Supreme Tribe of Ben–Hur v. Cauble, 255 U.S. 356 (1921). The Report noted that the "net effect" of § 1367(b) was to implement the "principal rationale" of *Kroger,* effecting only "one small change" in pre-*Finley* practice with respect to diversity actions: § 1367(b) would exclude "Rule 23(a) plaintiff-intervenors to the same extent as those sought to be joined as plaintiffs under Rule 19." (It is evident that the report here meant to refer to Rule 24, not Rule 23.)

As we have repeatedly held, the authoritative statement is the statutory text, not the legislative history or any other extrinsic material. Extrinsic materials have a role in statutory interpretation only to the extent they shed a reliable light on the enacting Legislature's understanding of otherwise ambiguous terms. Not all extrinsic materials are reliable sources of insight into legislative understandings, however, and legislative history in particular is vulnerable to two serious criticisms. First, legislative history is itself often murky, ambiguous, and contradictory. Judicial investigation of legislative history has a tendency to become, to borrow Judge Leventhal's memorable phrase, an exercise in " 'looking over a crowd and picking out your friends.' " See Wald, Some Observations on the Use of Legislative History in the 1981 Supreme Court Term, 68 Iowa L.Rev. 195, 214 (1983). Second, judicial reliance on legislative materials like committee reports, which are not themselves subject to the requirements of Article I, may give unrepresentative committee members—or, worse yet, unelected staffers and lobbyists—both the power and the incentive to attempt strategic manipulations of legislative history to secure results they were unable to achieve through the statutory text. We need not comment here on whether these problems are sufficiently prevalent to render legislative history inherently unreliable in all circumstances, a point on which Members of this Court have disagreed. It is clear, however, that in this instance both criticisms are right on the mark.

First of all, the legislative history of § 1367 is far murkier than selective quotation from the House Report would suggest. The text of § 1367 is based substantially on a draft proposal contained in a Federal Court Study Committee working paper, which was drafted by a Subcommittee chaired by Judge Posner. Report of the Subcommittee on the Role of the Federal Courts and Their Relationship to the States 567–68 (Mar. 12, 1990), reprinted in Judicial Conference of the United States, 1 Federal Courts Study Committee, Working Papers and Subcommittee Reports (July 1, 1990). See also Judicial Conference of the United States, Report of the Federal Courts Study Committee 47–48 (Apr. 2, 1990) (Study Committee Report) (echoing, in brief summary form, the Subcommittee Working Paper proposal and noting that the Subcommittee Working Paper "contains additional material on this subject"); House Report, at 27 ("[Section 1367] implements a recommendation of the Federal Courts Study Committee found on pages 47 and 48 of its report"). While the Subcommittee explained, in language echoed by the House Report, that its proposal "basically restores the law as it existed prior to *Finley*," Subcommittee Working Paper, at 561, it observed in a footnote that its proposal would overrule *Zahn* and that this would be a good idea, Subcommittee Working Paper, at 561, n.33. Although the Federal Courts Study Committee did not expressly adopt the Subcommittee's specific reference to *Zahn*, it neither explicitly disagreed with the Subcommittee's conclusion that this was the best reading of the proposed text nor substantially modified the proposal to avoid this result. Therefore, even if the House Report could fairly be read to reflect an understanding that the text of § 1367 did not overrule *Zahn*, the Subcommittee Working Paper on which § 1367 was based reflected the opposite understanding. The House Report is no more authoritative than the Subcommittee Working Paper. The utility of either can extend no further than the light it sheds on how the enacting Legislature understood the statutory text. Trying to figure out how to square the Subcommittee Working Paper's understanding with the House Report's understanding, or which is more reflective of the understanding of the enacting legislators, is a hopeless task.

Second, the worst fears of critics who argue legislative history will be used to circumvent the Article I process were realized in this case. The telltale evidence is the statement, by three law professors who participated in drafting § 1367, see House Report, at 27, n.13, that § 1367 "on its face" permits "supplemental jurisdiction over claims of class members that do not satisfy section 1332's jurisdictional amount requirement, which would overrule *[Zahn]*. [There is] a disclaimer of intent to accomplish this result in the legislative history.... It would have been better had the statute dealt explicitly with this problem, and the legislative history was an attempt to correct the oversight." Rowe, Burbank, & Mengler, Compounding or Creating Confusion About Supplemental Jurisdiction? A Reply to

Professor Freer, 40 Emory L.J. 943, 960 n.90 (1991). The professors were frank to concede that if one refuses to consider the legislative history, one has no choice but to "conclude that section 1367 has wiped *Zahn* off the books." So there exists an acknowledgment, by parties who have detailed, specific knowledge of the statute and the drafting process, both that the plain text of § 1367 overruled *Zahn* and that language to the contrary in the House Report was a post hoc attempt to alter that result. One need not subscribe to the wholesale condemnation of legislative history to refuse to give any effect to such a deliberate effort to amend a statute through a committee report.

In sum, even if we believed resort to legislative history were appropriate in these cases—a point we do not concede—we would not give significant weight to the House Report. The distinguished jurists who drafted the Subcommittee Working Paper, along with three of the participants in the drafting of § 1367, agree that this provision, on its face, overrules *Zahn*. This accords with the best reading of the statute's text, and nothing in the legislative history indicates directly and explicitly that Congress understood the phrase "civil action of which the district courts have original jurisdiction" to exclude cases in which some but not all of the diversity plaintiffs meet the amount in controversy requirement.

No credence, moreover, can be given to the claim that, if Congress understood § 1367 to overrule *Zahn,* the proposal would have been more controversial. We have little sense whether any Member of Congress would have been particularly upset by this result. This is not a case where one can plausibly say that concerned legislators might not have realized the possible effect of the text they were adopting. Certainly, any competent legislative aide who studied the matter would have flagged this issue if it were a matter of importance to his or her boss, especially in light of the Subcommittee Working Paper. There are any number of reasons why legislators did not spend more time arguing over § 1367, none of which are relevant to our interpretation of what the words of the statute mean.

D

Finally, we note that the Class Action Fairness Act (CAFA), Pub.L. 109–2, 119 Stat. 4, enacted this year, has no bearing on our analysis of these cases. Subject to certain limitations, the CAFA confers federal diversity jurisdiction over class actions where the aggregate amount in controversy exceeds $5 million. It abrogates the rule against aggregating claims, a rule this Court recognized in *Ben-Hur* and reaffirmed in *Zahn*. The CAFA, however, is not retroactive, and the views of the 2005 Congress are not relevant to our interpretation of a text enacted by Congress in 1990. The CAFA, moreover, does not moot the significance of our interpretation of § 1367, as many proposed exercises of supplemental jurisdiction, even in the class-action context, might not fall within the CAFA's ambit. The

CAFA, then, has no impact, one way or the other, on our interpretation of § 1367.

* * *

The judgment of the Court of Appeals for the Eleventh Circuit is affirmed. The judgment of the Court of Appeals for the First Circuit is reversed, and the case is remanded for proceedings consistent with this opinion.

It is so ordered.

■ JUSTICE STEVENS, with whom JUSTICE BREYER joins, dissenting.

Justice Ginsburg's carefully reasoned opinion demonstrates the error in the Court's rather ambitious reading of this opaque jurisdictional statute. She also has demonstrated that "ambiguity" is a term that may have different meanings for different judges, for the Court has made the remarkable declaration that its reading of the statute is so obviously correct—and Justice Ginsburg's so obviously wrong—that the text does not even qualify as "ambiguous." Because ambiguity is apparently in the eye of the beholder, I remain convinced that it is unwise to treat the ambiguity vel non of a statute as determinative of whether legislative history is consulted. Indeed, I believe that we as judges are more, rather than less, constrained when we make ourselves accountable to *all* reliable evidence of legislative intent.

The legislative history of 28 U.S.C. § 1367 provides powerful confirmation of Justice Ginsburg's interpretation of that statute. It is helpful to consider in full the relevant portion of the House Report, which was also adopted by the Senate:

> This section would authorize jurisdiction in a case like *Finley*, as well as essentially restore the pre-*Finley* understandings of the authorization for and limits on other forms of supplemental jurisdiction. In federal question cases, it broadly authorizes the district courts to exercise supplemental jurisdiction over additional claims, including claims involving the joinder of additional parties. In diversity cases, the district courts may exercise supplemental jurisdiction, except when doing so would be inconsistent with the jurisdictional requirements of the diversity statute. . . .
>
> Subsection 114(b) [§ 1367(b)] prohibits a district court in a case over which it has jurisdiction founded solely on the general diversity provision, 28 U.S.C. § 1332, from exercising supplemental jurisdiction in specified circumstances. [Footnote 16: "The net effect of subsection (b) is to implement the principal rationale of Owen Equipment & Erection Co. v. Kroger, 437 U.S. 365 (1978)."] In diversity-only actions the district courts may not hear plaintiffs' supplemental claims when exercising supplemental jurisdiction would encourage plaintiffs to evade the jurisdictional requirement of 28 U.S.C. § 1332 by the simple expedient of naming initially

only those defendants whose joinder satisfies section 1332's requirements and later adding claims not within original federal jurisdiction against other defendants who have intervened or been joined on a supplemental basis. In accord with case law, the subsection also prohibits the joinder or intervention of persons a plaintiffs if adding them is inconsistent with section 1332's requirements. The section is not intended to affect the jurisdictional requirements of 28 U.S.C. § 1332 in diversity-only class actions, as those requirements were interpreted prior to *Finley*. [Footnote 17: "See Supreme Tribe of Ben–Hur v. Cauble, 255 U.S. 356 (1921); Zahn v. International Paper Co., 414 U.S. 291 (1973)."]

Subsection (b) makes one small change in pre-*Finley* practice. Anomalously, under current practice, the same party might intervene as of right under Federal Rule of Civil Procedure 23(a) and take advantage of supplemental jurisdiction, but not come within supplemental jurisdiction if parties already in the action sought to effect the joinder under Rule 19. Subsection (b) would eliminate this anomaly, excluding Rule 23(a) plaintiff-intervenors to the same extent as those sought to be joined as plaintiffs under Rule 19.

H.R.Rep. No. 101–734, pp. 28–29 (1990) (hereinafter House Report or Report).

Not only does the House Report specifically say that § 1367 was not intended to upset *Zahn*, but its entire explanation of the statute demonstrates that Congress had in mind a very specific and relatively modest task—undoing this Court's 5-to-4 decision in *Finley*. In addition to overturning that unfortunate and much-criticized decision, the statute, according to the Report, codifies and preserves the "the pre-*Finley* understandings of the authorization for and limits on other forms of supplemental jurisdiction" with the exception of making "one small change in pre-*Finley* practice" which is not relevant here.

The sweeping purpose that the Court's decision imputes to Congress bears no resemblance to the House Report's description of the statute. But this does not seem to trouble the Court, for its decision today treats statutory interpretation as a pedantic exercise, divorced from any serious attempt at ascertaining congressional intent. Of course, there are situations in which we do not honor Congress' apparent intent unless that intent is made "clear" in the text of a statute—in this way, we can be certain that Congress considered the issue and intended a disfavored outcome. But that principle provides no basis for discounting the House Report, given that our cases have never recognized a presumption in *favor* of expansive diversity jurisdiction.

The Court's reasons for ignoring this virtual billboard of congressional intent are unpersuasive. That a subcommittee of the Federal Courts Study Committee believed that an earlier, substantially similar version of the statute overruled *Zahn* only highlights the fact that the statute is ambiguous. What is determinative is that the House Report explicitly rejected that broad reading of the statutory text. Such a report has special significance as an indicator of legislative intent. In Congress, committee reports are normally considered the authoritative explication of a statute's text and purposes, and busy legislators and their assistants rely on that explication in casting their votes.

The Court's second reason—its comment on the three law professors who participated in drafting § 1367—is similarly off the mark. In the law review article that the Court refers to, the professors were merely saying that the text of the statute was susceptible to an overly broad (and simplistic) reading, and that clarification in the House Report was therefore appropriate. See Rowe, Burbank, & Mengler, Compounding or Creating Confusion About Supplemental Jurisdiction? A Reply to Professor Freer, 40 Emory L.J. 943, 960, n. 90 (1991). Significantly, the reference to *Zahn* in the House Report does not at all appear to be tacked-on or out of place; indeed, it is wholly consistent with the Report's broader explanation of Congress' goal of overruling *Finley* and preserving pre-*Finley* law. To suggest that these professors participated in a "deliberate effort to amend a statute through a committee report" reveals an unrealistic view of the legislative process, not to mention disrespect for three law professors who acted in the role of public servants. To be sure, legislative history can be manipulated. But, in the situation before us, there is little reason to fear that an unholy conspiracy of "unrepresentative committee members" law professors, and "unelected staffers and lobbyists" endeavored to torpedo Congress' attempt to overrule (without discussion) two longstanding features of this Court's diversity jurisprudence.

After nearly 20 pages of complicated analysis, which explores subtle doctrinal nuances and coins various neologisms, the Court announces that § 1367 could not reasonably be read another way. That conclusion is difficult to accept. Given Justice Ginsburg's persuasive account of the statutory text and its jurisprudential backdrop, and given the uncommonly clear legislative history, I am confident that the majority's interpretation of § 1367 is mistaken. I respectfully dissent.

■ JUSTICE GINSBURG, with whom JUSTICE STEVENS, JUSTICE O'CONNOR, and JUSTICE BREYER join, dissenting.

... The Court reads § 1367 to overrule Clark v. Paul Gray, Inc., 306 U.S. 583, 589 (1939), and Zahn v. International Paper Co., 414 U.S. 291 (1973), thereby allowing access to federal court by co-plaintiffs or class members who do not meet the now in excess of $75,000 amount-in-controversy requirement, so long as at least one co-plaintiff, or the named class representative, has a jurisdictionally sufficient claim.

The Court adopts a plausibly broad reading of § 1367, a measure that is hardly a model of the careful drafter's art. There is another plausible reading, however, one less disruptive of our jurisprudence regarding supplemental jurisdiction. If one reads § 1367(a) to instruct, as the statute's text suggests, that the district court must first have "original jurisdiction" over a "civil action" before supplemental jurisdiction can attach, then *Clark* and *Zahn* are preserved, and supplemental jurisdiction does not open the way for joinder of plaintiffs, or inclusion of class members, who do not independently meet the amount-in-controversy requirement. For the reasons that follow, I conclude that this narrower construction is the better reading of § 1367.

I

... Shortly before the Court decided Finley v. United States, 490 U.S. 545, 548 (1989), Congress had established the Federal Courts Study Committee to take up issues relating to "the federal courts' congestion, delay, expense, and expansion." Judicial Conference of the United States, Report of the Federal Courts Study Committee 3 (Apr. 2, 1990). The Committee's charge was to conduct a study addressing the "crisis" in federal courts caused by the "rapidly growing" caseload.

Among recommendations, the Committee urged Congress to "authorize federal courts to assert pendent jurisdiction over parties without an independent federal jurisdictional base." If adopted, this recommendation would overrule *Finley*. Earlier, a subcommittee had recommended that Congress overrule both *Finley* and *Zahn*. Report of the Subcommittee on the Role of the Federal Courts and Their Relationship to the States 547, 561 n 33 (Mar. 12, 1990), reprinted in 1 Judicial Conference of the United States, Federal Courts Study Committee, Working Papers and Subcommittee Reports (July 1, 1990). In the subcommittee's view, "[f]rom a policy standpoint," *Zahn* "ma[de] little sense."[3] The full Committee, however, urged only the overruling of *Finley* and did not adopt the recommendation to overrule Zahn.

As a separate matter, a substantial majority of the Committee "strongly recommend[ed]" the elimination of diversity jurisdiction, save for "complex multi-state litigation, interpleader, and suits involving aliens." "[N]o other step," the Committee's Report maintained, "will do anywhere nearly as much to reduce federal caseload pressures and contain the growth of the federal judiciary."

Congress responded by adopting, as part of the Judicial Improvements Act of 1990, 104 Stat. 5089, recommendations of the Federal Courts Study Committee ranked by the House Committee on the Judiciary as "modest" and "noncontroversial." H.R.Rep. No. 101–734, pp. 15–16 (1990). Congress

---

3. Anomalously, in holding that each class member "must satisfy the jurisdictional amount," Zahn v. International Paper Co., 414 U.S. 291, 301 (1973), the *Zahn* Court did not refer to Supreme Tribe of Ben–Hur v. Cauble, 255 U.S. 356, 366 (1921), which established that in a class action, the citizenship of the named plaintiff is controlling. But see *Zahn,* 414 U.S., at 309–10 (Brennan, J., dissenting) (urging *Zahn's* inconsistency with *Ben-Hur*).

did not take up the Study Committee's immodest proposal to curtail diversity jurisdiction. It did, however, enact a supplemental jurisdiction statute, codified as 28 U.S.C. § 1367.

II

A

Section 1367, by its terms, operates only in civil actions "of which the district courts have original jurisdiction." The "original jurisdiction" relevant here is diversity-of-citizenship jurisdiction, conferred by § 1332. The character of that jurisdiction is the essential backdrop for comprehension of § 1367.

The Constitution broadly provides for federal-court jurisdiction in controversies "between Citizens of different States." Art. III, § 2, cl. 1. This Court has read that provision to demand no more than "minimal diversity," i.e., so long as one party on the plaintiffs' side and one party on the defendants' side are of diverse citizenship, Congress may authorize federal courts to exercise diversity jurisdiction. Further, the Constitution includes no amount-in-controversy limitation on the exercise of federal jurisdiction. But from the start, Congress, as its measures have been construed by this Court, has limited federal court exercise of diversity jurisdiction in two principal ways. First, unless Congress specifies otherwise, diversity must be "complete," i.e., all parties on plaintiffs' side must be diverse from all parties on defendants' side. Second, each plaintiff's stake must independently meet the amount-in-controversy specification: "When two or more plaintiffs, having separate and distinct demands, unite for convenience and economy in a single suit, it is essential that the demand of each be of the requisite jurisdictional amount." Troy Bank v. G.A. Whitehead & Co., 222 U.S. 39, 40 (1911).

The statute today governing federal court exercise of diversity jurisdiction in the generality of cases, § 1332, like all its predecessors, incorporates both a diverse-citizenship requirement and an amount-in-controversy specification.[5] ... This Court has long held that, in determining whether the amount-in-controversy requirement has been satisfied, a single plaintiff may aggregate two or more claims against a single defendant, even if the claims are unrelated. See, e.g., Edwards v. Bates County, 163 U.S. 269, 273

---

5. Endeavoring to preserve the "complete diversity" rule ..., the Court's opinion drives a wedge between the two components of 28 U.S.C. § 1332, treating the diversity-of-citizenship requirement as essential, the amount-in-controversy requirement as more readily disposable. Section 1332 itself, however, does not rank order the two requirements. What "[o]rdinary principl[e] of statutory construction" or "sound canon of interpretation" allows the Court to slice up § 1332 this way? In partial explanation, the Court asserts that amount in controversy can be analyzed claim-by-claim, but the diversity requirement cannot. It is not altogether clear why that should be so. The cure for improper joinder of a nondiverse party is the same as the cure for improper joinder of a plaintiff who does not satisfy the jurisdictional amount. In both cases, original jurisdiction can be preserved by dismissing the nonqualifying party.

(1896). But in multiparty cases, including class actions, we have unyieldingly adhered to the nonaggregation rule stated in *Troy Bank*.

This Court most recently addressed "[t]he meaning of [§ 1332's] 'matter in controversy' language" in *Zahn*. *Zahn*, like Snyder v. Harris, 394 U.S. 332 (1969) decided four years earlier, was a class action. In *Snyder*, no class member had a claim large enough to satisfy the jurisdictional amount. But in *Zahn*, the named plaintiffs had such claims. Nevertheless, the Court declined to depart from its "longstanding construction of the 'matter in controversy' requirement of § 1332." The *Zahn* Court stated:

> *Snyder* invoked the well-established rule that each of several plaintiffs asserting separate and distinct claims must satisfy the jurisdictional-amount requirement if his claim is to survive a motion to dismiss. This rule plainly mandates not only that there may be no aggregation and that the entire case must be dismissed where none of the plaintiffs claims [meets the amount-in-controversy requirement] but also requires that any plaintiff without the jurisdictional amount must be dismissed from the case, even though others allege jurisdictionally sufficient claims.

The rule that each plaintiff must independently satisfy the amount-in-controversy requirement, unless Congress expressly orders otherwise, was thus the solidly established reading of § 1332 when Congress enacted the Judicial Improvements Act of 1990, which added § 1367 to Title 28.

B

The Court divides ... on the impact of § 1367(a) on diversity cases controlled by § 1332. Under the majority's reading, § 1367(a) permits the joinder of related claims cut loose from the nonaggregation rule that has long attended actions under § 1332. Only the claims specified in § 1367(b) would be excluded from § 1367(a)'s expansion of § 1332's grant of diversity jurisdiction. And because § 1367(b) contains no exception for joinder of plaintiffs under Rule 20 or class actions under Rule 23, the Court concludes, *Clark* and *Zahn* have been overruled.[8]

The Court's reading is surely plausible, especially if one detaches § 1367(a) from its context and attempts no reconciliation with prior interpretations of § 1332's amount-in-controversy requirement. But § 1367(a)'s text, as the First Circuit held, can be read another way, one that would involve no rejection of *Clark* and *Zahn*.

---

8. Under the Court's construction of § 1367, Beatriz Ortega's family members can remain in the action because their joinder is merely permissive, see Fed. Rule Civ. Proc. 20. If, however, their presence was "needed for just adjudication," Rule 19, their dismissal would be required. The inclusion of those who may join, and exclusion of those who should or must join, defies rational explanation ....

As explained by the First Circuit ... , § 1367(a) addresses "civil action[s] of which the district courts have original jurisdiction," a formulation that, in diversity cases, is sensibly read to incorporate the rules on joinder and aggregation tightly tied to § 1332 at the time of § 1367's enactment. On this reading, a complaint must first meet that "original jurisdiction" measurement. If it does not, no supplemental jurisdiction is authorized. If it does, § 1367(a) authorizes "supplemental jurisdiction" over related claims. In other words, § 1367(a) would preserve undiminished, as part and parcel of § 1332 "original jurisdiction" determinations, both the "complete diversity" rule and the decisions restricting aggregation to arrive at the amount in controversy.[9] Section 1367(b)'s office, then, would be "to prevent the erosion of the complete diversity [and amount-in-controversy] requirement[s] that might otherwise result from an expansive application of what was once termed the doctrine of ancillary jurisdiction." See Pfander, Supplemental Jurisdiction and Section 1367: The Case for a Sympathetic Textualism, 148 U. Pa. L.Rev. 109, 114 (1999). In contrast to the Court's construction of § 1367, which draws a sharp line between the diversity and amount-in-controversy components of § 1332, the interpretation presented here does not sever the two jurisdictional requirements.

The more restrained reading of § 1367 just outlined would yield affirmance of the First Circuit's judgment ... and reversal of the Eleventh Circuit's judgment ... .It would not discard entirely, as the Court does, the judicially developed doctrines of pendent and ancillary jurisdiction as they existed when *Finley* was decided. Instead, it would recognize § 1367 essentially as a codification of those doctrines, placing them under a single heading, but largely retaining their substance, with overriding *Finley* the only basic change: Supplemental jurisdiction, once the district court has original jurisdiction, would now include "claims that involve the joinder or intervention of additional parties." § 1367(a).

Pendent jurisdiction ... applied only in federal-question cases and allowed plaintiffs to attach nonfederal claims to their jurisdiction-qualifying claims. Ancillary jurisdiction applied primarily, although not exclusively, in diversity cases and "typically involve[d] claims *by a defending party* haled into court against his will." *Kroger,* 437 U.S., at 376 (emphasis added). As the First Circuit observed, neither doctrine permitted a plaintiff to circumvent the dual requirements of § 1332 (diversity of citizenship and amount in controversy) "simply by joining her [jurisdictionally inadequate] claim in an action brought by [a] jurisdictionally competent diversity plaintiff."

Not only would the reading I find persuasive "alig[n] statutory supplemental jurisdiction with the judicially developed doctrines of pendent and

---

9. On this reading of § 1367(a), it is immaterial that § 1367(b) "does not withdraw supplemental jurisdiction over the claims of the additional parties at issue here." Because those claims would not come within § 1367(a) in the first place, Congress would have had no reason to list them in § 1367(b).

ancillary jurisdiction," it would also synchronize § 1367 with the removal statute, 28 U.S.C. § 1441. As the First Circuit carefully explained:

> Section 1441, like § 1367, applies only if the "civil action" in question is one "of which the district courts ... have original jurisdiction." § 1441(a). Relying on that language, the Supreme Court has interpreted § 1441 to prohibit removal unless the entire action, as it stands at the time of removal, could have been filed in federal court in the first instance. See, e.g., Syngenta Crop Protection, Inc. v. Henson, 537 U.S. 28, 33 (2002). Section 1441 has thus been held to incorporate the well-pleaded complaint rule;[11] the complete diversity rule; and rules for calculating the amount in controversy.

The less disruptive view I take of § 1367 also accounts for the omission of Rule 20 plaintiffs and Rule 23 class actions in § 1367(b)'s text. If one reads § 1367(a) as a plenary grant of supplemental jurisdiction to federal courts sitting in diversity, one would indeed look for exceptions in § 1367(b). Finding none for permissive joinder of parties or class actions, one would conclude that Congress effectively, even if unintentionally, overruled *Clark* and *Zahn*. But if one recognizes that the nonaggregation rule delineated in *Clark* and *Zahn* forms part of the determination whether "original jurisdiction" exists in a diversity case, then plaintiffs who do not meet the amount-in-controversy requirement would fail at the § 1367(a) threshold. Congress would have no reason to resort to a § 1367(b) exception to turn such plaintiffs away from federal court, given that their claims, from the start, would fall outside the court's § 1332 jurisdiction. See Pfander, 148 U. Pa. L.Rev., at 148.

Nor does the more moderate reading assign different meanings to "original jurisdiction" in diversity and federal-question cases. As the First Circuit stated:

> "[O]riginal jurisdiction" in § 1367(a) has the same meaning in every case: [An] underlying statutory grant of original jurisdiction must be satisfied. What differs between federal question and diversity cases is not the meaning of "original jurisdiction" but rather the [discrete] requirements of sections 1331 and 1332. Under § 1331, the sole issue is whether a federal question appears on the face of the plaintiff's well-pleaded complaint; the [citizenship] of the parties and the amounts they stand to recover [do not

---

11. The point of the Court's extended discussion of City of Chicago v. International College of Surgeons, 522 U.S. 156, 163 (1997), in the instant cases slips from my grasp. There was no disagreement in that case, and there is none now, that 28 U.S.C. § 1367(a) is properly read to authorize the exercise of supplemental jurisdiction in removed cases. *International College of Surgeons* was unusual in that the federal court there was asked to review a decision of a local administrative agency. Such review, it was unsuccessfully argued, was "appellate" in character, and therefore outside the ken of a court empowered to exercise "original" jurisdiction.

bear on that determination]. Section 1332, by contrast, predicates original jurisdiction on the identity of the parties (i.e., [their] complete diversity) and their [satisfaction of the amount-in-controversy specification]. [In short,] the 'original jurisdiction' language in § 1367 operates differently in federal-question and diversity cases not because the meaning of that term varies, but because the [jurisdiction-granting] statutes are different.

What is the utility of § 1367(b) under my reading of § 1367(a)? Section 1367(a) allows parties other than the plaintiff to assert *reactive* claims once entertained under the heading ancillary jurisdiction. ([E.g.,] compulsory counterclaims and impleader claims, over which federal courts routinely exercised ancillary jurisdiction). As earlier observed, § 1367(b) stops plaintiffs from circumventing § 1332's jurisdictional requirements by using another's claim as a hook to add a claim that the plaintiff could not have brought in the first instance. *Kroger* is the paradigm case. There, the Court held that ancillary jurisdiction did not extend to a plaintiff's claim against a nondiverse party who had been impleaded by the defendant under Rule 14. Section 1367(b), then, is corroborative of § 1367(a)'s coverage of claims formerly called ancillary, but provides exceptions to assure that accommodation of added claims would not fundamentally alter "the jurisdictional requirements of section 1332." See Pfander, supra, at 135–37.

While § 1367's enigmatic text[12] defies flawless interpretation,[13] the precedent-preservative reading, I am persuaded, better accords with the historical and legal context of Congress' enactment of the supplemental jurisdiction statute and the established limits on pendent and ancillary jurisdiction. It does not attribute to Congress a jurisdictional enlargement broader than the one to which the legislators adverted, and it follows the sound counsel that "close questions of [statutory] construction should be

---

12. The Court notes the passage this year of the Class Action Fairness Act (CAFA), only to dismiss that legislation as irrelevant. Subject to several exceptions and qualifications, CAFA provides for federal-court adjudication of state-law-based class actions in which diversity is "minimal" (one plaintiff's diversity from one defendant suffices), and the "matter in controversy" is an aggregate amount in excess of $5,000,000. Significant here, CAFA's enlargement of federal-court diversity jurisdiction was accomplished, "clearly and conspicuously," by amending § 1332.

13. If § 1367(a) itself renders unnecessary the listing of Rule 20 plaintiffs and Rule 23 class actions in § 1367(b), then it is similarly unnecessary to refer, as § 1367(b) does, to "persons proposed to be joined as plaintiffs under Rule 19." On one account, Congress bracketed such persons with persons "seeking to intervene as plaintiffs under Rule 24" to modify pre-§ 1367 practice. Before enactment of § 1367, courts entertained, under the heading ancillary jurisdiction, claims of Rule 24(a) intervenors "of right," but denied ancillary jurisdiction over claims of "necessary" Rule 19 plaintiffs. Congress may have sought simply to underscore that those seeking to join as plaintiffs, whether under Rule 19 or Rule 24, should be treated alike, i.e., denied joinder when "inconsistent with the jurisdictional requirements of section 1332." See H.R. Rep., at 29 ("Subsection (b) makes one small change in pre-*Finley* practice," i.e., it eliminates the Rule 19/Rule 24 anomaly.).

resolved in favor of continuity and against change." Shapiro, Continuity and Change in Statutory Interpretation, 67 N.Y.U.L.Rev. 921, 925 (1992).[14]

* * *

For the reasons stated, I would hold that § 1367 does not overrule *Clark* and Zahn. I would therefore affirm the judgment of the Court of Appeals for the First Circuit and reverse the judgment of the Court of Appeals for the Eleventh Circuit.

14. While the interpretation of § 1367 described in this opinion does not rely on the measure's legislative history, that history, as Justice Stevens has shown, is corroborative of the statutory reading set out above.

Page 586, add a footnote at the end of Note 6:

j. For general treatment of the *Semtek* issue, see Patrick Woolley, The Sources of Federal Preclusion Law after *Semtek*, 72 U. Cin. L. Rev. 527 (2003).

Page 587, add to citations in Note 7:

Robert T. Wasson, Jr., Resolving Separation of Powers and Federalism Problems Raised by *Erie*, the Rules of Decision Act, and the Rules Enabling Act: A Proposed Solution, 32 Capital U.L. Rev. 519 (2003).

CHAPTER VI

ABSTENTION

Page 641, omit footnote a, add a new Note 2, and renumber the remaining Notes:

2. The *Rooker-Feldman* Doctrine: *Exxon Mobil Corporation v. Saudi Basic Industries Corporation.* One related pair of decisions can be set aside at the outset. In Rooker v. Fidelity Trust Co., 263 U.S. 413 (1923), and District of Columbia Court of Appeals v. Feldman, 460 U.S. 462 (1983), the Court gave birth to a doctrine that it confined to a narrow role in Exxon Mobil Corporation v. Saudi Basic Industries Corporation, 544 U.S. ___ (2005).

Saudi Basic Industries Corporation (SABIC) sued Exxon Mobil in state court seeking a declaratory judgment that certain royalty charges were proper under a joint venture agreement. Two weeks later, Exxon Mobil sued SABIC in federal court alleging that it had been overcharged. In due course, it answered the state court complaint and filed counterclaims in state court asserting the same claims on which it had sued in federal court. The state court proceedings went to judgment first, resulting in a verdict of over $400 million in favor of Exxon Mobil. SABIC appealed to the state Supreme Court. A panel of that court affirmed the state court judgment, and rehearing en banc was denied.

Jurisdiction in the concurrent federal court proceedings was based on 28 U.S.C. § 1330, which authorizes federal courts to hear actions against foreign states. Prior to the state court trial, SABIC claimed sovereign immunity and moved to dismiss the federal action. The District Court denied the motion, and SABIC filed an interlocutory appeal.

By the time the Circuit Court heard the appeal, the state court jury had returned its verdict. As described by the Supreme Court, the Circuit Court on its own motion "raised the question whether 'subject matter jurisdiction over this case fails under the *Rooker-Feldman* doctrine because Exxon Mobil's claims have already been litigated in state court.' The court did not question the District Court's possession of subject-matter jurisdiction at the outset of the suit, but held that federal jurisdiction terminated when the Delaware Superior Court entered judgment on the jury verdict." The Supreme Court granted certiorari.[a]

---

[a]. At oral argument, SABIC declared its intention to seek certiorari from the Delaware Supreme Court decision upholding the jury verdict, but had not yet done so. The controversy was therefore still live, and not moot.

Speaking for a unanimous Court, Justice Ginsburg pointed out that "[s]ince *Feldman*, this Court has never applied *Rooker-Feldman* to dismiss an action for want of jurisdiction. The few decisions that have mentioned *Rooker* and *Feldman* have done so only in passing or to explain why those cases did not dictate dismissal."[b] She then explained the rationale for the doctrine and why it did not apply in this case:

> The *Rooker-Feldman* doctrine, we hold today, is confined to cases of the kind from which the doctrine acquired its name: cases brought by state-court losers complaining of injuries caused by state-court judgments rendered before the district court proceedings commenced and inviting district court review and rejection of those judgments. *Rooker-Feldman* does not otherwise override or supplant preclusion doctrine or augment the circumscribed doctrines that allow federal courts to stay or dismiss proceedings in deference to state-court actions. . . .
>
> *Rooker* and *Feldman* exhibit the limited circumstances in which this Court's appellate jurisdiction over state-court judgments, 28 U.S.C. § 1257, precludes a United States district court from exercising subject-matter jurisdiction in an action it would otherwise be empowered to adjudicate under a congressional grant of authority. In both cases, the losing party in state court filed suit in federal court after the state proceedings ended, complaining of an injury caused by the state-court judgment and seeking review and rejection of that judgment. Plaintiffs in both cases, alleging federal-question jurisdiction, called upon the District Court to overturn an injurious state-court judgment. Because § 1257, as long interpreted, vests authority to review a state court's judgment solely in this Court, the District Courts in *Rooker* and *Feldman* lacked subject-matter jurisdiction. . . .
>
> When there is parallel state and federal litigation, *Rooker-Feldman* is not triggered simply by the entry of judgment in state court. This Court has repeatedly held that "the pendency of an action in the state court is no bar to proceedings concerning the same matter in the Federal court having jurisdiction." McClellan v. Carland, 217 U.S. 268, 282 (1910). Comity or abstention doctrines may, in various circumstances, permit or require the federal court to stay or dismiss the federal action in favor of the state-court litigation. See, e.g., Colorado River Water Conservation Dist.

---

b. The doctrine was the subject of a Symposium in the Notre Dame Law Review. See Thomas D. Rowe, Jr., *Rooker-Feldman*: Worth Only the Powder to Blow It Up?, 74 Notre Dame L. Rev. 1081 (1999); Suzanna Sherry, Judicial Federalism in the Trenches: The *Rooker-Feldman* Doctrine in Action, 74 Notre Dame L. Rev. 1085 (1999); Barry Friedman & James E. Gaylord, *Rooker-Feldman*, from the Ground Up, 74 Notre Dame L. Rev. 1129 (1999); Susan Bandes, The *Rooker-Feldman* Doctrine: Evaluating Its Jurisdictional Status, 74 Notre Dame L. Rev. 1175 (1999); Jack M. Beermann, Comments on *Rooker-Feldman* or Let State Law Be Our Guide, 74 Notre Dame L. Rev. 1209 (1999).—[Footnote by eds.]

v. United States, 424 U.S. 800 (1976); Younger v. Harris, 401 U.S. 37 (1971); Burford v. Sun Oil Co., 319 U.S. 315 (1943); Railroad Comm'n of Tex. v. Pullman Co., 312 U.S. 496 (1941). But neither *Rooker* nor *Feldman* supports the notion that properly invoked concurrent jurisdiction vanishes if a state court reaches judgment on the same or related question while the case remains sub judice in a federal court.

Disposition of the federal action, once the state-court adjudication is complete, would be governed by preclusion law. The Full Faith and Credit Act, 28 U.S.C. § 1738, requires the federal court to "give the same preclusive effect to a state-court judgment as another court of that State would give." Parsons Steel, Inc. v. First Alabama Bank, 474 U.S. 518, 523 (1986). Preclusion, of course, is not a jurisdictional matter. In parallel litigation, a federal court may be bound to recognize the claim-and issue-preclusive effects of a state-court judgment, but federal jurisdiction over an action does not terminate automatically on the entry of judgment in the state court.

Nor does § 1257 stop a district court from exercising subject-matter jurisdiction simply because a party attempts to litigate in federal court a matter previously litigated in state court. If a federal plaintiff "present[s] some independent claim, albeit one that denies a legal conclusion that a state court has reached in a case to which he was a party ... , then there is jurisdiction and state law determines whether the defendant prevails under principles of preclusion." GASH Assocs. v. Village of Rosemont, 995 F.2d 726, 728 (7th Cir. 1993).

... Exxon Mobil plainly has not repaired to federal court to undo the Delaware judgment in its favor. Rather, it appears Exxon Mobil filed suit in Federal District Court (only two weeks after SABIC filed in Delaware and well before any judgment in state court) to protect itself in the event it lost in state court on grounds (such as the state statute of limitations) that might not preclude relief in the federal venue.[9] *Rooker-Feldman* did not prevent the District Court from exercising jurisdiction when Exxon Mobil filed the federal action, and it did not emerge to vanquish jurisdiction after Exxon Mobil prevailed in the Delaware courts.

Page 660, add at the end of footnote 13:

[For an example of a situation where a return to federal court was not permitted because "petitioners effectively asked the state court to resolve the same federal issues

9. The Court of Appeals criticized Exxon Mobil for pursuing its federal suit as an "insurance policy" against an adverse result in state court. There is nothing necessarily inappropriate, however, about filing a protective action.

they asked it to reserve," see San Remo Hotel, L.P. v. City and County of San Francisco, 545 U.S. ___ (2005).—Addition to Footnote by eds.]

Page 661, add a footnote at the end of the first question in Note 5:

m. For an argument that the *England* doctrine "can and should expand to achieve coherence in the law of federal jurisdiction," see Barry Friedman, Under the Law of Federal Jurisdiction: Allocating Cases Between Federal and State Courts, 104 Colum. L. Rev. 1211, 1264–79 (2004).

Page 736, rename Section 4 of Chapter VI "Anti–Injunction Acts" and add the following case at the end of Section 4:

Hibbs v. Winn

Supreme Court of the United States, 2004.
542 U.S. 88.

■ JUSTICE GINSBURG delivered the opinion of the Court.

Arizona law authorizes income-tax credits for payments to organizations that award educational scholarships and tuition grants to children attending private schools. See Ariz.Rev.Stat. Ann. § 43–1089 (West Supp. 2003). Plaintiffs below, respondents here, brought an action in federal court challenging § 43–1089, and seeking to enjoin its operation, on Establishment Clause grounds. The question presented is whether the Tax Injunction Act (TIA or Act), 28 U.S.C. § 1341, which prohibits a lower federal court from restraining "the assessment, levy or collection of any tax under State law," bars the suit. Plaintiffs-respondents do not contest their own tax liability. Nor do they seek to impede Arizona's receipt of tax revenues. Their suit, we hold, is not the kind § 1341 proscribes.

In decisions spanning a near half century, courts in the federal system, including this Court, have entertained challenges to tax credits authorized by state law, without conceiving of § 1341 as a jurisdictional barrier. On this first occasion squarely to confront the issue, we confirm the authority federal courts exercised in those cases.

It is hardly ancient history that States, once bent on maintaining racial segregation in public schools, and allocating resources disproportionately to benefit white students to the detriment of black students, fastened on tuition grants and tax credits as a promising means to circumvent Brown v. Board of Education, 347 U.S. 483 (1954). The federal courts, this Court among them, adjudicated the ensuing challenges, instituted under 42 U.S.C. § 1983, and upheld the Constitution's equal protection requirement. [Citations omitted.]

In the instant case, petitioner Hibbs, Director of Arizona's Department of Revenue, argues, in effect, that we and other federal courts were wrong in those civil-rights cases. The TIA, petitioner maintains, trumps § 1983; the Act, according to petitioner, bars all lower federal-court interference with state tax systems, even when the challengers are not endeavoring to avoid a tax imposed on them, and no matter whether the State's revenues would be raised or lowered should the plaintiffs prevail. The alleged jurisdictional bar, which petitioner asserts has existed since the TIA's enactment in 1937, was not even imagined by the jurists in the pathmarking civil-rights cases just cited, or by the defendants in those cases, litigants with every interest in defeating federal-court adjudicatory authority. Our prior decisions command no respect, petitioner urges, because they constitute mere "sub silentio holdings." We reject that assessment.

We examine in this opinion both the scope of the term "assessment" as used in the TIA, and the question whether the Act was intended to insulate state tax laws from constitutional challenge in lower federal courts even when the suit would have no negative impact on tax collection. Concluding that this suit implicates neither § 1341's conception of assessment nor any of the statute's underlying purposes, we affirm the judgment of the Court of Appeals.

I

Plaintiffs-respondents, Arizona taxpayers, filed suit in the United States District Court for the District of Arizona, challenging Ariz.Rev.Stat. Ann. § 43–1089 (West Supp.2003) as incompatible with the Establishment Clause. Section 43–1089 provides a credit to taxpayers who contribute money to "school tuition organizations" (STOs). An STO is a nonprofit organization that directs moneys, in the form of scholarship grants, to students enrolled in private elementary or secondary schools. STOs must disburse as scholarship grants at least 90 percent of contributions received, may allow donors to direct scholarships to individual students, may not allow donors to name their own dependents, must designate at least two schools whose students will receive funds, and must not designate schools that "discriminate on the basis of race, color, handicap, familial status or national origin." STOs are not precluded by Arizona's statute from designating schools that provide religious instruction or that give admissions preference on the basis of religion or religious affiliation. When taxpayers donate money to a qualified STO, § 43–1089 allows them, in calculating their Arizona tax liability, to credit up to $500 of their donation (or $625 for a married couple filing jointly).

In effect, § 43–1089 gives Arizona taxpayers an election. They may direct $500 (or, for joint-return filers, $625) to an STO, or to the Arizona Department of Revenue. As long as donors do not give STOs more than their total tax liability, their $500 or $625 contributions are costless.

The Arizona Supreme Court, by a 3-to-2 vote, rejected a facial challenge to § 43–1089 before the statute went into effect. That case took the form of a special discretionary action invoking the court's original jurisdiction. [This decision], it is undisputed, has no preclusive effect on the instant as-applied challenge to § 43–1089 brought by different plaintiffs.

Respondents' federal-court complaint against the Director of Arizona's Department of Revenue (Director) alleged that § 43–1089 "authorizes the formation of agencies that have as their sole purpose the distribution of State funds to children of a particular religious denomination or to children attending schools of a particular religious denomination." Respondents sought injunctive and declaratory relief, and an order requiring STOs to pay funds still in their possession "into the state general fund."

The Director moved to dismiss the action, relying on the TIA, which reads in its entirety:

> The district courts shall not enjoin, suspend or restrain the assessment, levy or collection of any tax under State law where a plain, speedy and efficient remedy may be had in the courts of such State.

The Director did not assert that a federal-court order enjoining § 43–1089 would interfere with the State's tax levy or collection efforts. He urged only that a federal injunction would restrain the "assessment" of taxes "under State law." Agreeing with the Director, the District Court held that the TIA required dismissal of the suit.

The Court of Appeals for the Ninth Circuit reversed.... We granted certiorari in view of the division of opinion on whether the TIA bars constitutional challenges to state tax credits in federal court. We now affirm the judgment of the Ninth Circuit.

II

Before reaching the merits of this case, we must address respondents' contention that the Director's petition for certiorari was jurisdictionally untimely under 28 U.S.C. § 2101(c) and our Rules. [The Court held the petition timely.]

III

To determine whether this litigation falls within the TIA's prohibition, it is appropriate, first, to identify the relief sought. Respondents seek prospective relief only. Specifically, their complaint requests "injunctive relief prohibiting [the Director] from allowing taxpayers to utilize the tax credit authorized by A.R.S. § 43–1089 for payments made to STOs that make tuition grants to children attending religious schools, to children attending schools of only one religious denomination, or to children selected on the basis of their religion." Respondents further ask for a "declaration that A.R.S. § 43–1089, on its face and as applied," violates the Establishment Clause "by affirmatively authorizing STOs to use State income-tax revenues to pay tuition for students attending religious schools or schools that discriminate on the basis of religion." Finally, respondents seek "[a]n order that [the Director] inform all [such] STOs that ... all funds in their possession as of the date of this Court's order must be paid into the state general fund." Taking account of the prospective nature of the relief requested, does respondents' suit, in 28 U.S.C. § 1341's words, seek to "enjoin, suspend or restrain the assessment, levy or collection of any tax under State law"? The answer to that question turns on the meaning of the term "assessment" as employed in the TIA.[1]

As used in the Internal Revenue Code (IRC), the term "assessment" involves a "recording" of the amount the taxpayer owes the Government. 26 U.S.C. § 6203. The "assessment" is "essentially a bookkeeping notation." Laing v. United States, 423 U.S. 161, 170 n.13 (1976). Section 6201(a) of the IRC authorizes the Secretary of the Treasury "to make . . . assessments of all taxes . . . imposed by this title." An assessment is made "by recording the liability of the taxpayer in the office of the Secretary in accordance with rules or regulations prescribed by the Secretary." § 6203.[2]

We do not focus on the word "assessment" in isolation, however. Instead, we follow "the cardinal rule that statutory language must be read in context [since] a phrase gathers meaning from the words around it." General Dynamics Land Systems, Inc. v. Cline, 540 U.S. 581, ___ (2004). In § 1341 and tax law generally, an assessment is closely tied to the collection of a tax, i.e., the assessment is the official recording of liability that triggers levy and collection efforts.

The rule against superfluities complements the principle that courts are to interpret the words of a statute in context. See 2A N. Singer, Statutes and Statutory Construction § 46.06, pp. 181–86 (rev. 6th ed. 2000) ("A statute should be construed so that effect is given to all its provisions, so that no part will be inoperative or superfluous, void or insignificant . . . ."). If, as the Director asserts, the term "assessment," by itself, signified "[t]he entire plan or scheme fixed upon for charging or taxing," the TIA would not need the words "levy" or "collection"; the term "assessment," alone, would do all the necessary work.

Earlier this Term, in United States v. Galletti, 541 U.S. 114 (2004), the Government identified "two important consequences" that follow from the IRS' timely tax assessment: "[T]he IRS may employ administrative enforcement methods such as tax liens and levies to collect the outstanding tax"; and "the time within which the IRS may collect the tax either administratively *or* by a 'proceeding in court' is extended [from 3 years] to 10 years after the date of assessment." The Government . . . made clear in

---

1. State taxation, for § 1341 purposes, includes local taxation.

2. The term "assessment" is used in a variety of ways in tax law. In the property-tax setting, the word usually refers to the process by which the taxing authority assigns a taxable value to real or personal property. To calculate the amount of property taxes owed, the tax assessor multiplies the assessed value by the appropriate tax rate. Income taxes, by contrast, are typically self-assessed in the United States. As anyone who has filed a tax return is unlikely to forget, the taxpayer, not the taxing authority, is the first party to make the relevant calculation of income taxes owed. The word "self-assessment," however, is not a technical term; as IRC § 6201(a) indicates, the Internal Revenue Service executes the formal act of income-tax assessment.

briefing *Galletti* that, under the IRC definition, the tax "assessment" serves as the trigger for levy and collection efforts. The Government did not describe the term as synonymous with the entire plan of taxation. Nor did it disassociate the word "assessment" from the company ("levy or collection") that word keeps.[3] Instead, and in accord with our understanding, the Government related "assessment" to the term's collection-propelling function....

IV

Congress modeled § 1341 upon earlier federal "statutes of similar import," laws that, in turn, paralleled state provisions proscribing "actions in State courts to enjoin the collection of State and county taxes." S.Rep. No. 1035, 75th Cong., 1st Sess., 1 (1937) (hereinafter S. Rep.). In composing the TIA's text, Congress drew particularly on an 1867 measure, sometimes called the Anti–Injunction Act (AIA), which bars "any court" from entertaining a suit brought "for the purpose of restraining the assessment or collection of any [federal] tax." Act of Mar. 2, 1867, ch. 169, § 10, 14 Stat. 475, now codified at 26 U.S.C. § 7421(a). See Jefferson County v. Acker, 527 U.S. 423, 434–35 (1999). While § 7421(a) "apparently has no recorded legislative history," Bob Jones Univ. v. Simon, 416 U.S. 725, 736 (1974), the Court has recognized, from the AIA's text, that the measure serves twin purposes: It responds to "the Government's need to assess and collect taxes as expeditiously as possible with a minimum of preenforcement judicial interference"; and it "'require[s] that the legal right to the disputed sums be determined in a suit for refund,'" ibid.[4] Lower federal courts have similarly comprehended § 7421(a). See, e.g., McGlotten v. Connally, 338 F.Supp. 448, 453–454 (D.D.C. 1972) (three-judge court) (§ 7421(a) does not bar action seeking to enjoin income-tax exemptions to fraternal orders that exclude nonwhites from membership, for in such an action, plaintiff "does not contest the amount of his own tax, nor does he seek to limit the amount of tax revenue collectible by the United States"); Tax Analysts and Advocates v. Shultz, 376 F.Supp. 889, 892 (D.D.C.1974) (§ 7421(a) does not bar challenge to IRS revenue ruling allowing contributors to political candidate committees to avoid federal gift tax on contributions in excess of $3,000 ceiling; while § 7421(a) "precludes suits to restrain the assessment or collection of taxes," the proscription does not apply when "plaintiffs seek not to restrain the Commissioner from collect-

---

3. The dissent is of two minds in this regard. On the one hand, it twice suggests that a proper definition of the term "assessment," for § 1341 purposes, is "the entire plan or scheme fixed upon for charging or taxing." On the other hand, the dissent would disconnect the word from the enforcement process ("levy or collection") that "assessment" sets in motion.

4. That Congress had in mind challenges to assessments triggering collections, i.e., attempts to prevent the collection of revenue, is borne out by the final clause of 26 U.S.C. § 7421(a), added in 1966: "whether or not such person is the person *against whom* such tax was assessed" (emphasis added).

ing taxes, but rather to *require* him to collect *additional* taxes according to the mandates of the law." (emphases in original)).

Just as the AIA shields federal tax collections from federal-court injunctions, so the TIA shields state tax collections from federal-court restraints. In both 26 U.S.C. § 7421(a) and 28 U.S.C. § 1341, Congress directed taxpayers to pursue refund suits instead of attempting to restrain collections. Third-party suits not seeking to stop the collection (or contest the validity) of a tax *imposed on plaintiffs,* as *McGlotten* and *Tax Analysts* explained, were outside Congress' purview. The TIA's legislative history is not silent in this regard. The Act was designed expressly to restrict "the jurisdiction of the district courts of the United States over suits relating to the collection of State taxes." S. Rep., p. 1.

Specifically, the Senate Report commented that the Act had two closely related, state-revenue-protective objectives: (1) to eliminate disparities between taxpayers who could seek injunctive relief in federal court—usually out-of-state corporations asserting diversity jurisdiction—and taxpayers with recourse only to state courts, which generally required taxpayers to pay first and litigate later; and (2) to stop taxpayers, with the aid of a federal injunction, from withholding large sums, thereby disrupting state government finances. In short, in enacting the TIA, Congress trained its attention on taxpayers who sought to avoid paying their tax bill by pursuing a challenge route other than the one specified by the taxing authority. Nowhere does the legislative history announce a sweeping congressional direction to prevent "federal-court interference with all aspects of state tax administration." Brief for Petitioner 20.[7]

The understanding of the Act's purposes and legislative history set out above underpins this Court's previous applications of the TIA. In California v. Grace Brethren Church, 457 U.S. 393 (1982), for example, we recognized that the principal purpose of the TIA was to "limit drastically" federal-court interference with "the collection of [state] taxes." True, the Court referred to the disruption of "state tax administration," but it did so specifically in relation to the "the collection of revenue." The complainants in *Grace Brethren Church* were several California churches and religious schools. They sought federal-court relief from an unemployment compensation tax that state law imposed on them. Their federal action, which bypassed state remedies, was exactly what the TIA was designed to ward off. The Director and the dissent endeavor to reconstruct *Grace Brethren Church* as precedent for the proposition that the TIA totally immunizes

---

7. The language of the TIA differs significantly from that of the Johnson Act, which provides in part: "The district courts shall not enjoin, suspend or restrain *the operation of, or compliance with,*" public-utility rate orders made by state regulatory bodies. 28 U.S.C. § 1342 (emphasis added). The TIA does not prohibit interference with "the operation of, or compliance with" state tax laws; rather, § 1341 proscribes interference only with those aspects of state tax regimes that are needed to produce revenue—i.e., assessment, levy, and collection.

from lower federal-court review "all aspects of state tax administration, and not just interference with the collection of revenue." The endeavor is unavailing given the issue before the Court in *Grace Brethren Church* and the context in which the words "state tax administration" appear.

The Director invokes several other decisions alleged to keep matters of "state tax administration" entirely free from lower federal-court "interference." Like *Grace Brethren Church,* all of them fall within § 1341's undisputed compass: All involved plaintiffs who mounted federal litigation to avoid paying state taxes (or to gain a refund of such taxes). Federal-court relief, therefore, would have operated to reduce the flow of state tax revenue. See Arkansas v. Farm Credit Servs. of Central Ark., 520 U.S. 821, 824 (1997) (corporations chartered under federal law claimed exemption from Arkansas sales and income taxation); National Private Truck Council, Inc. v. Oklahoma Tax Comm'n, 515 U.S. 582, 584 (1995) (action seeking to prevent Oklahoma from collecting taxes State imposed on nonresident motor carriers); Fair Assessment in Real Estate Assn., Inc. v. McNary, 454 U.S. 100, 105–06 (1981) (taxpayers, alleging unequal taxation of real property, sought, inter alia, damages measured by alleged tax overassessments); Rosewell v. LaSalle National Bank, 450 U.S. 503, 510 (1981) (state taxpayer, alleging her property was inequitably assessed, refused to pay state taxes).[8]

Our prior decisions are not fairly portrayed cut loose from their secure, state-revenue-protective moorings. See, e.g., *Grace Brethren Church,* 457 U.S., at 410 ("If federal declaratory relief were available to test state tax assessments, state tax administration might be thrown into disarray, and *taxpayers might escape the ordinary procedural requirements imposed by state law.* During the pendency of the federal suit *the collection of revenue under the challenged law might be obstructed, with consequent damage to the State's budget, and perhaps a shift to the State of the risk of taxpayer insolvency.*") (emphases added).[9]

In sum, this Court has interpreted and applied the TIA only in cases Congress wrote the Act to address, i.e., cases in which state taxpayers seek federal-court orders enabling them to avoid paying state taxes. We have

---

8. Petitioner urges, and the dissent agrees, that the TIA safeguards another vital state interest: the authority of state courts to determine what state law means. Respondents, however, have not asked the District Court to interpret any state law—there is no disagreement as to the meaning of Ariz.Rev. Stat. Ann. § 43–1089 (West Supp.2003), only about whether, as applied, the State's law violates the Federal Constitution. That is a question federal courts are no doubt equipped to adjudicate.

9. We note, furthermore, that this Court has relied upon "principles of comity," Brief for Petitioner 26, to preclude original federal-court jurisdiction only when plaintiffs have sought district-court aid in order to arrest or countermand state tax collection. See Fair Assessment in Real Estate Assn., Inc. v. McNary, 454 U.S. 100, 107–08 (1981) (Missouri taxpayers sought damages for increased taxes caused by alleged overassessments); Great Lakes Dredge & Dock Co. v. Huffman, 319 U.S. 293, 296–99 (1943) (plaintiffs challenged Louisiana's unemployment compensation tax).

read harmoniously the § 1341 instruction conditioning the jurisdictional bar on the availability of "a plain, speedy and efficient remedy" in state court. The remedy inspected in our decisions was not one designed for the universe of plaintiffs who sue the State. Rather, it was a remedy tailormade for taxpayers. See, *e.g., Rosewell,* 450 U.S., at 528 ("Illinois' legal remedy that provides property owners paying property taxes under protest a refund without interest in two years is a 'plain, speedy and efficient remedy' under the [TIA]"); *Grace Brethren Church,* 457 U.S., at 411 ("[A] state-court remedy is 'plain, speedy and efficient'" only if it "provides the taxpayer with a 'full hearing and judicial determination' at which she may raise any and all constitutional objections to the tax.").[10]

V

In other federal courts as well, § 1341 has been read to restrain state taxpayers from instituting federal actions to contest their liability for state taxes, but not to stop third parties from pursuing constitutional challenges to tax benefits in a federal forum. Relevant to the distinction between taxpayer claims that would reduce state revenues and third-party claims that would enlarge state receipts, Seventh Circuit Judge Easterbrook wrote trenchantly:

> Although the district court concluded that § 1341 applies to any federal litigation touching on the subject of state taxes, neither the language nor the legislative history of the statute supports this interpretation. The text of § 1341 does not suggest that federal courts should tread lightly in issuing orders that might allow local governments to raise additional taxes. The legislative history ... shows that § 1341 is designed to ensure that federal courts do not interfere with states' collection of taxes, so long as the taxpayers have an opportunity to present to a court federal defenses to the imposition and collection of the taxes. The legislative history is filled with concern that federal judgments were emptying state coffers and that corporations with access to the diversity jurisdiction could obtain remedies unavailable to resident taxpayers. *There was no articulated concern about federal courts' flogging state and local governments to collect additional taxes.* Dunn v. Carey, 808 F.2d 555, 558 (7th Cir. 1986) (emphasis added).

[Discussion of other lower federal court decisions has been omitted. Also omitted is discussion of "numerous federal-court decisions—including decisions of this Court reviewing lower federal-court judgments—[that]

---

10. Far from "ignor[ing]" the "plain, speedy and efficient remedy" proviso, as the dissent charges, we agree that this "codified exception" is key to a proper understanding of the Act. The statute requires the State to provide *taxpayers* with a swift and certain remedy when they resist tax collections. An action dependent on a court's discretion, for example, would not qualify as a fitting taxpayer's remedy.

have reached the merits of third-party constitutional challenges to tax benefits without mentioning the TIA."][12]

* * *

In a procession of cases not rationally distinguishable from this one, no Justice or member of the bar of this Court ever raised a § 1341 objection that, according to the petitioner in this case, should have caused us to order dismissal of the action for want of jurisdiction. [Citations omitted,] Consistent with the decades-long understanding prevailing on this issue, respondents' suit may proceed without any TIA impediment.[13]

For the reasons stated, the judgment of the United States Court of Appeals for the Ninth Circuit is

Affirmed.

■ JUSTICE STEVENS, concurring.

In Part IV of his dissent, Justice Kennedy observes that "years of unexamined habit by litigants and the courts" do not lessen this Court's obligation correctly to interpret a statute. It merits emphasis, however, that prolonged congressional silence in response to a settled interpretation of a federal statute provides powerful support for maintaining the status quo. In statutory matters, judicial restraint strongly counsels waiting for Congress to take the initiative in modifying rules on which judges and litigants have relied. In a contest between the dictionary and the doctrine of stare decisis, the latter clearly wins. The Court's fine opinion, which I join without reservation, is consistent with these views.

■ JUSTICE KENNEDY, with whom THE CHIEF JUSTICE, JUSTICE SCALIA, and JUSTICE THOMAS join, dissenting.

In this case, the Court shows great skepticism for the state courts' ability to vindicate constitutional wrongs. Two points make clear that the Court treats States as diminished and disfavored powers, rather than merely applies statutory text. First, the Court's analysis of the Tax Injunction Act (TIA or Act), 28 U.S.C. § 1341, contrasts with a literal reading of its terms. Second, the Court's assertion that legislative histories support the conclusion that "[t]hird-party suits not seeking to stop the collection

---

12. In school desegregation cases, as a last resort, federal courts have asserted authority to direct the imposition of, or increase in, local tax levies, even in amounts exceeding the ceiling set by state law. See Missouri v. Jenkins, 495 U.S. 33, 57 (1990); Liddell v. Missouri, 731 F.2d 1294, 1320 (8th Cir. 1984) (en banc); cf. Griffin v. School Bd. of Prince Edward Cty., 377 U.S. 218, 233 (1964). Controversial as such a measure may be, see Jenkins, 495 U.S., at 65–81 (Kennedy, J., concurring in part and concurring in judgment), it is noteworthy that § 1341 was not raised in those cases by counsel, lower courts, or this Court on its own motion.

13. In confirming that cases of this order may be brought in federal court, we do not suggest that "state courts are second rate constitutional arbiters." Instead, we underscore that adjudications of great moment discerning no § 1341 barrier cannot be written off as reflecting nothing more than "unexamined custom" or unthinking "habit."

(or contest the validity) of a tax *imposed on plaintiffs* ... were outside Congress' purview" in enacting the TIA and the anti-injunction provision on which the TIA was modeled is not borne out by those sources, as previously recognized by the Court. In light of these points, today's holding should probably be attributed to the concern the Court candidly shows animates it. See [passages] noting it was the federal courts that "upheld the Constitution's equal protection requirement" when States circumvented Brown v. Board of Education, 347 U.S. 483 (1954), by manipulating their tax laws. The concern, it seems, is that state courts are second rate constitutional arbiters, unequal to their federal counterparts. State courts are due more respect than this. Dismissive treatment of state courts is particularly unjustified since the TIA, by express terms, provides a federal safeguard: The Act lifts its bar on federal court intervention when state courts fail to provide "a plain, speedy, and efficient remedy." § 1341.

In view of the TIA's text, the congressional judgment that state courts are qualified constitutional arbiters, and the respect state courts deserve, I disagree with the majority's superseding the balance the Act strikes between federal and state court adjudication. I agree with the majority that the petition for certiorari was timely under 28 U.S.C. § 2101(c), and so submit this respectful dissent on the merits of the decision.

I

Today is the first time the Court has considered whether the TIA bars federal district courts from granting injunctive relief that would prevent States from giving citizens statutorily mandated state tax credits. There are cases, some dating back almost 50 years, which proceeded as if the jurisdictional bar did not apply to tax credit challenges; but some more recent decisions have said the bar is applicable. Compare, e.g., Mueller v. Allen, 463 U.S. 388 (1983); Committee for Public Ed. & Religious Liberty v. Nyquist, 413 U.S. 756 (1973); Griffin v. School Bd. of Prince Edward Cty., 377 U.S. 218 (1964), with, e.g., ACLU Foundation of La. v. Bridges, 334 F.3d 416 (5th Cir. 2003); In re Gillis, 836 F.2d 1001 (6th Cir. 1988). While unexamined custom favors the first position, the statutory text favors the latter. In these circumstances a careful explanation for the conclusion is necessary; but in the end the scope and purpose of the Act should be understood from its terms alone.

The question presented—whether the TIA bars the District Court from granting injunctive relief against the tax credit—requires two inquiries. First, the term assessment, as used in § 1341, must be defined. Second, we must determine if an injunction prohibiting the Director from allowing the credit would enjoin, suspend, or restrain an assessment.

The word assessment in the TIA is not isolated from its use in another federal statute. The TIA was modeled on the anti-injunction provision of the Internal Revenue Code (Code), 26 U.S.C. § 7421(a). That provision specifies, and has specified since 1867, that federal courts may not restrain or enjoin an "assessment or collection of any [federal] tax." The meaning of the term assessment in this Code provision is discernible by reference to other Code sections.

Chapter 63 of Title 26 addresses the subject of assessments and sheds light on the meaning of the term in the Code. Section 6201(a) first instructs that "[t]he Secretary [of the Internal Revenue Service] is ... required to make the ... assessments of all taxes ... imposed by this title...." Further it provides, "[t]he Secretary shall assess all taxes determined by the taxpayer or by the Secretary...." Section 6203 in turn sets forth a method for making an assessment: "The assessment shall be made by recording the liability of the taxpayer in the office of the Secretary."

Taken together, the provisions of Title 26 establish that an assessment, as that term is used in § 7421(a), must at the least encompass the recording of a taxpayer's ultimate tax liability. This is what the taxpayer owes the Government. See also Laing v. United States, 423 U.S. 161, 170 n.13 (1976) ("The 'assessment,' essentially a bookkeeping notation, is made when the Secretary or his delegate establishes an account against the taxpayer on the tax rolls"). Whether the Secretary or his delegate (today, the Commissioner) makes the recording on the basis of a taxpayer's self-reported filing form or instead chooses to rely on his own calculation of the taxpayer's liability (*e.g.*, via an audit) is irrelevant. The recording of the liability on the Government's tax rolls is itself an assessment.

The TIA was modeled on the anti-injunction provision; it incorporates the same terminology employed by the provision; and it employs that terminology for the same purpose. It is sensible, then, to interpret the TIA's terms by reference to the Code's use of the term. Cf. Lorillard v. Pons, 434 U.S. 575, 581 (1978) ("[W]here, as here, Congress adopts a new law incorporating sections of a prior law, Congress normally can be presumed to have had knowledge of the interpretation given to the incorporated law, at least insofar as it affects the new statute"). The Court of Appeals, which concluded that an assessment was the official estimate of the value of income or property used to calculate a tax or the imposition of a tax on someone, placed principal reliance for its interpretation on a dictionary definition. That was not entirely misplaced; but unless the definition is considered in the context of the prior statute, the advantage of that statute's interpretive guidance is lost.

Furthermore, the court defined the term in an unusual way. It relied on a dictionary that was unavailable when the TIA was enacted; it relied not on the definition of the term under consideration, "assessment," but on the definition of the term's related verb form, "assess"; and it examined only a portion of that terms' definition. In the dictionary used by the Court of Appeals, the verb is defined in two ways not noted by the court. One of the alternative definitions is quite relevant—"(2) to fix or determine the amount of (damages, a tax, a fine, etc.)." Further,

Had [the panel] looked in a different lay dictionary, [it] would have found a definition contrary to the one it preferred, such as "the entire plan or scheme fixed upon for charging or taxing." . . . Had the panel considered tax treatises and law dictionaries . . . it would have found much in accord with this broader definition. . . . Even the federal income tax code supports a broad reading of "assessment." Winn v. Killian, 321 F.3d 911, 912 (9th Cir. 2003) (Kleinfeld, J., dissenting from denial of rehearing en banc).

Guided first by the Internal Revenue Code, an assessment under § 1341, at a minimum, is the recording of taxpayers' liability on the State's tax rolls. The TIA, though a federal statute that must be interpreted as a matter of federal law, operates in a state-law context. In this respect, the Act must be interpreted so as to apply evenly to the 50 various state-law regimes and to the various recording schemes States employ. It is therefore irrelevant whether state officials record taxpayer liabilities with their own pen in a specified location, by collecting and maintaining taxpayers' self-reported filing forms, or in some other manner. The recordkeeping that equates to the determination of taxpayer liability on the State's tax rolls is the assessment, whatever the method. The Court seems to agree with this.

The dictionary definition of assessment provides further relevant information. Contemporaneous dictionaries from the time of the TIA's enactment define assessment in expansive terms. They would broaden any understanding of the term, and so the Act's bar. See, e.g., Webster's New International Dictionary 139 (1927) (providing three context relevant definitions for the term assessment: It is the act of apportioning or determining an amount to be paid; a valuation of property for the purpose of taxation; or the entire plan or scheme fixed upon for charging or taxing). See also United States v. Galletti, 541 U.S. __ (2004) (noting that under the Code the term assessment refers not only to recordings of tax liability but also to "the calculation . . . of a tax liability," including self-calculation done by the taxpayer). The Court need not decide the full scope of the term assessment in the TIA, however. For present purposes, a narrow definition of the term suffices. Applying the narrowest definition, the TIA's literal text bars district courts from enjoining, suspending, or restraining a State's recording of taxpayer liability on its tax rolls, whether the recordings are made by self-reported taxpayer filing forms or by a State's calculation of taxpayer liability.

The terms "enjoin, suspend, or restrain" require little scrutiny. No doubt, they have discrete purposes in the context of the TIA; but they also have a common meaning. They refer to actions that restrict assessments to varying degrees. It is noteworthy that the term "enjoin" has not just its meaning in the restrictive sense but also has meaning in an affirmative sense. The Black's Law Dictionary current at the TIA's enactment gives as a definition of the term, "to require; command; positively direct." Black's Law Dictionary 663 (3d ed.1933). That definition may well be implicated here, since an order invalidating a tax credit would seem to command States to collect taxes they otherwise would not collect. The parties, however, proceed on the assumption that enjoin means to bar. It is unobjectionable for the Court to make the assumption too, leaving the broader definition for later consideration.

Respondents argue the TIA does not bar the injunction they seek because even after the credit is enjoined, the Director will be able to record and enforce taxpayers' liabilities. In fact, respondents say, with the credit out of the way the Director will be able to record and enforce a higher level of liability and so profit the State. ("The amount of tax payable by some taxpayers would increase, but that can hardly be characterized as an injunction or restraint of the assessment process"). The argument, however, ignores an important part of the Act: "under State law." 28 U.S.C. § 1341 ("The district courts shall not enjoin, suspend or restrain the assessment . . . of any tax under State law"). The Act not only bars district courts from enjoining, suspending, or restraining a State's recording of taxpayer liabilities altogether; but it also bars them from enjoining, suspending, or restraining a State from recording the taxpayer liability that state law mandates.

Section 43–1089 is state law. It is an integral part of the State's tax statute; it is reflected on state tax forms; and the State Supreme Court has held that it is part of the calculus necessary to determine tax liability. A recording of a taxpayer's liability under state law must be made in accordance with § 43–1089. The same can be said with respect to each and every provision of the State's tax law. To order the Director not to record on the State's tax rolls taxpayer liability that reflects the operation of § 43–1089 (or any other state tax law provision for that matter) would be to bar the Director from recording the correct taxpayer liability. The TIA's language bars this relief and so bars this suit.

The Court tries to avoid this conclusion by saying that the recordings that constitute assessments under § 1341 must have a "collection-propelling function" and that the recordings at issue here do not have such a function. See also footnote 4 ("[T]he dissent would disconnect the word [assessment] from the enforcement process"). That is wrong. A recording of taxpayer liability on the State's tax rolls of course propels collection. In most cases the taxpayer's payment will accompany his filing, and thus will accompany the assessment so that no literal collection of moneys is necessary. As anyone who has paid taxes must know, however, if owed payment were not included with the tax filing, the State's recording of one's liability on the State's rolls would certainly cause subsequent collection efforts, for the filing's recording (i.e., the assessment) would propel collection by establishing the State's legal right to the taxpayer's moneys.

II

The majority offers prior judicial interpretations of the Code's similarly worded anti-injunction provision to support its contrary conclusions about the statutory text. That this Court and other federal courts have allowed nontaxpayer suits challenging tax credits to proceed in the face of the anti-injunction provision is not at all controlling. Those cases are quite distinguishable. Had the plaintiffs in those cases been barred from suit, there would have been no available forum at all for their claims. See McGlotten v. Connally, 338 F.Supp. 448, 453–54 (D.D.C.1972) (three-judge court) ("The preferred course of raising [such tax exemption and deduction] objections in a suit for refund is not available. In this situation we cannot read the statute to bar the present suit"). See also Tax Analysts and Advocates v. Shultz, 376 F.Supp. 889, 892 (D.D.C.1974) ("Since plaintiffs are not seeking to restrain the collection of taxes, and since they cannot obtain relief through a refund suit, [26 U.S.C.] § 7421(a) does not bar the injunctive relief they seek"). The Court ratified those decisions only insofar as they relied on this limited rationale as the basis for an exception to the statutory bar on adjudication. . . .

In contrast to the anti-injunction provision, the TIA on its own terms ensures an adequate forum for claims it bars. The TIA specially exempts actions that could not be heard in state courts by providing an exception for instances "where a plain, speedy, and efficient remedy may [not] be had in the courts of [the] State." 28 U.S.C. § 1341. . . . The practical effect is that a literal reading of the TIA provides for federal district courts to stand at the ready where litigants encounter legal or practical obstacles to challenging state tax credits in state courts. And this Court, of course, stands at the ready to review decisions by state courts on these matters.

The Court does not discuss this codified exception, yet the clause is crucial. It represents a congressional judgment about the balance that should exist between the respect due to the States (for both their administration of tax schemes and their courts' interpretation of tax laws) and the need for constitutional vindication. To ignore the provision is to ignore that Congress has already balanced these interests.

Respondents admit they would be heard in state court. Indeed a quite similar action previously was heard there. As a result, the TIA's exception does not apply. To proceed as if it does is to replace Congress' balancing of the noted interests with the Court's.

III

The Court and respondents further argue that the TIA's policy purposes and relatedly the federal anti-injunction provision's policy purposes (as discerned from legislative histories) justify today's holding. The two Acts, they say, reflect a unitary purpose: "In both . . . Congress directed taxpayers to pursue refund suits instead of attempting to restrain [tax] collections." See also [the Court's statement] that the Act's underlying purpose is to bar suits by "taxpayers who sought to avoid paying their tax bill." This purpose, the Court and respondents say, shows that the Act was not intended to foreclose relief in challenges to tax credits. The proposition rests on the premise that the TIA's sole purpose is to prevent district court orders that would decrease the moneys in state fiscs. Because the legislative histories of the Acts are not carefully limited in the manner that this reading suggests, the policy argument against a literal application of the Act's terms fails.

Taking the federal anti-injunction provision first, as has been noted before, "[its] history expressly reflects the congressional desire that all injunctive suits against the tax collector be prohibited." South Carolina v. Regan, 465 U.S. 367, 387 (1984) (O'Connor, J., concurring in judgment). The provision responded to "the grave dangers which accompany intrusion of the injunctive power of the courts into the administration of the revenue." Id., at 388. It "generally precludes judicial resolution of all abstract tax controversies," whether brought by a taxpayer or a nontaxpayer. Id., at 392. Thus, the provision's object is not just to bar suits that might "interrupt 'the process of collecting . . . taxes,'" but "[s]imilarly, the language and history evidence a congressional desire to prohibit courts from restraining any aspect of the tax laws' administration." Id., at 399.

The majority's reading of the TIA's legislative history is also inconsistent with the interpretation of this same history in the Court's earlier cases. The Court has made clear that the TIA's purpose is not only to protect the fisc but also to protect the State's tax system administration and tax policy implementation. California v. Grace Brethren Church, 457 U.S. 393 (1982), is a prime example.

In *Grace Brethren Church* the Court held that the TIA not only bars actions by individuals to stop tax collectors from collecting moneys (i.e., injunctive suits) but also bars declaratory suits. The Court explained that permitting declaratory suits to proceed would "defea[t] the principal purpose of the Tax Injunction Act: 'to limit drastically federal district court jurisdiction to interfere with so important a local concern as the collection of taxes.'" It continued:

> If federal declaratory relief were available to test state tax assessments, state tax administration might be thrown into disarray, and taxpayers might escape the ordinary procedural requirements imposed by state law. During the pendency of the federal suit the collection of revenue under the challenged law might be obstructed, with consequent damage to the State's budget, and perhaps a shift to the State of the risk of taxpayer insolvency. Moreover, federal constitutional issues are likely to turn on questions of state tax law, which, like issues of state regulatory law, are more properly heard in the state courts.

While this, of course, demonstrates that protecting the state fisc from damage is part of the TIA's purpose, it equally shows that actions that would throw the "state tax administration . . . into disarray" also implicate the Act and its purpose. The Court's concern with preventing administrative disarray puts in context its explanation that the TIA's principal concern is to limit federal district court interference with the "collection of taxes." The phrase, in this context, refers to the operation of the whole tax collection system and the implementation of entire tax policy, not just a part of it. While an order interfering with a specific collection suit disrupts one of the most essential aspects of a State's tax system, it is not the only way in which federal courts can disrupt the State's tax system:

> [T]he legislative history of the Tax Injunction Act demonstrates that Congress worried not so much about the form of relief available in the federal courts, as about divesting the federal courts of jurisdiction to interfere with state tax administration. *Grace Brethren Church*, supra, at 409 n.22.

The Court's decisions in Fair Assessment in Real Estate Assn., Inc. v. McNary, 454 U.S. 100 (1981), National Private Truck Council, Inc. v. Oklahoma Tax Comm'n, 515 U.S. 582 (1995) *(NPTC)*, and *Rosewell*, supra, make the same point. Though the majority says these cases support its holding because they "involved plaintiffs who mounted federal litigation to avoid paying state taxes," the language of these cases is too clear to be ignored and is contrary to the Court's holding today. In *Fair Assessment*, the Court observed that "[t]he [TIA] 'has its roots in equity practice, in principles of federalism, and in recognition of the imperative need of a State to administer its own fiscal operations.' This last consideration was [its] principal motivating force." In *NPTC*, the Court said, "Congress and this Court repeatedly have shown an aversion to federal interference with state tax administration. The passage of the [TIA] in 1937 is one manifestation of this aversion." [*NPTC* also summed] up this aversion, generated also from principles of comity and federalism, as creating a "background presumption that federal law generally will not interfere with administration of state taxes." In *Rosewell,* the Court described the Act's language as "broad" and "prophylactic" [and also said that] the TIA was "passed to limit federal-court interference in state tax matters."

The Act is designed to respect not only the administration of state tax systems but also state court authority to say what state law means. "[F]ederal constitutional issues are likely to turn on questions of state tax law, which, like issues of state regulatory law, are more properly heard in the state courts." *Grace Brethren Church*, supra, at 410. This too establishes that the TIA's purpose is not solely to ensure that the State's fisc is not decreased. There would be only a diminished interest in allowing state courts to say what the State's tax statutes mean if the Act protected just the state fisc. The TIA protects the responsibility of the States and their courts to administer their own tax systems and to be accountable to the citizens of the State for their policies and decisions. The majority objects that "there is no disagreement to the meaning of" state law in this case. As an initial matter, it is not clear that this is a fair conclusion. The litigation in large part turns on what state law requires and whether the product of those requirements violates the Constitution. More to the point, however, even if there were no controversy about the statutory framework the Arizona tax provision creates, the majority's ruling has implications far beyond this case and will most certainly result in federal courts in other States and in other cases being required to interpret state tax law in order to complete their review of challenges to state tax statutes.

Our heretofore consistent interpretation of the Act's legislative history to prohibit interference with state tax systems and their administration accords with the direct, broad, and unqualified language of the statute. The Act bars all orders that enjoin, suspend, or restrain the assessment of any tax under state law. In effecting congressional intent we should give full force to simple and broad proscriptions in the statutory language.

Because the TIA's language and purpose are comprehensive, arguments based on congressional silence on the question whether the TIA applies to actions that increase moneys a state tax system collects are of no moment. Whatever weight one gives to legislative histories, silence in the legislative record is irrelevant when a plain congressional declaration exists on a matter. "[W]hen terms are unambiguous we may not speculate on probabilities of intention." Merchants' Insurance Co. v. Ritchie, 72 U.S. (5 Wall.) 541, 545 (1867). Here, Congress has said district courts are barred from disrupting the State's tax operations. It is immaterial whether the State's collection is raised or lowered. A court order will thwart and replace the State's chosen tax policy if it causes either result. No authority supports the proposition that a State lacks an interest in reducing its citizens' tax burden. It is a troubling proposition for this Court to proceed on the assumption that the State's interest in limiting the tax burden on its citizens to that for which its law provides is a secondary policy, deserving of little respect from us.

IV

The final basis on which both the majority and respondents rest is that years of unexamined habit by litigants and the courts alike have resulted in federal courts' entertaining challenges to state tax credits. While we should not reverse the course of our unexamined practice lightly, our obligation is to give a correct interpretation of the statute. We are not obliged to maintain the status quo when the status quo is unfounded. The exercise of federal jurisdiction does not and cannot establish jurisdiction. See United States v. L.A. Tucker Truck Lines, Inc., 344 U.S. 33, 37–38 (1952): "[T]his Court is not bound by a prior exercise of jurisdiction in a case where it was not questioned and it was passed sub silentio." In this respect, the present case is no different than Federal Election Comm'n v. NRA Political Victory Fund, 513 U.S. 88 (1994). The case presented the question whether we had jurisdiction to consider a certiorari petition filed by the Federal Election Commission (FEC), and not by the Solicitor General on behalf of the FEC. The Court held that it lacked jurisdiction. Though that answer seemed to contradict the Court's prior practices, the Court said:

Nor are we impressed by the FEC's argument that it has represented itself before this Court on several occasions in the past without any question having been raised about its authority to do so.... The jurisdiction of this Court was challenged in none of these actions, and therefore the question is an open one before us.

See also Will v. Michigan Dept. of State Police, 491 U.S. 58, 63 n.4 (1989) (" '[T]his Court has never considered itself bound when a subsequent case finally brings the jurisdictional issue before us.' Hagans v. Lavine, 415 U.S. 528, 535 n.5 (1974)"). These cases make clear that our failure to consider a question hardly equates to a thing's being decided. As a consequence, I would follow the statutory language.

* * *

After today's decision, "[n]ontaxpaying associations of taxpayers, and most other nontaxpayers, will now be allowed to sidestep Congress' policy against [federal] judicial resolution of abstract [state] tax controversies." *Regan,* 465 U.S., at 394 (O'Connor, J., concurring in judgment). This unfortunate result deprives state courts of the first opportunity to hear such cases and to grant the relief the Constitution requires.

For the foregoing reasons, with respect, I dissent.

CHAPTER VII

HABEAS CORPUS

Page 739, add at the end of footnote c:

See also Daniel F. Piar, Using Coram Nobis to Attack Wrongful Convictions: A New Look at an Ancient Writ, 30 N. Ky. L. Rev. 505 (2003).

Page 739, add a new Note 3 and renumber the existing Note 3:

3. **Challenges to Executive Detention: The "Enemy Combatant" Cases.** As observed in footnote a on page 738 of the casebook, the ancient writ of habeas corpus—the form the Framers had in mind when they wrote the Suspension Clause—provided access to courts to review the legality of executive detention. Today, the most important form of habeas corpus provides collateral review for persons confined *after* judicial prosecution and conviction of crime. The issues raised by habeas as a means of collateral review are quite different from those that arise when the executive acts without judicial oversight. Moreover, post-conviction habeas is integrally related to this book's primary theme of federal-state relations, while habeas as a means of challenging executive detention rarely has such implications.

Nonetheless, it is appropriate to take note of three significant cases decided by the Supreme Court during its 2003 Term. All three involve the detention of persons alleged to be enemy combatants during military actions undertaken by the United States following the events of September 11, 2001. Each is summarized below.

(i) *Hamdi v. Rumsfeld.* The most complicated of the three is Hamdi v. Rumsfeld, 542 U.S. 507 (2004). Hamdi was detained and interrogated in Afganistan after U.S. Armed Forces entered that country to subdue al Qaeda and topple the Taliban regime. Hamdi was sent to the U.S. Naval Base in Guantanamo Bay, but later confined in a military brig in Virginia after it was discovered that he was an American citizen. As described by the Supreme Court, "[t]he Government contends that Hamdi is an 'enemy combatant,' and that this status justifies holding him in the United States indefinitely—without formal charges or proceedings—unless and until it makes the determination that access to counsel or further process is warranted."

Hamdi sought habeas in a Virginia federal district court, claiming that he had not been involved in military activities and seeking, inter alia, release from confinement. The Supreme Court unanimously agreed that Congress had not suspended the writ of habeas corpus, that habeas was therefore available, and that "due process" provided the standard by which appropriate relief was to be judged. But the Court divided on the meaning of "due process" in this context, as well as the important background question whether U.S. citizens could be detained at all as enemy combatants. The division can best be summarized by looking first at the separate but polar opposite opinions by Justices Thomas and Scalia.

Speaking for himself alone, Justice Thomas concluded that the President had authority to detain U.S. citizens determined by the Executive Branch to be enemy combatants, "an authority that includes making virtually conclusive factual findings." Courts "lack the capacity and responsibility to second-guess this determination." While habeas is available to test "whether the President has the asserted authority" to detain enemy combatants "at least while hostilities continue," "[i]n this context, due process requires nothing more than a good-faith executive detention."

By contrast, for Justice Scalia (joined by Justice Stevens) the choice was simple: The government had to try Hamdi for treason or some other offense, or let him go. Absent legislative suspension of the writ, the executive had no authority to detain an American citizen without filing and pursuing formal charges.

Writing for herself, Chief Justice Rehnquist, and Justices Kennedy and Breyer, Justice O'Connor took a middle ground. Her view was that Congress had legitimately authorized the detention of Hamdi as an "enemy combatant"[d] "for the duration of the hostilities," but that he was still entitled to due process. She continued:

> We ... hold that a citizen-detainee seeking to challenge his classification as an enemy combatant must receive notice of the factual basis for his classification, and a fair opportunity to rebut the Government's factual assertions before a neutral decisionmaker. These essential constitutional promises may not be eroded.
>
> At the same time, the exigencies of the circumstances may demand that, aside from these core elements, enemy combatant proceedings may be tailored to alleviate their uncommon potential to burden the Executive at a time of ongoing military conflict. Hearsay, for example, may need to be accepted as the most reliable available evidence from the Government in such a proceeding. Likewise, the Constitution would not be offended by a presumption in favor of the Government's evidence, so long as that presumption remained a rebuttable one and fair opportunity for rebuttal were provided. Thus, once the Government puts forth credible evidence that the habeas petitioner meets the enemy-combatant criteria, the onus could shift to the petitioner to rebut

---

d. For purposes of the decision, "enemy combatant" was defined as an individual who was "part of or supporting forces hostile to the United States or coalition partners" and was "engaged in an armed conflict against the United States."

that evidence with more persuasive evidence that he falls outside the criteria. A burden-shifting scheme of this sort would meet the goal of ensuring that the errant tourist, embedded journalist, or local aid worker has a chance to prove military error while giving due regard to the Executive once it has put forth meaningful support for its conclusion that the detainee is in fact an enemy combatant. . . .

There remains the possibility that the standards we have articulated could be met by an appropriately authorized and properly constituted military tribunal. . . . In the absence of such process, however, a court that receives a petition for a writ of habeas corpus from an alleged enemy combatant must itself ensure that the minimum requirements of due process are achieved.

Justice Souter, joined by Justice Ginsburg, provided the votes needed to vacate the proceedings below and remand to the federal habeas court for further proceedings in line with O'Connor's opinion. He thought the Executive did not have authority to detain an American citizen as an "enemy combatant" and that "[i]f the Government raises nothing further than the record now shows, . . . Hamdi [is entitled] to be released." Without more, this would have left a splintered series of opinions without majority support for a single judgment. Souter therefore concluded:

> Because I find Hamdi's detention . . . unauthorized . . . , I would not reach any questions of what process he may be due in litigating disputed issues in a proceeding under the habeas statute or prior to the habeas enquiry itself. For me, it suffices that the Government has failed to justify holding him in the absence of a further Act of Congress, criminal charges, [or] a showing that the detention conforms to the laws of war. . . . I would therefore vacate the judgment of the Court of Appeals and remand for proceedings consistent with this view.
>
> Since this disposition does not command a majority of the Court, however, the need to give practical effect to the conclusions of eight members of the Court rejecting the Government's position calls for me to join with the plurality in ordering remand on terms closest to those I would impose. Although I think litigation of Hamdi's status as an enemy combatant is unnecessary, the terms of the plurality's remand will allow Hamdi to offer evidence that he is not an enemy combatant, and he should at the least have the benefit of that opportunity.
>
> It should go without saying that in joining with the plurality to produce a judgment, I do not adopt the plurality's resolution of constitutional issues that I would not reach. It is not that I could disagree with the plurality's determinations (given the plurality's [conclusion that Hamdi may be detained as an "enemy combatant"]) that someone in Hamdi's position is entitled at a minimum

to notice of the Government's claimed factual basis for holding him, and to a fair chance to rebut it before a neutral decision maker; nor, of course, could I disagree with the plurality's affirmation of Hamdi's right to counsel. On the other hand, I do not mean to imply agreement that the Government could claim an evidentiary presumption casting the burden of rebuttal on Hamdi, or that an opportunity to litigate before a military tribunal might obviate or truncate enquiry by a court on habeas.

Subject to these qualifications, I join with the plurality in a judgment of the Court vacating the Fourth Circuit's judgment and remanding the case.

(ii) *Rumsfeld v. Padilla.* Padilla flew from Pakistan to Chicago's O'Hare Airport. He was arrested when he deplaned, initially on a material witness warrant issued by a New York federal district court. He was taken to New York for confinement, subsequently declared an "enemy combatant," and transported to a brig in South Carolina. Two days later, his attorney filed a habeas petition in New York. As the case came to the Supreme Court, the question was whether the petition had been properly filed in New York.

The Court held five to four that it was not. Rumsfeld v. Padilla, 542 U.S. 426 (2004). The majority opinion, written by Chief Justice Rehnquist, concluded that the proper respondent to the habeas petition was the Commander of the military prison in which Padilla was being held—"the equivalent," the opinion continued, "of the warden at the military brig." The New York federal court, moreover, did not have jurisdiction over the Commander located in South Carolina. This result followed from 28 U.S.C. § 2241(a), which authorizes federal courts to grant habeas "within their respective jurisdictions." The Court did not preclude a re-filing in South Carolina.

Justice Kennedy wrote a separate concurring opinion, joined by Justice O'Connor. Justice Stevens dissented in an opinion joined by Justices Souter, Ginsburg, and Breyer. In the view of the dissenters, Secretary Rumsfeld was a proper defendant, and he was within the in personam jurisdiction of the New York federal courts. The limitation to which the Court referred, the dissenters claimed, was one of venue, not subject matter jurisdiction. Venue in the New York federal court was not inappropriate.

(iii) *Rasul v. Bush.* Rasul v. Bush, 542 U.S. 466 (2004), involved two Australians and 12 Kuwaitis who were captured abroad and held as "enemy combatants" in Guantanamo Bay. They sought habeas in the Federal District Court for the District of Columbia. Speaking for the Supreme Court, Justice Stevens stated the issue as follows: "The question now before us is whether the habeas statute confers a right to judicial review of the legality of Executive detention of aliens in a territory over which the United States exercises plenary and exclusive jurisdiction, but not 'ultimate sovereignty.'" The fact that Guantanamo Bay was outside the territorial jurisdiction of any U.S. federal court was not an impediment:

> In the end, the answer to the question presented is clear. Petitioners contend that they are being held in federal custody in violation of the laws of the United States. No party questions the District Court's jurisdiction over petitioners' custodians. Section 2241, by its terms, requires nothing more. We therefore hold that § 2241 confers on the District Court jurisdiction to hear petitioners' habeas corpus challenges to the legality of their detention at the Guantanamo Bay Naval Base.

Justice Kennedy concurred in the judgment, reaching the same conclusion by a different route. Justice Scalia, joined by the Chief Justice and Justice Thomas, dissented.

Page 764, add to citations in the first full paragraph:

Barry Friedman, Under the Law of Federal Jurisdiction: Allocating Cases Between Federal and State Courts, 104 Colum. L. Rev. 1211, 1261–63 (2004).

Page 773, add to the citations in Note 4:

Bradley Scott Shannon, The Retroactive and Prospective Application of Judicial Decisions, 26 Harv. J.L. & Pub. Pol'y 811 (2003);

Page 796, add a footnote at the end of the first paragraph of Note 1:

a. The Court has exhibited considerable interest in policing Circuit Court application of the *Williams* standard. There were four such cases during the 2003 Term alone. See Yarborough v. Gentry, 540 U.S. 1 (2003)(unanimous per curiam); Mitchell v. Esparza, 540 U.S. 12 (2003) (unanimous per curiam); Yarborough v. Alvarado, 541 U.S. 652 (2004) (five-to-four division on application of *Miranda*); Holland v. Jackson, 542 U.S. 649 (2004) (per curiam; four Justices would have denied certiorari).

Page 797, add at the end of footnote a:

For defense of the contrary position, see Evan Tsen Lee, Section 2254(d) of the Federal Habeas Statute: Is it Beyond Reason?, 56 Hastings L.J. 283 (2004). See also Robert D. Sloane, AEDPA's "Adjudication on the Merits" Requirement: Collateral Review, Federalism, and Comity, 78 St. John's L. Rev. 615 (2004); Steven Semeraro, A Reasoning-Process Review Model for Federal Habeas Corpus, 94 J. Crim. L. & Criminology 897 (2004).

Page 798, add to the end of the first paragraph in footnote b:

The Court likewise found the "objectively unreasonable" and "prejudice" standards met in Rompilla v. Beard, 545 U.S. ___ (2005). *Rompilla* involved the Pennsylvania Supreme Court's application of *Strickland* in a capital case. Justice Kennedy dissented, joined by Chief Justice Rehnquist and Justices Scalia and Thomas.

Page 799, add a footnote at the end of Note 3:

c. The case reached the Supreme Court again in Beard v. Banks, 542 U.S. 406 (2004). The Court of Appeals held on remand that "the existing legal landscape compelled the decision in *Mills*. Accordingly, the court held that *Mills* applied retroactively to respondent and reinstated the remainder of its previous opinion, again granting respondent relief from his death sentence." In a five to four decision, the Supreme Court reversed. The majority held that *Mills* announced a "new" rule and that neither *Teague* exception applied. Habeas relief was therefore foreclosed: "Given our determination that the Court of Appeals erred in holding that *Mills* applied retroactively to respondent, we do not reach the question whether the Court of Appeals also erred in concluding that the Pennsylvania Supreme Court unreasonably applied *Mills*."

The Court also applied *Teague* in another case decided on the same day. Schriro v. Summerlin, 542 U.S. 348 (2004), held that Ring v. Arizona, 536 U.S. 584 (2002), does not apply retroactively to cases already final at the time it was decided. *Ring* held that "because Arizona law authorized the death penalty only if an aggravating factor was present, Apprendi v. New Jersey, 530 U.S. 466 (2000), required the existence of such a factor to be proved to a jury rather than to a judge." The majority noted that new "*substantive* rules generally apply retroactively. This includes decisions that narrow the scope of a criminal statute by interpreting its terms, as well as constitutional determinations that place particular conduct or persons covered by the statute beyond the State's power to punish." But *Ring* announced a new procedural rule, and new procedural rules "generally do not apply retroactively" unless they fit a *Teague* exception. The Court divided five to four (the same four dissented in *Banks*—Stevens, Souter, Ginsburg, and Breyer) over whether *Ring* announced a "watershed rule[] of criminal procedure implicating the fundamental fairness and accuracy of the criminal proceeding."

Page 801, add a footnote at the end of Note 4:

f. For a sequel decision applying the standard announced in *Slack* and *Miller-El*, see Tennard v. Dretke, 542 U.S. 274 (2004).

Page 802, add to the citations in Note 6:

Lyn Entzeroth, Federal Habeas Review of Death Sentences, Where Are We Now?: A Review of *Wiggins v. Smith* and *Miller-El v. Cockrell*, 39 Tulsa L. Rev. 49 (2003); Allan Ides, Habeas Standards of Review Under 28 U.S.C. § 2254(d)(1): A Commentary on Statutory Text and Supreme Court Precedent, 60 Wash. & Lee L. Rev. 677 (2003);

Page 870, add a new Note and renumber the remaining Notes:

8. *Castro v. United States.* Section 2255 is subject to the same repetitive application rules provided in § 2244(b) that are applicable to state habeas petitions. Castro v. United States, 540 U.S. 375 (2003), concerned ambiguity about the nature of a first application for relief. The question was whether it was properly regarded as a § 2255 proceeding so as to invoke the repetitive application rules when a second petition, a clear § 2255 motion, was filed.

The first claim for relief was filed pro se and called a motion for a new trial under Rule 33. The government argued that it was a § 2255 motion, and both the District and Circuit Courts mentioned both Rule 33 and § 2255 in denying relief. When the petitioner filed a second motion, this time styled a § 2255 proceeding, the District and Circuit Courts dismissed on the grounds that the conditions of § 2244(b) were not satisfied (Circuit Court approval for the filing had not been obtained).

The Supreme Court reversed. For the Court, Justice Breyer concluded "that the lower courts' recharacterization powers are limited in the following way:"

> The limitation applies when a court recharacterizes a pro se litigant's motion as a first § 2255 motion. In such circumstances the district court must notify the pro se litigant that it intends to recharacterize the pleading, warn the litigant that this recharacterization means that any subsequent § 2255 motion will be subject to the restrictions on "second or successive" motions, and provide the litigant an opportunity to withdraw the motion or to amend it so that it contains all the § 2255 claims he believes he has. If the court fails to do so, the motion cannot be considered to have become a § 2255 motion for purposes of applying to later motions the law's "second or successive" restrictions.

Justice Scalia, joined by Justice Thomas, concurred in the result. For them the best answer was that "because of the risk involved, pleadings should *never* be recharacterized into first § 2255 motions."

Page 883, add the following Notes:

NOTES ON THE AEDPA STATUTES OF LIMITATIONS

1. Introduction. The Supreme Court decided only 80 cases in full reported opinions during the term that ended in June 2005. Six of them involved statute of limitations questions under the Antiterrorism and Effective Death Penalty Act of 1996 (AEDPA). Two warrant only brief comment. The other four are summarized in succeeding notes, together with several additional decisions that provide necessary context.

(i) *Mayle v. Felix.* The question in Mayle v. Felix, 545 U.S. ___ (2005), was whether the expiration of the statute of limitations for new claims added in an amended petition is measured by the date of the original petition or the date the amendment is filed. Over a dissent by Justice Souter joined by Justice Stevens, the Court held the latter. Rule 15 of the Federal Rules of Civil Procedure provides that a claim asserted in an amended pleading "relates back to the date of the original pleading when ... the claim ... arose out of the conduct, transaction or occurrence set forth or attempted to be set forth in the original pleading." Unlike the much looser provisions of Rule 8(a) governing statements of claims in ordinary civil proceedings, Rule 2(c) of the Habeas Rules provides that a petition must "specify all the grounds for relief available to the petitioner" and must "state the facts supporting each ground." The model form available to habeas petitioners states, moreover, that "You must include in this petition all of the grounds for relief from the conviction or sentence that you challenge. ... If you fail to set forth all of the grounds in this petition, you may be barred from presenting additional grounds at a later date." This rule means what it says, the Court concluded, and operates to prevent the assertion of additional claims in an amended petition if the statute of limitations has expired when the amended petition is filed.

(ii) *Gonzalez v. Crosby.* In Gonzalez v. Crosby, 545 U.S. ___ (2005), the District Court had dismissed a habeas petition as time barred, but it failed to anticipate Artuz v. Bennett, 531 U.S. 4 (2000) (summarized below). After the decision in *Artuz*, the petitioner filed a motion under Rule 60(b)(6) of the Federal Rules of Civil Procedure, which permits relief from a final judgment on several grounds, the last of which is "any other reason justifying relief from the operation of the judgment." The Court held that a motion under Rule 60(b) was not a second or successive habeas petition requiring permission from the Circuit Court before it could be filed. But the petitioner was nonetheless not entitled to relief because a showing of "extraordinary circumstances" was required and the petitioner did not meet this standard. Justice Stevens dissented, joined by Justice Souter

2. **"Stay and Abeyance":** *Rhines v. Weber.* Rhines v. Weber, 544 U.S. ___ (2005), involved an aspect of the tolling problem that concerned the Justices who wrote separately in *Duncan v. Walker*. Rhines had been convicted of murder and sentenced to death. He filed a federal habeas petition containing 35 constitutional claims. He had filed a habeas petition in state court within three days of the denial of certiorari by the Supreme Court after his direct appeals. His federal petition was filed less than a month after the state petition was denied. He was thus well within—by more than 11 months—the one-year statute of limitations under AEDPA.[a]

Some 18 months later, the federal district court determined that eight of the 35 claims had not been exhausted. Since under *Duncan* the AEDPA statute of limitations was not tolled during the pendency of the federal action, the petitioner faced a problem. If he allowed dismissal as *Rose v. Lundy* required of a "mixed" petition, he could exhaust the eight claims but would be barred by AEDPA from returning to federal court on any of the 35 claims. Alternatively, he could proceed in federal court with the 27 exhausted claims only at the cost of foregoing federal review of the eight unexhausted claims.

Rhines responded by asking the district court to hold his pending federal petition in abeyance while he exhausted his state remedies on the eight claims, and then to let him return to federal court, if necessary, to litigate all 35 claims. The district court granted his motion, conditioned on the commencement of state proceedings within 60 days and a return to federal court, if necessary, within 60 days of the conclusion of those

---

a. Recall from *Duncan* that AEDPA provides that "The time during which a properly filed application for State post-conviction or other collateral review with respect to the pertinent judgment or claim is pending shall not be counted toward any period of limitation under this subsection." 28 U.S.C. § 2244(d)(2). The time began to run once direct review concluded, i.e., from the denial of certiorari by the Supreme Court. See 28 U.S.C. § 2244(d)(1)(A).

proceedings. The Court of Appeals held this procedure impermissible, and remanded for a determination of whether Rhines could proceed on his exhausted claims only. The Supreme Court adopted a middle ground.

Justice O'Connor's opinion for the Court summarized the landscape, and then addressed the question of a district court's power:

> District courts do ordinarily have authority to issue stays, where such a stay would be a proper exercise of discretion. AEDPA does not deprive district courts of that authority, but it does circumscribe their discretion. Any solution to this problem must therefore be compatible with AEDPA's purposes.

O'Connor then identified two relevant AEPDA purposes: to reduce delays in achieving finality for state court judgments; and to encourage litigation in state courts first. She continued:

> Stay and abeyance, if employed too frequently, has the potential to undermine these twin purposes. Staying a federal habeas petition frustrates AEDPA's objective of encouraging finality by allowing a petitioner to delay the resolution of the federal proceedings. It also undermines AEDPA's goal of streamlining federal habeas proceedings by decreasing a petitioner's incentive to exhaust all his claims in state court prior to filing his federal petition.
>
> For these reasons, stay and abeyance should be available only in limited circumstances. Because granting a stay effectively excuses a petitioner's failure to present his claims first to the state courts, stay and abeyance is only appropriate when the district court determines there was good cause for the petitioner's failure to exhaust his claims first in state court. Moreover, even if a petitioner had good cause for that failure, the district court would abuse its discretion if it were to grant him a stay when his unexhausted claims are plainly meritless. Cf. 28 U.S.C. § 2254(b)(2) ("An application for a writ of habeas corpus may be denied on the merits, notwithstanding the failure of the applicant to exhaust the remedies available in the courts of the State").
>
> Even where stay and abeyance is appropriate, the district court's discretion in structuring the stay is limited by the timeliness concerns reflected in AEDPA. A mixed petition should not be stayed indefinitely. Though, generally, a prisoner's "principal interest ... is in obtaining speedy federal relief on his claims," not all petitioners have an incentive to obtain federal relief as quickly as possible. In particular, capital petitioners might deliberately engage in dilatory tactics to prolong their incarceration and avoid execution of the sentence of death. Without time limits, petitioners could frustrate AEDPA's goal of finality by dragging out indefinitely their federal habeas review. Thus, district courts should

place reasonable time limits on a petitioner's trip to state court and back. See, e.g., Zarvela v. Artuz, 254 F.3d 374, 381 (2d Cir. 2001) ("[District courts] should explicitly condition the stay on the prisoner's pursuing state court remedies within a brief interval, normally 30 days, after the stay is entered and returning to federal court within a similarly brief interval, normally 30 days after state court exhaustion is completed"). And if a petitioner engages in abusive litigation tactics or intentional delay, the district court should not grant him a stay at all.

On the other hand, it likely would be an abuse of discretion for a district court to deny a stay and to dismiss a mixed petition if the petitioner had good cause for his failure to exhaust, his unexhausted claims are potentially meritorious, and there is no indication that the petitioner engaged in intentionally dilatory litigation tactics. In such circumstances, the district court should stay, rather than dismiss, the mixed petition. See *Rose v. Lundy,* 455 U.S., at 522 (the total exhaustion requirement was not intended to "unreasonably impair the prisoner's right to relief"). In such a case, the petitioner's interest in obtaining federal review of his claims outweighs the competing interests in finality and speedy resolution of federal petitions. For the same reason, if a petitioner presents a district court with a mixed petition and the court determines that stay and abeyance is inappropriate, the court should allow the petitioner to delete the unexhausted claims and to proceed with the exhausted claims if dismissal of the entire petition would unreasonably impair the petitioner's right to obtain federal relief. See id., at 520 (plurality opinion) ("[A petitioner] can always amend the petition to delete the unexhausted claims, rather than returning to state court to exhaust all of his claims").

Two Justices wrote separate opinions. Justice Stevens, joined by Justices Ginsburg and Breyer, joined the Court's opinion "on the understanding that its reference to 'good cause' for failing to exhaust state remedies more promptly is not intended to impose the sort of strict and inflexible requirement that would 'trap the unwary pro se prisoner.' " Justice Souter, also joined by Justices Ginsburg and Breyer, concurred in part and concurred in the judgment. He had "one reservation":

> [N]ot doctrinal but practical. Instead of conditioning stay-and-abeyance on "good cause" for delay, I would simply hold the order unavailable on a demonstration of "intentionally dilatory litigation tactics." The trickiness of some exhaustion determinations promises to infect issues of good cause when a court finds a failure to exhaust; pro se petitioners (as most habeas petitioners are) do not come well trained to address such matters. I fear that threshold enquiries into good cause will give the district courts too much trouble to be worth the time; far better to wait for the alarm to

sound when there is some indication that a petitioner is gaming the system.

3. "Properly Filed" State Applications: *Artuz v. Bennett*. As noted, the AEDPA provides that its one-year statute of limitations is tolled by the filing of a state application for post conviction relief. Specifically: "[t]he time during which a properly filed application for State postconviction or other collateral review with respect to the pertinent judgment or claim is pending shall not be counted toward any period of limitation under this subsection." 28 U.S.C. § 2244(d)(2). Artuz v. Bennett, 531 U.S. 4 (2000), presented "the question whether an application for state postconviction relief containing claims that are procedurally barred is 'properly filed' within the meaning of this provision."

In a unanimous opinion by Justice Scalia, the Court held the claim "properly filed":

> An application is "filed," as that term is commonly understood, when it is delivered to, and accepted by, the appropriate court officer for placement into the official record. And an application is "*properly* filed" when its delivery and acceptance are in compliance with the applicable laws and rules governing filings. These usually prescribe, for example, the form of the document, the time limits upon its delivery,[2] the court and office in which it must be lodged, and the requisite filing fee. In some jurisdictions the filing requirements also include, for example, preconditions imposed on particular abusive filers, or on all filers generally, cf. 28 U.S.C. § 2253(c) (1994 ed., Supp. IV) (conditioning the taking of an appeal on the issuance of a "certificate of appealability"). But in common usage, the question whether an application has been "properly filed" is quite separate from the question whether the claims *contained in the application* are meritorious and free of procedural bar. . . .
>
> The state procedural bars at issue in this case . . . simply prescribe a rule of decision for a court confronted with claims that were "previously determined on the merits upon an appeal from the judgment" of conviction or that could have been raised on direct appeal but were not: "[T]he court must deny" such claims for relief. Neither provision purports to set forth a condition to filing, as opposed to a condition to obtaining relief.

4. "Properly Filed" State Applications: *Pace v. DiGuglielmo*. The question reserved in footnote 2 in *Artuz* was presented in Pace v. DiGuglielmo, 544 U.S. ___ (2005). The Court divided five to four on the answer.

---

2. We express no view on the question whether the existence of certain exceptions to a timely filing requirement can prevent a late application from being considered improperly filed.

Pace was sentenced to life without parole in 1986. He filed no direct appeal, and between 1986 and 1992 unsuccessfully undertook his first round of state post conviction proceedings. Four years later, in November of 1996, he filed a second state post conviction application. This petition was dismissed as untimely by the Pennsylvania Superior Court on December 3, 1998,[b] and the Pennsylvania Supreme Court denied review on July 29, 1999.

Pace filed a petition for federal relief on December 24, 1999. AEDPA became effective on April 24, 1996. By consensus in the Courts of Appeals, prisoners whose convictions occurred prior to that date had one year to seek federal relief. Pace was untimely in federal court if the state proceeding did not toll the federal statute of limitations. But he was timely if it did.

Chief Justice Rehnquist wrote for the majority:

> As in *Artuz,* we are guided by the "common usage" and "commo[n] underst[anding]" of the phrase "properly filed." In common understanding, a petition filed after a time limit, and which does not fit within any exceptions to that limit, is no more "properly filed" than a petition filed after a time limit that permits no exception. The purpose of AEDPA's statute of limitations confirms this commonsense reading. On petitioner's theory, a state prisoner could toll the statute of limitations at will simply by filing untimely state postconviction petitions. This would turn § 2244(d)(2) into a de facto extension mechanism, quite contrary to the purpose of AEDPA, and open the door to abusive delay. ... When a postconviction petition is untimely under state law, "that [is] the end of the matter" for purposes of § 2244(d)(2).

Pace had argued that "any condition that must be applied on a claim-by-claim basis, such as Pennsylvania's time limit, cannot be a 'condition to filing'" within *Artuz*. But this, Rehnquist said, was inconsistent with AEDPA's text, "which refers not just to a 'properly filed application,' but to a 'properly filed application ... *with respect to the pertinent judgment or claim.*'"

Pace also challenged the fairness of the Court's interpretation:

> He claims that a "petitioner trying in good faith to exhaust state remedies may litigate in state court for years only to find out at the end that he was never 'properly filed,'" and thus that his

---

b. Pennsylvania adopted a new post conviction statute in 1995 that contained, for the first time, a one-year statute of limitations running from the time a conviction became final. There were four exceptions: if earlier filing was prevented by governmental interference; if the claim was based on a new constitutional rule that was made retroactive; if the claim was based on new facts that could not have been discovered through due diligence; or if a prisoner's *first* petition was presented within one year of the effective date of the statute. Pace filed a state petition within a year of the effective date of the new statute, but it was his *second* state petition, not his *first*. The Superior Court found none of the exceptions applicable.

federal habeas petition is time barred. A prisoner seeking state postconviction relief might avoid this predicament, however, by filing a "protective" petition in federal court and asking the federal court to stay and abey the federal habeas proceedings until state remedies are exhausted. See Rhines v. Weber, 544 U.S. ___ (2005). A petitioner's reasonable confusion about whether a state filing would be timely will ordinarily constitute "good cause" for him to file in federal court. *Ibid.* ("[I]f the petitioner had good cause for his failure to exhaust, his unexhausted claims are potentially meritorious, and there is no indication that the petitioner engaged in intentionally dilatory tactics," then the district court likely "should stay, rather than dismiss, the mixed petition").

Rehnquist concluded by addressing one final contention:

> We now turn to petitioner's argument that he is entitled to *equitable* tolling for the time during which his untimely PCRA petition was pending in the state courts.[8] Generally, a litigant seeking equitable tolling bears the burden of establishing two elements: (1) that he has been pursuing his rights diligently, and (2) that some extraordinary circumstance stood in his way. Petitioner argues that he has satisfied the extraordinary circumstance test. He reasons that Third Circuit law at the time he sought relief required him to exhaust his state remedies and thus seek PCRA relief, even if it was unlikely the state court would reach the merits of his claims, and that state law made it appear as though he might gain relief, despite the petition's untimeliness. Thus, he claims, "state law and Third Circuit exhaustion law created a trap" on which he detrimentally relied as his federal time limit slipped away. Even if we were to accept petitioner's theory, he would not be entitled to relief because he has not established the requisite diligence.
>
> Petitioner's PCRA petition set forth three claims: that his sentence was "illegal"; that his plea was invalid because he did not understand his life sentence was without the possibility of parole; and that he received ineffective assistance of counsel at "all levels of representation." The first two of these claims were available to petitioner as early as 1986. Indeed, petitioner asserted a version of his invalid plea claim in his [first state] petition. The third claim—ineffective assistance of counsel—related only to events occurring in or before 1991.
>
> Yet petitioner waited years, without any valid justification, to assert these claims . . . .Had petitioner advanced his claims within

---

8. We have never squarely addressed the question whether equitable tolling is applicable to AEDPA's statute of limitations. Because respondent assumes that equitable tolling applies and because petitioner is not entitled to equitable tolling under any standard, we assume without deciding its application for purposes of this case.

a reasonable time of their availability, he would not now be facing any time problem, state or federal. And not only did petitioner sit on his rights for years *before* he filed his [state] petition, but he also sat on them for five more months *after* his [state] proceedings became final before deciding to seek relief in federal court. Under long-established principles, petitioner's lack of diligence precludes equity's operation.

Joined by Justices Souter, Ginsburg, and Breyer, Justice Stevens dissented. Stevens argued that "[t]he Court's interpretation of § 2244(d)(2) is not compelled by the text of that provision and will most assuredly frustrate its purpose." He continued:

> The Court's interpretation of "properly filed" in this context conflicts with the meaning we gave the phrase in *Artuz*. . . . It would be much wiser simply to apply *Artuz*'s rule to state time bars that . . . operate like a procedural bar. In this case, the [state] time bar's enumerated exceptions, which require state courts to review the claims elucidated in postconviction petitions and to determine whether particular claims trigger the applicability of the exceptions, plainly function like a procedural bar. . . .
>
> Application of the *Artuz* rule in this context is clearly consonant with the statutory text. A time bar is nothing more than a species of the larger category of procedural bars that may preclude consideration of the merits of the state petition, and may raise questions that are equally difficult to decide. . . . Because most state laws respecting untimely filings of postconviction petitions function in a manner identical to the procedural bar at issue in *Artuz,* there is no justification for giving special treatment to any state rule based on untimeliness. . . .
>
> The Court's principal justification for its rule is the fear that allowing statutory tolling in this context would allow prisoners to extend the federal statute of limitations indefinitely by repeatedly filing meritless state petitions. That fear is misguided for two reasons. First, it ignores a basic fact that we have recognized repeatedly—a "prisoner's principal interest, of course, is in obtaining speedy federal relief on his claims." Rose v. Lundy, 455 U.S. 509, 520 (1982). [For most prisoners] delaying the initiation of federal postconviction relief will almost assuredly maximize their periods of incarceration.
>
> Second, the Court's concern is premised on the incorrect assumption that the phrase "properly filed" has no meaningful content unless all untimely petitions are by definition improper. The reason that assumption is wrong is because any claim that a state application has tolled the limitations period will always depend on the district court's finding that the petition was "properly filed." In my view, it would be entirely appropriate, and

consistent with the text and purposes of AEDPA, to define "properly filed" as excluding any filings deemed by the district court to be repetitious or abusive. If an application for postconviction review is not filed in good faith—filed, in other words, explicitly to prolong the federal statute of limitations—it would be improper under AEDPA, and statutory tolling would not be appropriate. Federal and state courts have considerable experience identifying and preventing the kind of dilatory pleadings that concern the Court today. There is no reason that courts could not engage in similar analyses to prevent state prisoners from prolonging indefinitely the AEDPA statute of limitations.[6]

Unfortunately, the most likely consequence of the Court's new rule will be to increase, not reduce, delays in the federal system. The inevitable result of today's decision will be a flood of protective filings in the federal district courts. As the history of this case demonstrates, litigants, especially those proceeding pro se, cannot predict accurately whether a state court will find their application timely filed. Because a state court's timeliness ruling cannot be predicted with certainty, prisoners who would otherwise run the risk of having the federal statute of limitations expire while they are exhausting their state remedies will have no choice but to file premature federal petitions accompanied by a request to stay federal proceedings pending the exhaustion of their state remedies. The Court admits that this type of protective filing will result from its holding. I fail to see any merit in a rule that knowingly and unnecessarily "add[s] to the burdens on the district courts in a way that simple tolling ... would not." Duncan v. Walker, 533 U.S. 167, 192 (2001) (Breyer, J., dissenting).

Beyond increasing the burdens faced by district courts, the Court's tacit encouragement of countless new protective filings will diminish the "statutory incentives to proceed first in state court" and thereby "increase the risk of the very piecemeal litigation that the exhaustion requirement is designed to reduce." Id., at 180. Congress enacted § 2254(d)(2), along with § 2254(b), to "encourage litigants *first* to exhaust all state remedies and *then* to file their federal habeas petitions as soon as possible." Id., at 181. The Court's rule turns that statutory goal on its head—in essence, encouraging all petitioners who have doubts regarding the timeliness of their state petitions to file simultaneously for relief in federal and state court. *Artuz* appropriately prevented such a

---

6. Such an inquiry is consistent with *Artuz*, which distinguished between properly filed applications and individual claims contained within those applications. An application filed intentionally to prolong the federal statute of limitations would be improper in its entirety. Indeed, it is difficult to imagine how one particular claim in an application could be improperly motivated to delay federal proceedings, while another claim was "properly filed" under AEDPA.

result with respect to procedural bars. Because I see no reason to depart from that sound approach, I would hold that Pace's application was "properly filed" under AEDPA.^c

5. The "Due Diligence" Exception: *Johnson v. United States*.
The AEDPA also adopts a one-year statute of limitations for the operation of § 2255. It operates from the date the conviction becomes final, with three exceptions, the third of which starts the period from "the date on which the facts supporting the claim or claims presented could have been discovered through the exercise of due diligence." 28 U.S.C. § 2255 ¶ 6(4).[d] Johnson v. United States, 544 U.S. ___ (2005), involved the meaning of this provision. It was decided five to four, by unusual combinations of Justices.

In 1994 Johnson pleaded guilty in federal court to a conspiracy involving cocaine distribution. He received an enhanced sentence as a career offender. He filed a state habeas application in 1998 challenging the validity of seven prior Georgia convictions. He asserted that he had not knowingly, intelligently, and voluntarily waived his right to counsel when he pleaded guilty in those cases. The state court found no record of an affirmative waiver, and entered an order of vacatur setting aside all seven convictions.

One of these convictions provided the basis for his federal career offender sentence, so he then sought under § 2255 to have that sentence set aside. His § 2255 petition was untimely under AEDPA unless it fit within the exception quoted above.

(i) *Custis v. United States* and *Daniels v. United States*.
Understanding the landscape against which *Johnson* was decided requires consideration of two prior decisions. Custis v. United States, 511 U.S. 485 (1994), held that prior state convictions on which a federal enhanced sentence was based could not be collaterally attacked in the federal sentencing proceeding. As the Court explained *Custis* in *Johnson*:

> We thought that Congress had not meant to make it so easy to challenge final judgments—that every occasion to enhance a sentence for recidivism would turn a federal sentencing court into a forum for difficult and time-consuming reexaminations of stale state proceedings. We recognized only one exception to this rule that collateral attacks were off-limits, and that was for challenges

---

c. Stevens had added in an earlier footnote: "Because I would hold that Pace was entitled to statutory tolling, I need not answer the question whether the Court of Appeals erred by reversing the District Court's decision to grant Pace equitable tolling."—[Footnote by eds.]

d. The other two exceptions start the clock from: "the date on which the impediment to making a motion created by governmental action in violation of the Constitution or laws of the United States is removed, if the movant was prevented from making a motion by such governmental action" or "the date on which the right asserted was initially recognized by the Supreme Court, if that right has been newly recognized by the Supreme Court and made retroactively applicable to cases on collateral review."

to state convictions allegedly obtained in violation of the right to appointed counsel, an exception we thought necessary to avoid undermining Gideon v. Wainwright, 372 U.S. 335 (1963). As to challenges falling outside of that exception, we pointed out that a defendant who successfully attacked his state conviction in state court or on federal habeas review could then "apply for reopening of any federal sentence enhanced by the state sentences."

Daniels v. United States, 532 U.S. 374 (2001), was also summarized by the Court in *Johnson*:

> *Daniels* ... extended *Custis* to hold, subject to the same exception for *Gideon* claims, that a federal prisoner may not attack a predicate state conviction through a § 2255 motion challenging an enhanced federal sentence, and again we stressed considerations of administration and finality. Again, too, we acknowledged that a prisoner could proceed under § 2255 after successful review of the prior state conviction on federal habeas under § 2254 or favorable resort to any postconviction process available under state law. We simply added that if the prior conviction was no longer open to direct or collateral attack in its own right, the federal prisoner could do nothing more about his sentence enhancement.[e]

(ii) *Johnson*. The question was whether Johnson was time-barred from seeking § 2255 relief after the Georgia courts set aside the prior convictions on which his federal enhanced sentence was based. The answer, on Justice Souter's analysis for the Court, involved two steps. The first concerned the meaning of the word "facts" in the relevant AEDPA exception.[f] Johnson argued that the relevant "fact" was entry of the state vacatur order. The government claimed that the relevant "facts" were "the facts on which he based his challenge to the validity of the state convictions."[g]

---

e. The Court added two footnotes to its discussion of *Daniels*. One recognized the possibility of a slight opening in addition to the *Gideon* exception: "The *Daniels* Court allowed that 'there may be rare cases in which no channel of review was actually available to a defendant with respect to a prior conviction, due to no fault of his own,' in which case a prisoner might be able to use a motion under § 2255 to challenge the prior conviction as well as the federal sentence based on it. As in *Daniels,* the circumstances of this case do not call for further exploration of that possibility." The other recognized that "[h]indsight after *Daniels* reveals that Johnson's claim likely would have brought his challenge within the *Gideon* exception, entitling him to attack the state conviction collaterally in a timely § 2255 motion after enhancement of his federal sentence, even without having first resorted to state court."—[Footnote by eds.]

f. Section 2255 says "the date on which the *facts* supporting the claim or claims presented could have been discovered through the exercise of due diligence." (Emphasis added.)

g. This was a change from the government's argument in the Court of Appeals. The dissent characterized it as "[s]eeking a new rationale to imprison petitioner for an additional eight years on the basis of a prior Georgia conviction all of us know to be void . . ."

The Court thought neither argument wholly persuasive. One problem with the government's argument was that it led to an absurdity: Taken literally, it could require a defendant to file a § 2255 proceeding before federal criminal proceedings were even commenced. But Johnson's argument had problems too:

> A ... serious problem is Johnson's position that his § 2255 petition is timely under paragraph four as long as he brings it within a year of learning he succeeded in attacking the prior conviction, no matter how long he may have slumbered before starting the successful proceeding. If Johnson were right about this, a petitioner might wait a long time before raising any question about a predicate conviction, as this very case demonstrates. Of course it may well be that Johnson took his time because his basic sentence had years to run before the period of enhancement began. But letting a petitioner wait for as long as the enhancement makes no difference to his actual imprisonment, while the predicate conviction grows increasingly stale and the federal outcome is subject to question, is certainly at odds with the provision in paragraph four that the one year starts running when the operative fact "could have been discovered through the exercise of due diligence." And by maximizing the time that judgments are open to question, a rule allowing that kind of delay would thwart one of AEDPA's principal purposes . . . .
>
> We think ... however ... that notice of the order vacating the predicate conviction is the event that starts the one year running. Our job here is to find a sensible way to apply paragraph four when the truth is that with *Daniels* not yet on the books AEDPA's drafters probably never thought about the situation we face here. Of course it is peculiar to speak of "discovering" the fact of the very eventuality the petitioner himself has brought about, but when that fact is necessary to the § 2255 claim, and treating notice of it as the trigger produces a more reasonable scheme than the alternatives, the scheme should be reconciled with the statutory language if it can be. And here the fit is painless, if short on style.
>
> While it sounds odd to speak of discovering a fact one has generated, a petitioner does not generate the fact of vacatur all by himself. He does, after all, have to learn of the court's response in the state proceeding, and receiving notice of success can surely qualify as a kind of discovery falling within the statutory language.

But the second step in Justice Souter's analysis accommodated the Court's concern with Johnson's argument:

> That leaves us with the question of how to implement the statutory mandate that a petitioner act with due diligence in discovering the crucial fact of the vacatur order that he himself

seeks. The answer is that diligence can be shown by prompt action on the part of the petitioner as soon as he is in a position to realize that he has an interest in challenging the prior conviction with its potential to enhance the later sentence. The important thing is to identify a particular time when the course of the later federal prosecution clearly shows that diligence is in order. That might be the date the federal indictment is disclosed, the date of judgment, or the date of finality after direct appeal. Picking the first date would require the quickest response and serve finality best, but it would produce some collateral litigation that federal acquittals would prove to have been needless, and it shares the same disconnection from the existence of a § 2255 claim as the Government's view of the relevant "facts." If we picked the third date, collateral litigation would be minimized, but finality would come late. This shapes up as a case for choosing the bowl of porridge between the one too hot and the one too cold, and settling on the date of judgment as the moment to activate due diligence seems best to reflect the statutory text and its underlying concerns. After the entry of judgment, the subject of the § 2255 claim has come into being, the significance of inaction is clear, and very little litigation would be wasted, since most challenged federal convictions are in fact sustained.

The dissent, like Johnson, would dispense with any due diligence requirement in seeking the state vacatur order itself, on the ground that the States can impose their own limitation periods on state collateral attacks, as most States do. But the United States has an interest in the finality of sentences imposed by its own courts; § 2255 is, after all, concerned directly with federal cases. As to those federal cases, due diligence is not a "requirement of [our] own design," but an explicit demand in the text of § 2255, one that reflects AEDPA's core purposes. The requirement of due diligence must therefore demand something more than the dissent's willingness to accept no diligence at all, if the predicate conviction occurred in a State that itself imposes no limit of time for collaterally attacking its convictions.

The dissent suggests that due diligence is satisfied by prompt discovery of the existence of the order vacating the state conviction. Where one "discovers" a fact that one has helped to generate, however, whether it be the result of a court proceeding or of some other process begun at the petitioner's behest, it does not strain logic to treat required diligence in the "discovery" of that fact as entailing diligence in the steps necessary for the existence of that fact. . . .

We accordingly apply the fourth paragraph in the situation before us by holding that from November 29, 1994, the date the

District Court entered judgment in his federal case, Johnson was obliged to act diligently to obtain the state-court order vacating his predicate conviction. Had he done so, the 1–year limitation period would have run from the date he received notice of that vacatur.[8]

Applying this standard, the Court held that Johnson had not exercised due diligence. He offered no explanation for his delay in seeking relief, other than the fact that he was an unsophisticated pro se litigant. As to this the Court observed: "But we have never accepted pro se representation alone or procedural ignorance as an excuse for prolonged inattention when a statute's clear policy calls for promptness . . . ."

Justice Kennedy dissented. He was joined by Justices Stevens, Scalia, and Ginsburg. Kennedy agreed that the order of vacatur was the "fact" that triggered the limitations period. But he disagreed on the Court's due diligence requirement. He summarized his reasoning as follows:

> In my view the Court's new rule of prevacatur diligence is inconsistent with the statutory language; is unnecessary since States are quite capable of protecting themselves against undue delay in commencing state proceedings to vacate prior judgments; introduces an imprecise and incongruous deadline into the federal criminal process; is of sufficient uncertainty that it will require further litigation before its operation is understood; and, last but not least, drains scarce defense resources away from the prisoner's federal criminal case in some of its most critical stages. For these reasons, I submit my respectful dissent.

He elaborated:

> If the State has allowed the vacatur subject to its own rules respecting timely motions or applications and if petitioner has acted diligently in discovering entry of that vacatur, the proper conclusion is that he may bring a § 2255 petition within one year of obtaining the vacatur, or one year of reasonably discovering it. The only way the majority's construction can fit the statute is if the controlling fact is the circumstance giving rise to the vacatur, not the vacatur itself. Yet the majority resists that proposition, for

---

8. Once a petitioner diligently has initiated state-court proceedings, any delay in those proceedings that is not attributable to the petitioner will not impair the availability of the paragraph four limitation rule, once those proceedings finally conclude. We further recognize that the facts underlying the challenge to the state-court conviction might themselves not be discoverable through the exercise of due diligence until after the date of the federal judgment. In such circumstances, once the facts become discoverable and the prisoner proceeds diligently to state court, the limitations period will run from the date of notice of the eventual state-court vacatur. Finally, we note that a petitioner who has been inadequately diligent can still avail himself of paragraph four if he can show that he filed the § 2255 motion within a year of the date he would have received notice of vacatur if he had acted promptly, though this may be a difficult showing.

> it measures the 1-year period from the date the vacatur is ordered.
> . . .
>
> [The majority] is troubled by the prospect that a petitioner "might wait a long time before raising any question about a predicate conviction . . . ." Even if this concern were a sufficient basis for adding the majority's prevacatur diligence requirement to the statute and creating a two-tier diligence structure, the concern is overstated. In most instances, States can, and do, impose diligence by limiting the time for requesting a vacatur of a prior state conviction. It was represented at oral argument that all but about six States impose a limitation by statute or laches. Even in those six States, furthermore, it is not clear that equitable defenses would not apply.
>
> Any States that do not impose time limitations are free to do so if deemed necessary to protect the integrity of their own judgments, so a federal time limit is not required. This is illustrated by the instant case. When Johnson sought state relief, Georgia imposed no limitation on a petitioner's ability to obtain a vacatur. Since then, however, Georgia has enacted a 4-year limitations period for proceeding to obtain a vacatur. The majority's apparent concern that, absent its interpretation of § 2255, petitioners have some incentive to delay proceedings to vacate a conviction seems quite unfounded.
>
> The majority's construction, furthermore, can allow for the same delay it seeks to avoid. After all, the Court holds that the due diligence requirement is triggered only by a federal judgment. Consider a simple hypothetical. Suppose that a petitioner suffers a state conviction in 1980, and, despite learning in 1985 that his conviction is constitutionally infirm, does nothing. Suppose further he is sentenced for a federal crime in 2000. Under the majority's view, the petitioner's obligation to question his state conviction is not triggered until 2000, a full 15 years after he knew the basis for vacatur. Despite the adaptation it makes to § 2255, the majority has failed to create an incentive for petitioner to act promptly in instituting state proceedings. The incentive exists under state law, and the Court does not need to supplement it.

The dissent then shifted to different grounds of attack:

> The error of the majority's position is further revealed by its selection of what I consider to be an incorrect date for triggering the prevacatur diligence requirement. It holds that the triggering event is set at the date of petitioner's federal judgment.
>
> This rule of the Court's own contrivance is adopted, in my respectful submission, without full appreciation for the dynamic of the criminal process and its demands on counsel. Assuming for the

moment that some event in the federal court should start the time period for pursuing state relief, surely the entry of judgment is ill chosen. This means the judgment is a mandatory beginning point for collateral proceedings to correct a judgment and sentence not yet final.

If the Court wants to invent its own rule and use an event in the federal criminal proceeding to commence a limitations period (and I disagree with both propositions), the date the judgment becomes final, not the date of judgment in the trial court, is the proper point of beginning.

The law, and the decisions of this Court, put extraordinary demands on defense counsel. Immediately after a judgment, defense counsel must concentrate on ensuring that evidence of trial misconduct does not disappear and that grounds for appeal are preserved and presented. Today the Court says defense counsel must divert scarce resources from these heavy responsibilities to commence collateral proceedings to attack state convictions.

In this case seven different convictions in Georgia may have been relevant. In other cases convictions that might enhance have been entered in different States. It is most troubling for a Court that insists on high standards of performance for defense counsel now to instruct that collateral proceedings must be commenced in one or more States during the critical time immediately after judgment and before appeal.

If the Court is to insist upon its own second tier of diligence, the dynamics of the criminal system and ordinary rules for determining when collateral proceedings become necessary should instruct us that, for federal purposes, this tier begins when the federal conviction becomes final. This also ensures that the federal court does not make demands on counsel and on state courts that are pointless if the federal conviction is overturned. . . .

Aside from diverting resources from a petitioner's federal case, the majority's approach creates new uncertainty, giving rise to future litigation. It leaves unsaid what standard will be used for measuring whether a petitioner acted promptly, forcing litigants and lawyers to scramble to state court in the hopes they satisfy the Court's vague prevacatur diligence requirement. The Court tells us nothing about what to make of existing state standards regarding diligence. Assume a State has a 4–year limitations period for bringing a vacatur action and a petitioner acts within two years of his state conviction. Do we look to state law as a benchmark for what should be presumed to be diligent? The murkiness of the Court's new rule will set in motion satellite litigation on this and related points.

In lieu of adopting an interpretation that creates more problems than it avoids, I would hold that the order vacating a prior state conviction is the fact supporting a § 2255 claim, and the statute is satisfied if the § 2255 proceeding is commenced within one year of its entry, unless the petitioner shows it was not reasonably discovered until later in which case that date will control when the statute begins to run.

6. The Retroactive New Rule Exception: *Dodd v. United States*. One of the other exceptions to the rule that the one-year statute of limitations starts to run from the date the defendant's conviction becomes final starts the clock from "the date on which the right asserted was initially recognized by the Supreme Court, if that right has been newly recognized by the Supreme Court and made retroactively applicable to cases on collateral review." 28 U.S.C. § 2255, ¶ 6(3). The meaning of this provision was at issue in another five-to-four decision, Dodd v. United States, 545 U.S. ___ (2005).

Richardson v. United States, 526 U.S. 813 (1999), held that a jury must agree unanimously on each of the predicate crimes that satisfy the multiple crime requirement needed for conviction of engaging in a continuing criminal enterprise in violation of 21 U.S.C. § 848. As is its usual practice, the Court did not state in *Richardson* whether this was a new rule to be applied retroactively. *Richardson* was decided on June 1, 1999. The Eleventh Circuit held it retroactive on April 19, 2002.

Dodd's conviction became final on August 6, 1997. He raised a *Richardson* claim in a § 2255 petition filed on April 4, 2001. If the statute of limitations exception was triggered by the date of the Circuit Court retroactivity holding, his petition was timely. If it was triggered by the date of the *Richardson* decision, it was not.

Justice O'Connor's opinion for the Court chose the latter date:

> We believe that the text of ¶ 6(3) settles this dispute. It unequivocally identifies one, and only one, date from which the 1-year limitation period is measured: "the date on which the right asserted was initially recognized by the Supreme Court." We "must presume that [the] legislature says in a statute what it means and means in a statute what it says there." Connecticut Nat. Bank v. Germain, 503 U.S. 249, 253–54 (1992). What Congress has said in ¶ 6(3) is clear: an applicant has one year from the date on which the right he asserts was initially recognized by this Court. . . .
>
> Dodd's reliance on the second clause to identify the operative date is misplaced. That clause—"if that right has been newly recognized by the Supreme Court and made retroactively applicable to cases on collateral review"—imposes a condition on the applicability of this subsection. . . . It . . . limits ¶ 6(3)'s application

to cases in which applicants are seeking to assert rights "newly recognized by the Supreme Court and made retroactively applicable to cases on collateral review." That means that ¶ 6(3)'s date—"the date on which the right asserted was initially recognized by the Supreme Court"—does not apply at all if the conditions in the second clause—the right "has been newly recognized by the Supreme Court and made retroactively applicable to cases on collateral review"—have not been satisfied. As long as the conditions in the second clause are satisfied so that ¶ 6(3) applies in the first place, that clause has no impact whatsoever on the date from which the 1-year limitation period in ¶ 6(3) begins to run. Thus, if this Court decides a case recognizing a new right, a federal prisoner seeking to assert that right will have one year from this Court's decision within which to file his § 2255 motion. He may take advantage of the date in the first clause of ¶ 6(3) only if the conditions in the second clause are met.

Joined by Justices Souter, Ginsburg, and Breyer, Justice Stevens dissented. He thought the Court's interpretation "anomalous" because:

> If, as I believe Congress thought to be the case, this Court made a decision concerning a new rule's retroactive application at the same time it recognized the new right, the statutory scheme would make perfect sense: Petitioners, whether filing an initial habeas petition or a second or successive petition, would have one year from this Court's decision to file a petition for a writ taking advantage of that decision. Within a relatively short amount of time, those claims would be adjudicated, and the statute's goals of finality would be duly served. In practice, however, this Court does not ordinarily make retroactivity judgments at the time a new right is recognized. [T]he statute implicates two relevant events: this Court's recognition of a new right (which, according to the majority, triggers the limitation period) and the declaration that the right can be applied retroactively (which allows a petitioner to proceed with the claim). Because a significant amount of time may elapse during the interval between the triggering event and the point at which a petitioner may actually be able to file an action seeking relief under the statute, there is a real risk that the 1-year limitation period will expire before the cause of action accrues. In my judgment, the probable explanation for statutory text that creates this risk is Congress' apparent assumption that our recognition of the new right and our decision to apply it retroactively would be made at the same time. Otherwise it seems nonsensical to assume that Congress deliberately enacted a statute that recognizes a cause of action, but wrote the limitation period in a way that precludes an individual from ever taking advantage of the cause of action. . . .

Under the majority's interpretation, the statute of limitations ... expired on June 1, 2000, one year after we recognized the new rule. The Eleventh Circuit, however, did not decide whether *Richardson* was retroactive until April 19, 2002. Thus, Dodd would not, under the majority's interpretation, have been able to raise his claim at all, since the statute of limitations expired before he could have taken advantage of ¶ 6(3)'s 1–year grace period. Even for those prisoners who are incarcerated in a jurisdiction in which the new rule is quickly held to be retroactive, at least part of the 1–year period in which to file a claim taking advantage of the retroactive rule will run before the petition raising the claim can be filed. ...

To avoid this result, I would interpret ¶ 6(3) to begin to run only when the Supreme Court has initially recognized the new right *and* when that right has been held to be retroactive. Under this interpretation, the statute of limitation would not begin to run until the prisoner was actually able to file a petition under ¶ 6(3), which is the only interpretation Congress could have intended. Although in enacting AEDPA Congress was clearly concerned with finality, ¶ 6(3) is an explicit exception to that general preference. Congress surely intended to allow habeas petitioners to take advantage of the new rights that this Court deems retroactive. Otherwise, there would have been no reason to include that section in the statute.

Stevens also advanced a second reason for his interpretation:

In addition to creating the perverse result that the statute of limitations will run before a prisoner can file an initial habeas petition, the Court's myopic reading of ¶ 6(3) effectively nullifies 28 U.S.C. § 2244(b)(2)(A), which allows prisoners to file second or successive applications based on a retroactive rule. [T]he majority recognizes in what amounts to a dramatic understatement [that] its interpretation of ¶ 6(3) "makes it difficult for applicants filing second or successive § 2255 motions to obtain relief." Because of the way ¶ ¶ 6(3) and 8(2) interact, a prisoner can only file a second or successive petition based on a newly recognized rule that has been made retroactive if this Court has held the rule to be retroactive within one year of recognizing it. Unfortunately for such prisoners, however, this Court has never done so since Teague v. Lane, 489 U.S. 288 (1989), was decided. Because of the need for percolation, and the time it takes for cases to come to this Court from the courts below, it seems unlikely (to say the least) that we would ever do so. Therefore, the majority's interpretation of ¶ 6(3) effectively nullifies ¶ 8(2). It is, of course, a basic canon of statutory construction that we will not interpret a congressional statute in such a manner as to effectively nullify an entire section.

... It is a strange principle that requires strict adherence to the text of one provision while allowing another to have virtually no real world application. It would seem far wiser to give *both* sections the meaning that Congress obviously intended.

Justice O'Connor responded to this point as follows:

We recognize that the statute of limitations in ¶ 6(3) makes it difficult for applicants filing second or successive § 2255 motions to obtain relief. The limitation period in ¶ 6(3) applies to "all motions" under § 2255, initial motions as well as second or successive ones. Section 2255, ¶ 8(2), narrowly restricts an applicant's ability to file a second or successive motion. An applicant may file a second or successive motion only in limited circumstances, such as where he seeks to take advantage of "a new rule of constitutional law, made retroactive to cases on collateral review by the Supreme Court, that was previously unavailable." Dodd points out that this Court rarely decides that a new rule is retroactively applicable within one year of initially recognizing that right. Thus, because of the interplay between ¶ ¶ 8(2) and 6(3), an applicant who files a second or successive motion seeking to take advantage of a new rule of constitutional law will be time barred except in the rare case in which this Court announces a new rule of constitutional law and makes it retroactive within one year.

Although we recognize the potential for harsh results in some cases, we are not free to rewrite the statute that Congress has enacted. "[W]hen the statute's language is plain, the sole function of the courts—at least where the disposition required by the text is not absurd—is to enforce it according to its terms." Hartford Underwriters Ins. Co. v. Union Planters Bank, N. A., 530 U.S. 1, 6 (2000). See also Tyler v. Cain, 533 U.S. 656, 663, n.5 (2001) ("[E]ven if we disagreed with the legislative decision to establish stringent procedural requirements for retroactive application of new rules, we do not have license to question the decision on policy grounds"). The disposition required by the text here, though strict, is not absurd. It is for Congress, not this Court, to amend the statute if it believes that the interplay of ¶ ¶ 8(2) and 6(3) of § 2255 unduly restricts federal prisoners' ability to file second or successive motions.

In a footnote, Stevens added one more observation:

I should note an additional point of disagreement with the majority (and with petitioner). In reaching its result, the Court relies on an assumption made by both parties and not challenged in this Court: namely, that the decision to make a new rule retroactive for purposes of this section can be made by any lower court. While I recognize that every Circuit to have addressed the issue has made the same assumption, I am satisfied that . . . the requirement that "the right has been newly recognized by the Supreme Court and made retroactively applicable to cases on collateral review" is met only if the *Supreme Court* has made the right retroactive.

Courts that have reached the contrary conclusion have principally relied on the fact that 28 U.S.C. § 2244(b)(2)(A) contains an explicit requirement that a new rule be "made retroactive . . . *by the Supreme Court.*" (Emphasis added.) Thus, the argument goes, the absence of "by the Supreme Court" after "made retroactive" must have some meaning. However, in that clause there is only one verb that the prepositional phrase "by the Supreme Court" can modify, whereas in the relevant clause of § 2255, ¶ 6(3), there are two: newly recognized and made retroactive. The more natural reading of ¶ 6(3) is that the prepositional phrase "by the Supreme Court" modifies *both* verbs of the subordinate clause. This reading comports with Congress' general direction that this Court, and not the lower courts, should provide the final answer to questions of interpretation arising under [AEDPA]. See, e.g., 28 U.S.C. § 2254(d)(1) (requiring that a state-court decision be contrary to "clearly established Federal law, *as determined by the Supreme Court of the United States* "(emphasis added)). Additionally, it avoids difficult questions of which court can make a retroactivity determination, sets a uniform date by which lower courts can make determinations as to whether a petition is timely, and means that only those cases made retroactive by this Court can form the basis for a petition that can gain the benefit of tolling under § 2255, ¶ 6(3). Finally, it is the only interpretation that gives full effect to § 2255, ¶ 8(2), which allows prisoners who have already completed one round of federal habeas review to seek additional relief on the basis of such a new rule.

Ultimately, this reading has no direct bearing on the question presented in this case. While my view that this Court must make the retroactivity determination informs my belief that Congress had a mistaken understanding of how ¶ 6(3) would operate in practice, I would conclude that the 1–year limitation period begins to run when both requirements of ¶ 6(3) are met regardless of which court makes the retroactivity decision.

Justices Souter, Ginsburg, and Breyer did not join this footnote. In a separate opinion joined by Justice Breyer, Justice Ginsburg explained:

Petitioner and respondent assume, for the purpose at hand, that a controlling decision whether a right operates retroactively may be made by a court of appeals. We have no cause in this case to question that assumption. I therefore do not subscribe to Justice Stevens' statements that only this Court has the prerogative to make the retroactivity determination. I would await full adversarial presentation before expressing an opinion on that issue.

Page 915, add to citations in Note 2:

Roger Berkowitz, Error–Centricity, Habeas Corpus, and the Rule of Law as the Law of Rulings, 64 La. L. Rev. 477 (2004) ("this paper shows how the great writ of habeas corpus is in danger of losing its once mythical connection to justice") .

Page 916, add to the list of citations in Note 2:

George C. Thomas, III, Gordon G. Young, Keith Sharfman, and Kate B. Briscoe, Is it Ever Too Late for Innocence? Finality, Efficiency, and Claims of Innocence, 64 U. Pitt. L. Rev. 263 (2003);

Page 916, add at the end of Note 2:

For different takes on the factual innocence question, see Brandon L. Garrett, Innocence, Harmless Error, and Federal Wrongful Conviction Law, 2005 Wis. L. Rev. 35 (exploring wrongful conviction suits under § 1983); D. Michael Risinger, Unsafe Verdicts: The Need for Reformed Standards for the Trial and Review of Factual Innocence Claims, 41 Hous. L. Rev. 1281 (2004) (proposing reforms in the trial and direct review process); Laura Denvir Stith, A Contrast of State and Federal Court Authority to Grant Habeas Relief, 38 Val. U. L. Rev. 421 (2004) (Missouri Supreme Court Judge exploring one state's decision to inquire more broadly into actual innocence claims in state habeas proceedings than federal habeas law would allow).

Page 926, insert the following case after *Bousley*:

Dretke v. Haley

Supreme Court of the United States. 2004.
541 U.S. 386.

■ JUSTICE O'CONNOR delivered the opinion of the Court.

Out of respect for finality, comity, and the orderly administration of justice, a federal court will not entertain a procedurally defaulted constitutional claim in a petition for habeas corpus absent a showing of cause and prejudice to excuse the default. We have recognized a narrow exception to the general rule when the habeas applicant can demonstrate that the alleged constitutional error has resulted in the conviction of one who is actually innocent of the underlying offense or, in the capital sentencing context, of the aggravating circumstances rendering the inmate eligible for the death penalty. Murray v. Carrier, 477 U.S. 478 (1986); Sawyer v. Whitley, 505 U.S. 333 (1992). The question before us is whether this exception applies where an applicant asserts "actual innocence" of a noncapital sentence. Because the District Court failed first to consider alternative grounds for relief urged by respondent, grounds that might obviate any need to reach the actual innocence question, we vacate the judgment and remand.

I

In 1997, respondent Michael Wayne Haley was arrested after stealing a calculator from a local Wal–Mart and attempting to exchange it for other merchandise. Respondent was charged with, and found guilty at trial of, theft of property valued at less than $1,500, which, because respondent already had two prior theft convictions, was a "state jail felony" punishable by a maximum of two years in prison. Tex. Penal Code Ann. § 31.03(e)(4)(D) (Supp.2004). The State also charged respondent as a habitual felony offender. The indictment alleged that respondent had two prior felony convictions and that the first—a 1991 conviction for delivery of amphetamine—"became final prior to the commission" of the second—a 1992 robbery. The timing of the first conviction and the second offense is significant: Under Texas' habitual offender statute, only a defendant convicted of a felony who "has previously been finally convicted of two felonies, *and* the second previous felony conviction is for an offense that occurred subsequent to the first previous conviction having become final, ... shall be punished for a second-degree felony." § 12.42(a)(2) (emphasis added). A second degree felony carries a minimum sentence of 2 and a maximum sentence of 20 years in prison. § 12.33(a).

Texas provides for bifurcated trials in habitual offender cases. If a defendant is found guilty of the substantive offense, the State, at a separate penalty hearing, must prove the habitual offender allegations beyond a reasonable doubt. During the penalty phase of respondent's trial, the State introduced records showing that respondent had been convicted of delivery of amphetamine on October 18, 1991, and attempted robbery on September 9, 1992. The record of the second conviction, however, showed that respondent had committed the robbery on October 15, 1991—three days *before* his first conviction became final. Neither the prosecutor, nor the defense attorney, nor the witness tendered by the State to authenticate the records, nor the trial judge, nor the jury, noticed the 3–day discrepancy. Indeed, the defense attorney chose not to cross-examine the State's witness or to put on any evidence.

The jury returned a verdict of guilty on the habitual offender charge and recommended a sentence of 16½ years; the court followed the recommendation. Respondent appealed. Appellate counsel did not mention the 3–day discrepancy nor challenge the sufficiency of the penalty-phase evidence to support the habitual offender enhancement. The State Court of Appeals affirmed respondent's conviction and sentence; the Texas Court of Criminal Appeals refused respondent's petition for discretionary review.

Respondent thereafter sought state postconviction relief, arguing for the first time that he was ineligible for the habitual offender enhancement based on the timing of his second conviction. The state habeas court refused to consider the merits of that claim because respondent had not raised it, as required by state procedural law, either at trial or on direct appeal. The state habeas court rejected respondent's related ineffective assistance of counsel claim, saying only that "counsel was not ineffective" for failing to object to or to appeal the enhancement. The Texas Court of Criminal Appeals summarily denied respondent's state habeas application.

In August 2000, respondent filed a timely pro se application for a federal writ of habeas corpus pursuant to 28 U.S.C. § 2254, renewing his sufficiency of the evidence and ineffective assistance of counsel claims. The State conceded that respondent was "correct in his assertion that the enhancement paragraphs as alleged in the indictment do not satisfy section 12.42(a)(2) of the Texas Penal Code." Rather than agree to resentencing, however, the State argued that respondent had procedurally defaulted the sufficiency of the evidence claim by failing to raise it before the state trial court or on direct appeal. The Magistrate Judge, to whom the habeas application had been referred, recommended excusing the procedural default and granting the sufficiency of the evidence claim because respondent was "'actually innocent' of a sentence for a second-degree felony." Because she recommended relief on the erroneous enhancement claim, the Magistrate Judge did not address respondent's related ineffective assistance of counsel challenges. The District Court adopted the Magistrate Judge's report, granted the application, and ordered the State to resentence respondent "without the improper enhancement."

The Court of Appeals for the Fifth Circuit affirmed, holding narrowly that the actual innocence exception "applies to noncapital sentencing procedures involving a career offender or habitual felony offender." The Fifth Circuit thus joined the Fourth Circuit in holding that the exception should not extend beyond allegedly erroneous recidivist enhancements to other claims of noncapital factual sentencing error: "[T]o broaden the exception further would 'swallow' the 'cause portion of the cause and prejudice requirement' and it 'would conflict squarely with Supreme Court authority indicating that generally more than prejudice must exist to excuse procedural default.'" Finding the exception satisfied, the panel then granted relief on the merits of respondent's otherwise defaulted sufficiency of the evidence claim. In so doing, the panel assumed that challenges to the sufficiency of noncapital sentencing evidence are cognizable on federal habeas under Jackson v. Virginia, 443 U.S. 307 (1979).

The Fifth Circuit's decision exacerbated a growing divergence of opinion in the Courts of Appeals regarding the availability and scope of the actual innocence exception in the noncapital sentencing context. Compare [two cases holding that there is "no actual innocence exception for noncapital sentencing error"] with [one case holding that the "actual innocence exception applies in noncapital sentencing context when error is related to finding of predicate act forming the basis for enhancement''] and [another holding that the "actual innocence exception applies in noncapital sentencing context where error relates to a recidivist enhancement'']. We granted the State's request for a writ of certiorari, and now vacate and remand.

II

The procedural default doctrine, like the abuse of writ doctrine, "refers to a complex and evolving body of equitable principles informed and controlled by historical usage, statutory developments, and judicial decisions." McCleskey v. Zant, 499 U.S. 467, 489 (1991). A corollary to the habeas statute's exhaustion requirement, the doctrine has its roots in the general principle that federal courts will not disturb state court judgments based on adequate and independent state law procedural grounds. Wainwright v. Sykes, 433 U.S. 72, 81 (1977); Brown v. Allen, 344 U.S. 443, 486–87 (1953). But, while an adequate and independent state procedural disposition strips this Court of certiorari jurisdiction to review a state court's judgment, it provides only a strong prudential reason, grounded in "considerations of comity and concerns for the orderly administration of justice," not to pass upon a defaulted constitutional claim presented for federal habeas review. Francis v. Henderson, 425 U.S. 536, 538–39 (1976); see also Fay v. Noia, 372 U.S. 391, 399 (1963) ("[T]he doctrine under which state procedural defaults are held to constitute an adequate and independent state law ground barring direct Supreme Court review is not to be extended to limit the power granted the federal courts under the federal habeas statute''). That being the case, we have recognized an equitable exception to the bar when a habeas applicant can demonstrate cause and prejudice for the procedural default. The cause and prejudice requirement shows due regard for States' finality and comity interests while ensuring that "fundamental fairness [remains] the central concern of the writ of habeas corpus." Strickland v. Washington, 466 U.S. 668, 697 (1984).

The cause and prejudice standard is not a perfect safeguard against fundamental miscarriages of justice. Murray v. Carrier, 477 U.S. 478 (1986), thus recognized a narrow exception to the cause requirement where a constitutional violation has "probably resulted" in the conviction of one who is "actually innocent" of the substantive offense. We subsequently extended this exception to claims of capital sentencing error in Sawyer v. Whitley, 505 U.S. 333 (1992). Acknowledging that the concept of "actual innocence" did not translate neatly into the capital sentencing context, we limited the exception to cases in which the applicant could show "by clear and convincing evidence that, but for constitutional error, no reasonable juror would have found the petitioner eligible for the death penalty under the applicable state law."

We are asked in the present case to extend the actual innocence exception to procedural default of constitutional claims challenging noncapital sentencing error. We decline to answer the question in the posture of this case and instead hold that a federal court faced with allegations of actual innocence, whether of the sentence or of the crime charged, must first address all nondefaulted claims for comparable relief and other grounds for cause to excuse the procedural default.

This avoidance principle was implicit in *Carrier* itself, where we expressed confidence that, "for the most part, 'victims of fundamental miscarriage of justice will meet the cause-and-prejudice standard.'" Our confidence was bolstered by the availability of ineffective assistance of counsel claims—either as a ground for cause or as a free-standing claim for relief—to safeguard against miscarriages of justice. The existence of such safeguards, we observed, "may properly inform this Court's judgment in determining '[w]hat standards should govern the exercise of the habeas court's equitable discretion' with respect to procedurally defaulted claims." *Carrier*, supra, at 496.

Petitioner here conceded at oral argument that respondent has a viable and "significant" ineffective assistance of counsel claim. ("[W]e agree at this point there is a very significant argument of ineffective assistance of counsel"); [the petitioner also agreed] "not [to] raise any procedural impediment" to consideration of the merits of respondent's ineffective assistance claim on remand. Success on the merits would give respondent all of the relief that he seeks—i.e., resentencing. It would also provide cause to excuse the procedural default of his sufficiency of the evidence claim.

Contrary to the dissent's view, it is precisely because the various exceptions to the procedural default doctrine are judge-made rules that courts as their stewards must exercise restraint, adding to or expanding them only when necessary. To hold otherwise would be to license district courts to riddle the cause and prejudice standard with ad hoc exceptions whenever they perceive an error to be "clear" or departure from the rules expedient. Such an approach, not the rule of restraint adopted here, would have the unhappy effect of prolonging the pendency of federal habeas applications as each new exception is tested in the courts of appeals. And because petitioner has assured us that it will not seek to reincarcerate respondent during the pendency of his ineffective assistance claim, ("[T]he state is willing to allow the ineffective assistance claim to be litigated before proceeding to reincarcerate [respondent]"), the negative consequences for respondent of our judgment to vacate and remand in this case are minimal.

While availability of other remedies alone would be sufficient justification for a general rule of avoidance, the many threshold legal questions often accompanying claims of actual innocence provide additional reason for restraint. For instance, citing Jackson v. Virginia, 443 U.S. 307 (1979), respondent here seeks to bring through the actual innocence gateway his constitutional claim that the State's penalty-phase evidence was insufficient to support the recidivist enhancement. But the constitutional hook in

Jackson was In re Winship, 397 U.S. 358 (1970), in which we held that due process requires proof of each element of a criminal offense beyond a reasonable doubt. We have not extended *Winship's* protections to proof of prior convictions used to support recidivist enhancements. Almendarez-Torres v. United States, 523 U.S. 224 (1998); see also Apprendi v. New Jersey, 530 U.S. 466, 488–90 (2000) (reserving judgment as to the validity of *Almendarez-Torres*); Monge v. California, 524 U.S. 721, 734 (1998) (Double Jeopardy Clause does not preclude retrial on a prior conviction used to support recidivist enhancement). Respondent contends that *Almendarez-Torres* should be overruled or, in the alternative, that it does not apply because the recidivist statute at issue required the jury to find not only the existence of his prior convictions but also the additional fact that they were sequential. These difficult constitutional questions, simply assumed away by the dissent are to be avoided if possible.

To be sure, not all claims of actual innocence will involve threshold constitutional issues. Even so, as this case and the briefing illustrate, such claims are likely to present equally difficult questions regarding the scope of the actual innocence exception itself. Whether and to what extent the exception extends to noncapital sentencing error is just one example. The judgment of the Court of Appeals is vacated, and the case is remanded for further proceedings consistent with this opinion.

It is so ordered.

■ JUSTICE STEVENS, with whom JUSTICE KENNEDY and JUSTICE SOUTER join, dissenting.

The unending search for symmetry in the law can cause judges to forget about justice. This should be a simple case.

Respondent was convicted of the theft of a calculator. Because of his prior theft convictions, Texas law treated respondent's crime as a "state jail felony," which is punishable by a maximum sentence of two years in jail. But as a result of a congeries of mistakes made by the prosecutor, the trial judge, and his attorney, respondent was also erroneously convicted and sentenced under Texas' habitual offender law. Respondent consequently received a sentence of more than 16 years in the penitentiary. The State concedes that respondent does not qualify as a habitual offender and that the 16-year sentence was imposed in error.[3] Respondent has already served more than 6 years of that sentence—a sentence far in excess of the 2-year maximum that Texas law authorizes for respondent's crime.

Because, as all parties agree, there is no factual basis for respondent's conviction as a habitual offender, it follows inexorably that respondent has been denied due process of law. Thompson v. Louisville, 362 U.S. 199 (1960); Jackson v. Virginia, 443 U.S. 307 (1979). And because that constitutional error clearly and concededly resulted in the imposition of an unau-

---

3. "[I]t's almost a law school hypothetical, because the error is so clean."

thorized sentence, it also follows that respondent is a "victim of a miscarriage of justice," Wainwright v. Sykes, 433 U.S. 72, 91 (1977), entitled to immediate and unconditional release.

The Magistrate Judge, the District Court, and the Court of Appeals all concluded that respondent is entitled to such relief. Not a word in any federal statute or any provision of the Federal Rules of Procedure provides any basis for challenging that conclusion. The Court's contrary determination in this case rests entirely on a procedural rule of its own invention. But having also invented the complex jurisprudence that requires a prisoner to establish "cause and prejudice" as a basis for overcoming procedural default, the Court unquestionably has the authority to recognize a narrow exception for the unusual case that is as clear as this one.

Indeed, in the opinion that first adopted the cause and prejudice standard, the Court explained its purpose as providing "an adequate guarantee" that a procedural default would "not prevent a federal habeas court from adjudicating for the first time the federal constitutional claim of a defendant who in the absence of such an adjudication will be the victim of a miscarriage of justice." The Court has since held that in cases in which the cause and prejudice standard is inadequate to protect against fundamental miscarriages of justice, the cause and prejudice requirement "must yield to the imperative of correcting a fundamentally unjust incarceration." Engle v. Isaac, 456 U.S. 107, 135 (1982).

If there were some uncertainty about the merits of respondent's claim that he has been incarcerated unjustly, it might make sense to require him to pursue other avenues for comparable relief before deciding the claim.[4] But in this case, it is universally acknowledged that respondent's incarceration is unauthorized. The miscarriage of justice is manifest. Since the "imperative of correcting a fundamentally unjust incarceration" will lead to the issuance of the writ regardless of the outcome of the cause and prejudice inquiry, the Court's ruling today needlessly postpones final adjudication of respondent's claim and perversely prolongs the very injustice that the cause and prejudice standard was designed to prevent.

That the State has decided to oppose the grant of habeas relief in this case, even as it concedes that respondent has already served more time in prison than the law authorized, might cause some to question whether the State has forgotten its overriding "obligation to serve the cause of justice."

---

4. Because it is not always easy to discern the difference between "constitutional claims that call into question the reliability of an adjudication of legal guilt," to which the cause and prejudice requirement applies, and claims that a constitutional violation "probably resulted in the conviction of one who is actually innocent," for which failure to show cause is excused, a court reviewing a claim of actual innocence must generally proceed with caution. But that type of caution is plainly unwarranted in a case in which constitutional error has concededly resulted in the imposition of an unlawful sentence. In such a case, there is simply no risk that entertaining the habeas applicant's procedurally defaulted claim will result in an unwarranted encroachment on the principles of comity and finality that underlie the procedural default doctrine.

But this Court is surely no less at fault. In its attempt to refine the boundaries of the judge-made doctrine of procedural default, the Court has lost sight of the basic reason why the "writ of habeas corpus indisputably holds an honored position in our jurisprudence." *Engle,* 456 U.S., at 126. Habeas corpus is, and has for centuries been, a "bulwark against convictions that violate fundamental fairness." Ibid. Fundamental fairness should dictate the outcome of this unusually simple case.

I respectfully dissent.

■ JUSTICE KENNEDY, dissenting.

For the reasons Justice Stevens sets forth, the Respondent should be entitled to immediate relief, and I join his dissenting opinion. The case also merits this further comment concerning the larger obligation of state or federal officials when they know an individual has been sentenced for a crime he did not commit.

In 1997, Michael Haley was sentenced to serve 16 years and 6 months in prison for violating the Texas habitual offender law. Texas officials concede Haley did not violate this law. They agree that Haley is guilty only of theft, a crime with a 2-year maximum sentence. Yet, despite the fact that Haley served more than two years in prison for his crime, Texas officials come before our Court opposing Haley's petition for relief. They wish to send Haley back to prison for a crime they agree he did not commit.

The rigors of the penal system are thought to be mitigated to some degree by the discretion of those who enforce the law. The clemency power is designed to serve the same function. Among its benign if too-often ignored objects, the clemency power can correct injustices that the ordinary criminal process seems unable or unwilling to consider. These mechanisms hold out the promise that mercy is not foreign to our system. The law must serve the cause of justice.

These mitigating elements seem to have played no role in Michael Haley's case. Executive discretion and clemency can inspire little confidence if officials sworn to fight injustice choose to ignore it. Perhaps some would say that Haley's innocence is a mere technicality, but that would miss the point. In a society devoted to the rule of law, the difference between violating or not violating a criminal statute cannot be shrugged aside as a minor detail.

It may be that Haley's case provides a convenient mechanism to vindicate an important legal principle. Beyond that, however, Michael Haley has a greater interest in knowing that he will not be reincarcerated for a crime he did not commit. It is not clear to me why the State did not exercise its power and perform its duty to vindicate that interest in the first place.

CHAPTER VIII

STATE SOVEREIGN IMMUNITY AND THE 11TH AMENDMENT

Page 931, add a footnote at the end of Note 4:

f. For a critical reexamination of *Hans* in its historical context, see Edward R. Purcell, Jr., The Particularly Dubious Case of *Hans v. Louisiana*: An Essay on Law, Race, History, and "Federal Courts," 81 N.C.L. Rev. 1927 (2003). For analysis of state consent to suit and the (arguably distinct) doctrine of state waiver of sovereign immunity, see Jonathan R. Siegel, Waivers of State Sovereign Immunity and the Ideology of the Eleventh Amendment, 52 Duke L. J. 1167 (2003). Siegel recounts the history of consent and waiver and proposes that waiver doctrine be reformed to allow consideration of the interests of other parties litigating against a state.—[Footnote by eds.]

Page 944, add before the last paragraph of Note 5:

Another genuinely original argument appears in John F. Manning, The Eleventh Amendment and the Reading of Precise Constitutional Texts, 113 Yale L.J. 1663 (2004). Manning criticizes the Court's willingness to read the 11th Amendment to mean much more than it says. In reading "precise constitutional texts," he argues, the Court should adhere to the approach of statutory interpretation and "[hew] closely to the rules embedded in the enacted text, rather than adjusting that text to make it more consistent with its apparent purposes." In Manning's view, the "strong purposivism" that characterizes 11th Amendment jurisprudence ignores the precise political compromise reflected in the text. He also argues, contra Caleb Nelson (see above), that the 11th Amendment's literal narrowness may carry a negative implication against broader exceptions to the judicial power under Article III.

Page 966, add to the end of footnote a:

See also Lauren K. Robel, Sovereignty and Democracy: The States' Obligations to Their Citizens under Federal Statutory Law, 78 Ind. L.J. 543 (2003), which "explores how states should make ... waiver decisions, and what constraints—both political and legal—states face in doing so."

Page 1026, add a new Note 4 and renumber the remaining Notes:

4. *Tennessee v. Lane.* *Board of Trustees of the University of Alabama v. Garrett* involved Title I of the Americans with Disabilities Act, which concerns employment. The Act contains an unambiguously clear statement of congressional intent to hold states liable, but the Court, following the analysis of *City of Boerne v. Flores* found that the statute could not be justified as remedial legislation under § 5 of the Fourteenth Amendment. Consequently, the attempt to impose damages liability on states lay beyond Congress's power.

In Tennessee v. Lane, 541 U.S. 509 (2004), the Court followed the same analysis to reach the opposite conclusion—in this instance with respect to Title II of the ADA, which concerns public services and programs.[d] Plaintiffs were paraplegics who complained of state courthouses without elevator facilities. One of them crawled up two flights of stairs to answer criminal charges. When he returned to the courthouse for a hearing, he refused to repeat that effort or to be carried by officers to the courtroom. In consequence, he was arrested and jailed for failing to appear.

Speaking through Justice Stevens, the Court found several reasons to distinguish *Garrett*. For one thing, the underlying constitutional rights were different. *Garrett* involved the equal protection right to like treatment for persons similarly situated, a right triggering "mere rationality" review. *Lane* implicated that right and others, including the due process right of access to the courts and the Sixth Amendment's confrontation clause. These claims, said the Court, were "subject to a more searching standard of judicial review" than mere rationality. Consequently, remedial legislation seeking to prevent these harms would be more closely related to an underlying constitutional violation. Of course, many claims arising under Title II of the ADA would not involve access to the courts, but the Court refused to allow the possibility that some other applications of the statute might be invalid to affect its resolution of this case.

Another reason for distinguishing *Garrett* was the greater evidentiary support before Congress when the ADA was passed. According to the majority, most of the evidence concerning disability discrimination by governments concerned public services and public accommodations, which are governed by Title II, rather than employment, which is the subject of Title I. Congress made an explicit finding that "discrimination against individuals with disabilities persists in such critical areas as ... access to public services." 42 U.S.C. § 1201(a)(3). The "extensive record" that underlay this finding made it "clear beyond peradventure that inadequate provision of public services and access to public facilities was an appropriate subject for prophylactic legislation" under § 5.

Neither of these grounds proved persuasive to four dissenters. Speaking for himself and for Justices Kennedy and Thomas, the Chief Justice reprised the "congruence and proportionality" analysis of *City of Boerne* and found Title II wanting. In particular, Rehnquist objected to the Court's reliance on wide-ranging evidence of societal discrimination against the disabled. He thought the proper inquiry whether Congress had identified a "history and pattern" of discrimination regarding access to the courts. Besides, he argued, the mere fact of an architecturally inaccessible courthouse, at least for older buildings, did not make out a constitutional violation. As he put it, "the fact that the State may need to assist an

---

d. Specifically, the statute provides that "no qualified individual with a disability shall, by reason of such disability, be excluded from participation in or be denied the benefits of the services, programs or activities of a public entity...." 42 U.S.C. § 12131.

individual to attend a hearing has no bearing on whether the individual successfully exercises his due process right to be present at the proceeding." Viewed in this way, the congressional record behind Title II revealed a "near-total lack of actual constitutional violations." Consequently, Rehnquist found that Title II could not be justified as remedial legislation but amounted to an attempt by Congress to enact substantive legislation imposing new liability on the states.

Justice Scalia also dissented, but on broader grounds. He regretted having signed on to the "congruence and proportionality" test in *City of Boerne* and later cases and announced his willingness to learn from experience:

> The "congruence and proportionality" standard, like all such flabby tests, is a standing invitation to judicial arbitrariness and policy-driven decisionmaking. Worse still, it casts the Court in the role of Congress's taskmaster. Under it, the courts (and ultimately this Court) must regularly check Congress's homework to make sure that it has identified sufficient constitutional violations to make its remedy congruent and proportional. As a general matter, we are ill advised to adopt or adhere to constitutional rules that bring us into constant conflict with a coequal branch of Government. When conflict is unavoidable, we should not come to do battle with the United States Congress armed only with a test ("congruence and proportionality") that has no demonstrable basis in the text of the Constitution and cannot objectively be shown to have been met or failed. . . .
>
> I would replace "congruence and proportionality" with another test—one that provides a clear, enforceable limitation supported by the text of § 5. Section 5 grants Congress the power "to *enforce*, by appropriate legislation," the other provisions of the Fourteenth Amendment (emphasis added). . . . [O]ne does not, within any normal meaning of the term, "enforce" a prohibition by issuing a still broader prohibition directed to the same end. One does not, for example, "enforce" a 55–mile-per-hour speed limit by imposing a 45–mile-per-hour speed limit—even though that is indeed directed to the same end of automotive safety and will undoubtedly result in many fewer violations of the 55–mile-per-hour limit. And one does not "enforce" the right of access to the courts at issue in this case by requiring that disabled persons be provided access to *all* of the "services, programs, or activities" furnished or conducted by the State. 42 U.S.C. § 12132. That is simply not what the power to enforce means—or ever meant. . . .

In short, Scalia concluded, "Nothing in § 5 allows Congress to go *beyond* the provisions of the Fourteenth Amendment to proscribe, prevent, or 'remedy' conduct that does not *itself* violate any provision of the Fourteenth Amendment."

Finally, Scalia attempted to reconcile his approach with the precedents, or rather most of them, by excepting racial discrimination: "Giving § 5 more expansive scope with regard to measures directed against racial discrimination by the States accord to practices that are distinctively violative of the principal purpose of the Fourteenth Amendment a priority of attention that this Court envisioned from the beginning, and that has repeatedly been reflected in our opinions." Scalia therefore announced his willingness to continue a "permissive" standard for remedial legislation when race is involved, but otherwise to insist on direct "enforcement" of the provisions of the Fourteenth Amendment, rather than allowing broadly prophylactic legislation addressed to the same general ends.

Page 1036, add at the end of the carry-over paragraph:

Marcia L. McCormick, Federalism Re–Constructed: The Eleventh Amendment's Illogical Impact on Congress' Power, 37 Ind. L. Rev. 345 (2004) arguing that cases construing the 11th Amendment and those cases construing Section 5 of the 14th Amendment combine to impose dangerous and unwarranted limitations on Congress's power to remedy civil rights violations by the states; Ann Althouse, Vanguard States, Laggard States: Federalism and Constitutional Rights, 152 U. Pa. L. Rev. 1745 (2004) (analyzing recent decisions in terms of a concern for the behavior of "laggard states" and the impact of such perceptions on judicial views of federalism).

Page 1036, add to the citations in the first full paragraph:

Michael E. Solimine, Formalism, Pragmatism, and the Conservative Critique of the Eleventh Amendment, 101 Mich. L. Rev. 1463 (2003) (wide-ranging review essay of John Noonan's book, Narrowing the Nation's Power: The Supreme Court Sides With the States).

Page 1047, add a footnote at the end of the Note on *Verizon Maryland*:

a. For analysis of *Verizon Maryland* as a case lying at the fault line between suits to enjoin enforcement of state statutes said to be preempted by a federal statute (where a cause of action is assumed under *Ex parte Young*) and suits to enjoin state executive action said to be preempted by a federal statute (where the plaintiff must show statutory standing), see David Sloss, Constitutional Remedies for Statutory Violations, 89 Iowa L. Rev. 355 (2004).

Page 1047, add the following at the end of the Note on *Verizon Maryland, Inc. v. Public Service Commission*.

The inference to be drawn from *Verizon Maryland* seems to have been confirmed in Frew v. Hawkins, 540 U.S. 431 (2004). At issue was the enforceability of a consent decree against state officials. Plaintiffs sued state agencies and officers alleging that a Texas Medicaid program failed to meet the requirements of federal law. They sought only injunctive relief. The state agencies were dismissed from the suit on 11th Amendment grounds, but the officials agreed to a (highly detailed) consent decree regulating the Texas program. Two years later, the plaintiffs were back in federal court alleging failure to comply. In response, the officers claimed that the 11th Amendment precluded enforcement against them.

The Fifth Circuit accepted this claim, but the Supreme Court unanimously reversed. Speaking through Justice Kennedy, the Court had no trouble finding the consent decree enforceable through injunctions directed against state officers. Pennhurst State School and Hospital v. Halderman, 465 U.S. 89 (1984), was distinguished on the ground that it involved only violations of state law. Here the consent decree was entered into by state officers in order to comply with federal law. Hence, it was enforceable under *Ex parte Young*.

CHAPTER IX

42 U.S.C. § 1983

Page 1103, add at the end of Note 10:

For thoughtful criticism of this approach, see Thomas Healy, The Rise of Unnecessary Constitutional Rulings, 83 N.C.L. Rev. 847 (2005) (arguing, on the basis of an extensive review of lower court decisions, that "unnecessary" merits rulings in qualified immunity cases are unlikely to result in the establishment of new rights).

Page 1106, add new main case and Notes at the end of the page:

Brosseau v. Haugen
Supreme Court of the United States, 2004.
543 U.S. ___, 125 S.Ct. 596.

■ PER CURIAM.

Officer Rochelle Brosseau, a member of the Puyallup, Washington, Police Department, shot Kenneth Haugen in the back as he attempted to flee from law enforcement authorities in his vehicle. Haugen subsequently filed this action in the United States District Court for the Western District of Washington pursuant to 42 U.S.C. § 1983. He alleged that the shot fired by Brosseau constituted excessive force and violated his federal constitutional rights. The District Court granted summary judgment to Brosseau after finding she was entitled to qualified immunity. The Court of Appeals for the Ninth Circuit reversed. Following the two-step process set out in Saucier v. Katz, 533 U.S. 194 (2001), the Court of Appeals found, first, that Brosseau had violated Haugen's Fourth Amendment right to be free from excessive force and, second, that the right violated was clearly established and thus Brosseau was not entitled to qualified immunity. Brosseau then petitioned for writ of certiorari, requesting that we review both of the Court of Appeals' determinations. We grant the petition on the second, qualified immunity question and [summarily] reverse.

The material facts, construed in a light most favorable to Haugen, are as follows. On the day before the fracas, Glen Tamburello went to the police station and reported to Brosseau that Haugen, a former crime partner of his, had stolen tools from his shop. Brosseau later learned that there was a felony no-bail warrant out for Haugen's arrest on drug and other offenses. The next morning, Haugen was spray-painting his Jeep Cherokee in his mother's driveway. Tamburello learned of Haugen's whereabouts, and he and cohort Matt Atwood drove a pickup truck to Haugen's mother's house to pay Haugen a visit. A fight ensued, which was witnessed by a neighbor who called 911.

Brosseau heard a report that the men were fighting in Haugen's mother's yard and responded. When she arrived, Tamburello and Atwood were attempting to get Haugen into Tamburello's pickup. Brosseau's arrival created a distraction, which provided Haugen the opportunity to get away. Haugen ran through his mother's yard and hid in the neighborhood. Brosseau requested assistance, and, shortly thereafter, two officers arrived with a K–9 to help track Haugen down....

An officer radioed from down the street that a neighbor had seen a man in her backyard. Brosseau ran in that direction, and Haugen appeared. He ran past the front of his mother's house and then turned and ran into the driveway. With Brosseau still in pursuit, he jumped into the driver's side of the Jeep and closed and locked the door. Brosseau believed that he was running to the Jeep to retrieve a weapon.

Brosseau arrived at the Jeep, pointed her gun at Haugen, and ordered him to get out of the vehicle. Haugen ignored her command and continued to look for the keys so that he could get the Jeep started. Brosseau repeated her commands and hit the driver's side window several times with her handgun, which failed to deter Haugen. On the third or fourth try, the window shattered. Brosseau unsuccessfully attempted to grab the keys and struck Haugen on the head with the barrel and butt of her gun. Haugen, still undeterred, succeeded in starting the Jeep. As the Jeep started or shortly after it began to move, Brosseau jumped back and to the left. She fired one shot through the rear driver's side window at a forward angle, hitting Haugen in the back. She later explained that she shot Haugen because she was " 'fearful for the other officers on foot who [she] believed were in the immediate area, [and] for the occupied vehicles in [Haugen's] path and for any other citizens who might be in the area.' "

Despite being hit, Haugen, in his words, " 'st[ood] on the gas' " ... ; swerved across the neighbor's lawn; and continued down the street. After about a half block, Haugen realized that he had been shot and brought the Jeep to a halt. He suffered a collapsed lung and was airlifted to a hospital. He survived the shooting and subsequently pleaded guilty to the felony of "eluding." Wash. Rev. Code § 46.61.024 (1994). By so pleading, he admitted that he drove his Jeep in a manner indicating "a wanton or wilful disregard for the lives ... of others." He subsequently brought this § 1983 action against Brosseau.

* * *

When confronted with a claim of qualified immunity, a court must ask first [whether the Constitution has been violated]. As the Court of Appeals recognized, the constitutional question in this case is governed by the principles enunciated in Tennessee v. Garner, 471 U.S. 1 (1985), and

Graham v. Connor, 490 U.S. 386 (1989). These cases establish that claims of excessive force are to be judged under the Fourth Amendment's "objective reasonableness" standard. Specifically, with regard to deadly force, we explained in *Garner* that it is unreasonable for an officer to "seize an unarmed, nondangerous suspect by shooting him dead." But "[w]here the officer has probably cause to believe that the suspect poses a threat of serious physical harm, either to the officer or to others, it is not constitutionally unreasonable to prevent escape by using deadly force."

We express no view as to the correctness of the Court of Appeals' decision on the constitutional question itself. We believe that, however that question is decided, the Court of Appeals was wrong on the issue of qualified immunity.[3]

Qualified immunity shields an officer from suit when she makes a decision that, even if constitutionally deficient, reasonably misapprehends the law governing the circumstances she confronted. . . . It is important to emphasize that this inquiry "must be undertaken in light of the specific context of the case, not as a broad proposition." *Saucier v. Katz*, 533 U.S., at 206. As we previously said in this very context:

> [T]here is no doubt that *Graham v. Connor*, supra, clearly establishes the general proposition that use of force is contrary to the Fourth Amendment if it is excessive under objective standards of reasonableness. Yet that is not enough. Rather, we emphasized in Anderson v. Creighton, 483 U.S. 635, 640 (1987), "that the right the official is alleged to have violated must have been 'clearly established' in a more particularized, and hence more relevant, sense: The contours of the right must be sufficiently clear that a reasonable official would understand that what he is doing violates that right.". . . .

The Court of Appeals acknowledged this statement of law, but then proceeded to find fair warning in the general tests set out in *Graham* and *Garner*. In so doing, it was mistaken. . . .

We therefore turn to ask whether, at the time of Brosseau's actions, it was "clearly established" in this more "particularized" sense that she was violating Haugen's Fourth Amendment right. The parties point us to only a handful of cases relevant to the "situation [Brosseau] confronted": whether to shoot a disturbed felon, set on avoiding capture through vehicular flight, when persons in the immediate area are at risk from that flight.[4] Specifical-

---

3. We have no occasion in this case to reconsider our instruction in Saucier v. Katz, 533 U.S. 194, 201 (2001), that lower courts decide the constitutional question prior to deciding the qualified immunity question. We exercise our summary reversal procedure here simply to correct a clear misapprehension of the qualified immunity standard.

4. The parties point us to a number of other cases in this vein that postdate the conduct in question. These decisions, of course, could not have given fair notice to Brosseau and are of no use in the clearly established inquiry.

ly, Brosseau points us to Cole v. Bone, 993 F.2d 1328 (8th Cir. 1993), and Smith v. Freland, 954 F.2d 343 (6th Cir. 1992).

In these cases, the courts found no Fourth Amendment violation when an officer shot a fleeing suspect who presented a risk to others. *Smith* is closer to this case. There, the officer and suspect engaged in a car chase, which appeared to be at an end when the officer cornered the suspect at the back of a dead-end residential street. The suspect, however, freed his car and began speeding down the street. At this point, the officer fired a shot, which killed the suspect. The court held the officer's decision was reasonable and thus did not violate the Fourth Amendment. It noted that the suspect, like Haugen here, "had proven he would do almost anything to avoid capture" and that he posed a major threat to, among others, the officers at the end of the street.

Haugen points us to Estate of Starks v. Enyard, 5 F.3d 230 (7th Cir. 1993), where the court found summary judgment inappropriate on a Fourth Amendment claim involving a fleeing suspect. There, the court concluded that the threat created by the fleeing suspect's failure to brake when an officer suddenly stepped in front of his just-started car was not a sufficiently grave threat to justify the use of deadly force.

These ... cases taken together undoubtedly show that this are is one in which the result depends very much on the facts of each case. None of them squarely governs the case here; they do suggest that Brosseau's actions fell in the " 'hazy border between excessive and acceptable force.' " *Saucier v. Katz*, 533 U.S., at 206. The cases by no means "clearly establish" that Brosseau's conduct violated the Fourth Amendment.

The judgment of the United States Court of Appeals for the Ninth Circuit is therefore reversed, and the case is remanded for further proceedings consistent with this opinion.

■ JUSTICE BREYER, with whom JUSTICE SCALIA and JUSTICE GINSBURG join, concurring.

I join the Court's opinion but write separately to express my concern about the matter to which the Court refers in footnote 3, namely, the way in which lower courts are required to evaluate claims of qualified immunity under the Court's decision in Saucier v. Katz, 533 U.S. 194 (2001). As the Court notes, *Saucier* requires lower courts to decide (1) the constitutional question prior to deciding (2) the qualified immunity question. I am concerned that the current rule rigidly requires the courts unnecessarily to decide difficult constitutional questions when there is available an easier basis for the decision (e.g., qualified immunity) that will satisfactorily resolve the case before the court. Indeed, when courts' dockets are crowded, a rigid "order of battle" makes little administrative sense and can sometimes lead to a constitutional decision that is effectively insulated from review, see Bunting v. Mellen, 541 U.S. 1019 (2004) (Scalia, J., dissenting from denial of certiorari). For these reasons, I think we should reconsider this issue.

■ JUSTICE STEVENS dissenting.

In my judgment, the answer to the constitutional question presented by this case is clear: Under the Fourth Amendment, it was objectively unreasonable for Officer Brosseau to use deadly force against Kenneth Haugen in an attempt to prevent his escape. What is not clear is whether Brosseau is nonetheless entitled to qualified immunity because it might not have been apparent to a reasonably well trained officer in Brosseau's shoes that killing Haugen to prevent his escape was unconstitutional. In my opinion that question should be answered by a jury....

An officer is entitled to qualified immunity, despite having engaged in constitutionally deficient conduct, if, in doing so, she did not violate "clearly established statutory or constitutional rights of which a reasonable person would have known." Harlow v. Fitzgerald, 457 U.S. 800, 818 (1982). The requirement that the law be clearly established is designed to ensure that officers have fair notice of what conduct is proscribed. See Hope v. Pelzer, 536 U.S. 730, 739 (2002). Accordingly, we have recognized that "general statements of the law are not inherently incapable of giving fair and clear warning," United States v. Lanier, 520 U.S. 259, 271 (1997), and have firmly rejected the notion that "an official action is protected by qualified immunity unless the very action in question has previously been held unlawful." Anderson v. Creighton, 483 U.S. 635, 640 (1987).

Thus, the Court's search for relevant case law applying the Tennessee v. Garner, 471 U.S. 1 (1985), standard to materially similar facts is both unnecessary and ill-advised. See *Hope*, 536 U.S., at 741 ("Although earlier cases involving 'fundamentally similar' facts can provide especially strong support for a conclusion that the law is clearly established, they are not necessary to such a finding").

Rather than uncertainty about the law, it is uncertainty about the likely consequences of Haugen's flight—or, more precisely, uncertainly about how a reasonable officer making the split-second decision to use deadly force would have assessed the foreseeability of a serious accident—that prevents me from answering the question of qualified immunity that this case presents. This is a quintessentially "fact-specific" question, not a question that judges should try to answer "as a matter of law." Although it is preferable to resolve the qualified immunity question at the earliest possible stage of litigation, this preference does not give judges license to take inherently factual questions away from the jury. ...

In sum, the constitutional limits on an officer's use of deadly force have been well settled in this Court's jurisprudence for nearly two decades, and, in this case, Officer Brosseau acted outside of those clearly delineated bounds. Nonetheless, in my judgment, there is a genuine factual question as to whether a reasonably well-trained officer standing in Brosseau's shoes could have concluded otherwise, and the question plainly falls within the purview of the jury.

For these reasons, I respectfully dissent.

NOTES ON "CLEARLY ESTABLISHED LAW"

1. Required Similarity Between Challenged Conduct and Prior Precedent: *Hope v. Pelzer*. Use of deadly force by police officers—the act challenged in *Brosseau*—is a sufficiently common occurrence that there will be many opportunities for fleshing out the circumstances in which an officer's actions are unreasonable. But how are courts to assess whether the law is "clearly established" in more unusual circumstances?

The Supreme Court addressed that issue in Hope v. Pelzer, 536 U.S. 730 (2002). The case concerned the Alabama Department of Corrections' (ADOC) use of a "hitching post" to punish state prison inmates who refused to work or disrupted work squads. (Alabama was apparently the only state to use this practice.) According to his complaint, Hope was handcuffed to a hitching post on two occasions. The first time, he was attached to the post for two hours. Due to his height, his arms were pinioned above shoulder height and "[w]henever he tried moving his arms to improve his circulation, the handcuffs cut into his wrists, causing pain and discomfort." The second time, Hope was required to remove his shirt before being handcuffed to the post, and he remained at the post for seven hours. He was given water only once or twice, was denied any bathroom breaks, was taunted by guards, and suffered sunburn.

Hope filed a § 1983 suit against three guards involved in the first incident, one of whom was also involved in the second. Both the District Court and the Court of Appeals held that the guards were entitled to qualified immunity. The Court of Appeals agreed with Hope that the alleged conduct would violate the Eighth Amendment. Nonetheless, because the facts in the cases on which Hope relied, "though analogous," were not "materially similar," they did not create clearly established law.

The Supreme Court reversed the grant of qualified immunity. Justice Stevens's opinion for the Court agreed that Alabama's practices violated the Eighth Amendment. Given the facts as alleged by Hope, the guards' actions involved the "unnecessary and wanton infliction of pain" that Whitley v. Albers, 475 U.S. 312 (1986), had held violative of the Cruel and Unusual Punishment Clause. With respect to qualified immunity, the Court held that the Eleventh Circuit's requirement that § 1983 plaintiffs point to a decision involving "materially similar" facts was a "rigid gloss on the qualified immunity standard ... not consistent with our cases." Such a requirement, the Court stated, was not necessary "to ensure that before they are subjected to suit, officers are on notice their conduct is unlawful."

The Court drew a parallel to its decision in United States v. Lanier, 520 U.S. 259 (1997), which involved criminal prosecution under 18 U.S.C. § 242 of a state-court judge who sexually assaulted a number of women. Section 242 makes it a crime for a state official to "willfully" deprive a person of rights protected by the Constitution. Lanier argued that he had not received "fair warning" that his conduct violated the statute because no prior case had held that sexual assaults committed under color of state law violated the Fourth Amendment. The Supreme Court disagreed, noting that it had repeatedly upheld convictions under § 242 despite factual differences between the instant prosecutions and prior precedents:

> Our opinion in *Lanier* thus makes clear that officials can still be on notice that their conduct violates established law even in novel factual circumstances. Indeed, in *Lanier*, we expressly rejected a requirement that previous cases be "fundamentally similar." Although earlier cases involving "fundamentally similar" facts can provide especially strong support for a conclusion that the law is clearly established, they are not necessary to such a finding. The same is true of cases with "materially similar" facts. Accordingly, pursuant to *Lanier* the salient question that the Court of Appeals ought to have asked is whether the state of the law in 1995 gave respondents fair warning that their alleged treatment of Hope was unconstitutional.

The Court held that it did. It pointed to a 1974 court of appeals decision, binding on the Eleventh Circuit, that had held unconstitutional several forms of corporal punishment inflicted within the Mississippi prison system, including "handcuffing inmates to the fence and to cells for long periods of time, . . . and forcing inmates to stand, sit or lie on crates, stumps, or otherwise maintain awkward positions for prolonged periods":

> [For] the purpose of providing fair notice to reasonable officers administering punishment for past misconduct, [there is no] reason to draw a constitutional distinction between a practice of handcuffing an inmate to a fence for prolonged periods and handcuffing him to a hitching post for seven hours. The Court of Appeals' conclusion to the contrary exposes the danger of a rigid, overreliance on factual similarity. As the Government submits in its brief amicus curiae: "No reasonable officer could have concluded that the constitutional holding of [Gates v. Collier, 501 F.2d 1291 (5th Cir. 1974)] turned on the fact that inmates were handcuffed to fences or the bars of cells, rather than a specially designed metal bar designated for shackling. If anything, the use of a designated hitching post highlights the constitutional problem." Brief for United States as Amicus Curiae 22. In light of *Gates*, the unlawfulness of the alleged conduct should have been apparent to the respondents.

The Court further viewed the "reasoning, though not the holding" of Ort v. White, 813 F.2d 318 (11th Cir. 1987), as "sen[ding] the same message to reasonable officers in that Circuit." *Ort* had reasoned that while temporary denials of drinking water to inmates who refused to work might be characterized as "necessary coercive measures undertaken to obtain compliance with a reasonable prison rule," denials of water as punishment would raise serious constitutional issues, and would violate the Constitution if they threatened the inmate's health.

> Relevant to the question whether *Ort* provided fair warning to respondents that their conduct violated the Constitution is a regulation promulgated by ADOC in 1993. The regulation ... provides that an activity log should be completed for each ... inmate, detailing his responses to offers of water and bathroom breaks every 15 minutes. Such a log was completed and maintained for petitioner's shackling in May, but the record contains no such log for the seven-hour shackling in June and the record indicates that the periodic offers contemplated by the regulation were not made. The regulation also states that an inmate "will be allowed to join his assigned squad" whenever he tells an officer "that he is ready to go to work." [Findings in an earlier case], as well as the record in this case, indicate that this important provision of the regulation was frequently ignored by corrections officers. If regularly observed, a requirement that would effectively give the inmate the keys to the handcuffs that attached him to the hitching post would have made this case more analogous to the practice upheld in *Ort*, rather than the kind of punishment *Ort* described as impermissible. A course of conduct that tends to prove that the requirement was merely a sham, or that respondents could ignore it with impunity, provides equally strong support for the conclusion that they were fully aware of the wrongful character of their conduct. ...
>
> Our conclusion that "a reasonable person would have known," Harlow v. Fitzgerald, 457 U.S. 800, 818 (1982), of the violation is buttressed by the fact that the [United States Department of Justice (DOJ)] specifically advised the ADOC of the unconstitutionality of its practices before the incidents in this case took place.... The ADOC replied that it thought the post could permissibly be used "to preserve prison security and discipline." In response, the DOJ informed the ADOC that, "although an emergency situation may warrant drastic action by corrections staff, our experts found that the 'rail' is being used systematically as an improper punishment for relatively trivial offenses. Therefore, we have concluded that the use of the 'rail' is without penological justification." Although there is nothing in the record indicating that the DOJ's views were communicated to respondents, this exchange lends support to the view that reasonable

officials in the ADOC should have realized that the use of the hitching post under the circumstances alleged by Hope violated the Eighth Amendment prohibition against cruel and unusual punishment.

The obvious cruelty inherent in this practice should have provided respondents with some notice that their alleged conduct violated Hope's constitutional protection against cruel and unusual punishment. Hope was treated in a way antithetical to human dignity—he was hitched to a post for an extended period of time in a position that was painful, and under circumstances that were both degrading and dangerous.

Justice Thomas, joined by Chief Justice Rehnquist and Justice Scalia, dissented:

In evaluating whether it was clearly established in 1995 that respondents' conduct violated the Eighth Amendment, the Court of Appeals properly noted that "it is important to analyze the facts in [the prior cases relied upon by petitioner where courts found Eighth Amendment violations], and determine if they are materially similar to the facts in the case in front of us." The right not to suffer from "cruel and unusual punishments" is an extremely abstract and general right. In the vast majority of cases, the text of the Eighth Amendment does not, in and of itself, give a government official sufficient notice of the clearly established Eighth Amendment law applicable to a particular situation. Rather, one must look to case law....

Such cases give government officials the best indication of what conduct is unlawful in a given situation....

Previous litigation over Alabama's use of the restraining bar, however, did nothing to warn reasonable Alabama prison guards that attaching a prisoner to a restraining bar was unlawful, let alone that the illegality of such conduct was clearly established. In fact, the outcome of those cases effectively forecloses petitioner's claim that it should have been clear to respondents in 1995 that handcuffing petitioner to a restraining bar violated the Eighth Amendment....

In the face of these decisions, and the absence of contrary authority, I find it impossible to conclude that respondents either were "plainly incompetent" or "knowingly violating the law" when they affixed petitioner to the restraining bar. Malley v. Briggs, 475 U.S. 335, 341 (1986). A reasonably competent prison guard attempting to obey the law is not only entitled to look at how courts have recently evaluated his colleagues' prior conduct, such judicial decisions are often the only place that a guard can look for guidance, especially in a situation where a State stands alone in adopting a particular policy.

Moreover, if the application of this Court's general Eighth Amendment jurisprudence to the use of a restraining bar was as "obvious" as the Court claims, one wonders how Federal District Courts in Alabama could have repeatedly arrived at the opposite conclusion, and how respondents, in turn, were to realize that these courts had failed to grasp the "obvious." . . . .

The Department of Justice report referenced by the Court does nothing to demonstrate that it should have been clear to respondents that attaching petitioner to a restraining bar violated his Eighth Amendment rights. To begin with, the Court concedes that there is no indication the Justice Department's recommendation that the ADOC stop using the restraining bar was ever communicated to respondents, prison guards in the small town of Capshaw, Alabama. In any event, an extraordinarily well-informed prison guard in 1995, who had read both the Justice Department's report and Federal District Court decisions addressing the use of the restraining bar, could have concluded only that there was a dispute as to whether handcuffing a prisoner to a restraining bar constituted an Eighth Amendment violation, not that such a practice was clearly unconstitutional.

2. Unintended Effects of the *Saucier* Sequencing Requirement: *Bunting v. Mellen*. Note that in *Brosseau*, three Justices expressed concern at the requirement that lower courts invariably adhere to *Saucier*'s requirement of first determining the constitutionality of the defendant's conduct before asking whether the law was clearly established at the time of the defendant's actions. The bases for their concern were illustrated in Bunting v. Mellen, 541 U.S. 1019 (2004). The underlying case concerned a First Amendment challenge by two cadets at the Virginia Military Institute, a state institution of higher education, to the school's practice of conducting a prayer before the cadets' evening meal. The cadets sued Bunting, the Superintendent of VMI, seeking declaratory and injunctive relief, as well as nominal damages. The District Court entered summary judgment in favor of the plaintiffs, awarding them declaratory relief and enjoining Bunting from continuing to sponsor the prayer. But it found that Bunting was entitled to qualified immunity on plaintiffs' damages claims because his arguments were not "so obviously incorrect that a reasonable government official in [his] place should have known that his actions violated [the plaintiffs'] rights under the Establishment Clause."

Both sides appealed—the superintendent challenging the District Court's award of declaratory and injunctive relief, and the cadets challenging the District Court's decision on qualified immunity. In the meantime, the cadets had graduated and Bunting had retired as superintendent. The Court of Appeals therefore vacated as moot the district court's judgment awarding them declaratory and injunctive relief. With respect to the damages claim, the Court of Appeals affirmed, agreeing with the District Court that the supper prayer violated the Establishment Clause of the First Amendment, but that Bunting was nevertheless entitled to qualified immunity.

Bunting and Peay, the new Superintendent of VMI, petitioned for certiorari, seeking review of the determination that the supper prayer was unconstitutional. The Court denied the petition, but five Justices expressed their views regarding the interaction of the *Saucier* sequencing principle and appellate review. Justice Scalia, joined by the Chief Justice, dissented from the denial of certiorari. He noted that the "*Saucier* constitutional-question-first procedure played a central role in the proceedings below." The Court of Appeals' ruling created the kind of conflict with decisions of other courts of appeals that would normally make the case a strong candidate for certiorari:

> But it is questionable whether Bunting's request for review can be entertained, since he won judgment in the court below. For although the statute governing our certiorari jurisdiction permits application by "any party" to a case in a federal court of appeals, 28 U.S.C. § 1254(1), our practice reflects a "settled refusal" to entertain an appeal by a party on an issue as to which he prevailed. We sit, after all, not to correct errors in dicta; "this Court reviews judgments, not statements in opinions." California v. Rooney, 483 U.S. 307, 311 (1987) (per curiam) (internal quotation marks omitted).
>
> I think it plain that this general rule should not apply where a favorable judgment on qualified-immunity grounds would deprive a party of an opportunity to appeal the unfavorable (and often more significant) constitutional determination. That constitutional determination is not mere dictum in the ordinary sense, since the whole reason we require it to be set forth (despite the availability of qualified immunity) is to clarify the law and thus make unavailable repeated claims of qualified immunity in future cases....
>
> Not only is the denial of review unfair to the litigant (and to the institution that the litigant represents) but it undermines the purpose served by initial consideration of the constitutional question, which is to clarify constitutional rights without undue delay. See, e.g., Wilson v. Layne, 526 U.S., 603, 609 (1999); County of Sacramento v. Lewis, 523 U.S. 833, 841–42, n.5 (1998)....
>
> This situation should not be prolonged. We should either make clear that constitutional determinations are not insulated from our review (for which purpose this case would be an appropriate vehicle), or else drop any pretense at requiring the ordering in every case.

By contrast, Justice Stevens, joined by Justices Ginsburg and Breyer, voted to deny certiorari in the case and reiterated the view that the "'perceived procedural tangle' described by Justice Scalia's dissent is a byproduct of an unwise judge-made rule under which courts must decide whether the plaintiff has alleged a constitutional violation before addressing the question whether the defendant state actor is entitled to qualified immunity." They would therefore relax the "inflexible rule requiring the premature adjudication of constitutional issues." And they argued further that the Court lacked jurisdiction over the petition for certiorari because Bunting "had retired from his position as Superintendent of VMI, and will suffer no direct injury if VMI is unable to continue the prayer. Thus, there no longer is a live controversy between Bunting and respondents regarding the constitutionality of the prayer. As for the other named petitioner, new Superintendent Peay, there never was a live controversy. Peay was added to the case (apparently in error) after the Court of Appeals issued its decision vacating the District Court's award of injunctive and declaratory relief. At that point, the only issue was Bunting's individual-capacity liability—an issue in which Peay obviously has no interest. VMI itself is not a party."

Page 1129, add to footnote b:

David Jacks Achtenberg, Taking History Seriously: Municipal Liability under 42 U.S.C. § 1983 and the Debate over Respondeat Superior, 73 Fordham L. Rev. 2183 (2005) (exploring in detail both the common-law antecedents of *Monell* and the application to that question of the common-law decisions-making process).

Page 1259, add a new Note:

12. *City of Rancho Palos Verdes v. Abrams*. The restrictive approach of *Gonzaga University* was reaffirmed in City of Rancho Palos Verdes v. Abrams, 544 U.S. ___ (2005). Plaintiff Abrams sued his locality, claiming that the denial of a zoning permit for a radio antenna on his property violated restrictions imposed on localities by the Telecommunications Act of 1996. Writing for a nearly unanimous Court, Justice Scalia began with the familiar admonition that the statute must create individually enforceable rights in the class of beneficiaries to which the plaintiff belongs. That showing, however, creates only a rebuttable presumption that the right is enforceable under § 1983. The presumption is rebutted if the defendant shows that Congress "did not intend" that the newly created right be enforceable under § 1983, and a lack of congressional intent is the "ordinary inference" from a different statutory enforcement scheme. In the case of the Telecommunications Act, individual enforcement is explicitly authorized but on a shorter timetable, arguably without compensatory damages, and certainly without attorneys fees. These differences in remedy precluded application of § 1983, absent legislation indication of a purpose to provide that relief. Justice Breyer, joined by Justices O'Connor, Souter, and Ginsburg, concurred to say that context would sometimes be important in determining whether Congress intended to exclude enforcement under § 1983. Only Justice Stevens dissented.

CHAPTER X

REMEDIAL INTERACTIONS

Page 1336, move Notes 3 and 4 as indicated below, and add the following:

NOTES ON SUBSEQUENT *PREISER* LITIGATION

1. ***Edwards v. Balisok.*** [Here read Note 3 on page 1336.]

2. ***Wilkinson v. Dotson.*** William Dotson and Rogerico Johnson were serving lengthy prison sentences in Ohio state prisons. Dotson was sentenced to life in 1981. He sought parole in 2000. The parole board denied relief and postponed further consideration for five years. Johnson began a 10–30 year term in 1992. He was considered and rejected for parole in 1999.

In both cases the parole board applied standards that were adopted in 1998, well after the two prisoners committed their offenses and were convicted and sentenced. Both sought an injunction under § 1983 on the ground that retroactive application of the 1998 guidelines denied them due process and violated the Ex Post Facto clause. The District Court held the case cognizable only under habeas. The Court of Appeals disagreed. In an opinion by Justice Breyer, the Supreme Court agreed with the Circuit Court. Wilkinson v. Dotson, 544 U.S. ___ (2005).

In the course of holding that the suit could proceed under § 1983, Justice Breyer summarized the prior cases and applied their principles:

> Throughout the legal journey from *Preiser* to *Balisok*, the Court has focused on the need to ensure that state prisoners use only habeas corpus (or similar state) remedies when they seek to invalidate the duration of their confinement—either directly through an injunction compelling speedier release or indirectly through a judicial determination that necessarily implies the unlawfulness of the State's custody. Thus, *Preiser* found an implied exception to § 1983's coverage where the claim seeks—not where it simply "relates to"—"core" habeas corpus relief, i.e., where a state prisoner requests present or future release. ... *Heck* specifies that a prisoner cannot use § 1983 to obtain damages where success would necessarily imply the unlawfulness of a (not previously invalidated) conviction or sentence. And *Balisok* ... demonstrates that habeas remedies do not displace § 1983 actions where success in the civil rights suit would not necessarily vitiate the

legality of (not previously invalidated) state confinement. These cases, taken together, indicate that a state prisoner's § 1983 action is barred (absent prior invalidation)—no matter the relief sought (damages or equitable relief), no matter the target of the prisoner's suit (state conduct leading to conviction or internal prison proceedings)—if success in that action would necessarily demonstrate the invalidity of confinement or its duration.

Applying these principles to the present case, we conclude that respondents' claims are cognizable under § 1983, i.e., they do not fall within the implicit habeas exception. Dotson and Johnson seek relief that will render invalid the state procedures used to deny parole eligibility (Dotson) and parole suitability (Johnson). Neither respondent seeks an injunction ordering his immediate or speedier release into the community. And . . . a favorable judgment will not "necessarily imply the invalidity of [their] conviction[s] or sentence[s]." *Heck*, 512 U.S., at 487. Success for Dotson does not mean immediate release from confinement or a shorter stay in prison; it means at most new eligibility review, which at most will speed consideration of a new parole application. Success for Johnson means at most a new parole hearing at which Ohio parole authorities may, in their discretion, decline to shorten his prison term. Because neither prisoner's claim would necessarily spell speedier release, neither lies at "the core of habeas corpus." *Preiser*, 411 U.S., at 489. Finally, the prisoners' claims for future relief (which, if successful, will not necessarily imply the invalidity of confinement or shorten its duration) are yet more distant from that core.

Justice Scalia joined the Court's opinion but wrote separately "to note that a contrary holding would require us to broaden the scope of habeas relief beyond recognition." He continued:

It is one thing to say that permissible habeas relief, as our cases interpret the statute, includes ordering a "quantum change in the level of custody," Graham v. Broglin, 922 F.2d 379, 381 (7th Cir. 1991) (Posner, J.), such as release from incarceration to parole. It is quite another to say that the habeas statute authorizes federal courts to order relief that neither terminates custody, accelerates the future date of release from custody, nor reduces the level of custody. That is what is sought here: the mandating of a new parole hearing that may or may not result in release, prescription of the composition of the hearing panel, and specification of the procedures to be followed. A holding that this sort of judicial immersion in the administration of discretionary parole lies at the "core of habeas" would utterly sever the writ from its common-law roots. The dissent suggests that because a habeas court may issue a conditional writ ordering a prisoner released unless the State conducts a new sentencing proceeding, the court may also issue a conditional writ ordering release absent a new parole proceeding. But the prisoner who shows that his sentencing was unconstitutional is actually entitled to release, because the judgment pursuant to which he is confined has been invalidated; the conditional writ serves only to "delay the release ... in order to provide the State an opportunity to correct the constitutional violation." Hilton v. Braunskill, 481 U.S. 770, 775 (1987). By contrast, the validly sentenced prisoner who shows only that the State made a procedural error in denying discretionary parole has not established a right to release, and so cannot obtain habeas relief—conditional or otherwise. Conditional writs enable habeas courts to give States time to replace an invalid judgment with a valid one, and the consequence when they fail to do so is always release. Conditional writs are not an all-purpose weapon with which federal habeas courts can extort from the respondent custodian forms of relief short of release, whether a new parole hearing or a new mattress in the applicant's cell.

Justice Thomas joined the Scalia opinion. Justice Kennedy was the lone dissenter.

3. ***Nelson v. Campbell***. Nelson v. Campbell, 541 U.S. 637 (2004), involved the following problem:

> Three days before his scheduled execution by lethal injection, petitioner David Nelson filed a civil rights action in District Court, pursuant to 42 U.S.C. § 1983, alleging that the use of a "cutdown" procedure to access his veins would violate the Eighth Amendment. Petitioner, who had already filed one unsuccessful federal habeas application, sought a stay of execution so that the District Court could consider the merits of his constitutional claim. The question before us is whether § 1983 is an appropriate vehicle for petitioner's Eighth Amendment claim seeking a temporary stay and permanent injunctive relief.

The Circuit Court held that the claim sounded in habeas, and dismissed because it was a repetitive application that fit no exception allowing it to go forward. "Thus," the Supreme Court noted, "the 11th Circuit held that petitioner was without recourse to challenge the constitutionality of the cut-down procedure in Federal District Court."

In an opinion by Justice O'Connor, the Supreme Court held unanimously that the petitioner's § 1983 claim could go forward. Because petitioner had compromised veins due to years of drug abuse, unusual medical procedures were necessary in order to carry out the execution. Petitioner's claim carefully stated that he was not objecting to the fact of execution by legal injection, but only to the particular "cut-down" procedure by which it was proposed to be administered.[b] The Court responded:

> We have not yet had occasion to consider whether civil rights suits seeking to enjoin the use of a particular method of execution—e.g., lethal injection or electrocution—fall within the core of federal habeas corpus or, rather, whether they are properly viewed as challenges to the conditions of a condemned inmate's death sentence. Neither the "conditions" nor the "fact or duration" label is particularly apt. A suit seeking to enjoin a particular means of effectuating a sentence of death does not directly call into question the "fact" or "validity" of the sentence itself—by simply altering its method of execution, the State can go forward with the sentence. On the other hand, imposition of the death penalty presupposes a means of carrying it out. In a State such as Alabama, where the legislature has established lethal injection as the preferred method of execution, a constitutional challenge seeking to permanently enjoin the use of lethal injection may amount to a challenge to the fact of the sentence itself. A finding of unconstitutionality would require statutory amendment or variance, imposing significant costs on the State and the administration of its penal system. And while it makes little sense to talk of the "duration" of a death sentence, a State retains a significant interest in meting out a sentence of death in a timely fashion.
>
> We need not reach here the difficult question of how to categorize method-of-execution claims generally. Respondents at oral argument conceded that § 1983 would be an appropriate vehicle for an inmate who is not facing execution to bring a "deliberate indifference" challenge to the constitutionality of the cut-down procedure if used to gain venous access for purposes of providing medical treatment. Tr. of Oral Arg. 40 ("I don't disagree . . . that a cut-down occurring for purposes of venous access, wholly divorced from an execution, is indeed a valid conditions of confinement claim"); see also Estelle v. Gamble, 429 U.S. 97, 104 (1976) ("We therefore conclude that deliberate indifference to serious medical needs of prisoners constitutes the 'unnecessary and wanton infliction of pain' proscribed by the Eighth Amend-

---

b. At one point, petitioner was told that "prison personnel would . . . make a 2-inch incision in petitioner's arm or leg; the procedure would take place one hour before the scheduled execution; and only local anesthesia would be used. There was no assurance that a physician would perform or even be present for the procedure." By contrast, petitioner submitted an affidavit from a reputable physician to the effect that "the cut-down is a dangerous and antiquated medical procedure to be performed only by a trained physician in a clinical environment with the patient under deep sedation. In light of safer and less-invasive contemporary means of venous access, [the Doctor] concluded that 'there is no comprehensible reason for the State of Alabama to be planning to employ the cut-down procedure to obtain intravenous access, unless there exists an intent to render the procedure more painful and risky than it otherwise needs to be.'"

ment"). We see no reason on the face of the complaint to treat petitioner's claim differently solely because he has been condemned to die.

Respondents counter that, because the cut-down is part of the execution procedure, petitioner's challenge is, in fact, a challenge to the fact of his execution. They offer the following argument: A challenge to the use of lethal injection as a method of execution sounds in habeas; venous access is a necessary prerequisite to, and thus an indispensable part of, any lethal injection procedure; therefore, a challenge to the State's means of achieving venous access must be brought in a federal habeas application. Even were we to accept as given respondents' premise that a challenge to lethal injection sounds in habeas, the conclusion does not follow. That venous access is a necessary prerequisite does not imply that a particular means of gaining such access is likewise necessary. Indeed, the gravamen of petitioner's entire claim is that use of the cut-down would be *gratuitous*. Merely labeling something as part of an execution procedure is insufficient to insulate it from a § 1983 attack.

If as a legal matter the cut-down were a statutorily mandated part of the lethal injection protocol, or if as a factual matter petitioner were unable or unwilling to concede acceptable alternatives for gaining venous access, respondents might have a stronger argument that success on the merits, coupled with injunctive relief, would call into question the death sentence itself. But petitioner has been careful throughout these proceedings, in his complaint and at oral argument, to assert that the cut-down, as well as the warden's refusal to provide reliable information regarding the cut-down protocol, are *wholly unnecessary* to gaining venous access. Petitioner has alleged alternatives that, if they had been used, would have allowed the State to proceed with the execution as scheduled. App. 17 (complaint) (proffering as "less invasive, less painful, faster, cheaper, and safer" the alternative procedure of "percutaneous central line placement"); id., at 37–38 (affidavit of Dr. Mark Heath) (describing relative merits of the cut-down and percutaneous central line placement). No Alabama statute requires use of the cut-down and respondents have offered no duly-promulgated regulations to the contrary.

If on remand and after an evidentiary hearing the District Court concludes that use of the cut-down procedure as described in the complaint is necessary for administering the lethal injection, the District Court will need to address the broader question, left open here, of how to treat method-of-execution claims generally. An evidentiary hearing will in all likelihood be unnecessary, however, as the State now seems willing to implement petitioner's proposed alternatives. See Tr. of Oral Arg. 45–46 ("I think there is no disagreement here that percutaneous central line placement is the preferred method and will, in fact, be used, a cut-down to be used only if actually necessary").

We note that our holding here is consistent with our approach to civil rights damages actions, which, like method-of-execution challenges, fall at the margins of habeas. Although damages are not an available habeas remedy, we have previously concluded that a § 1983 suit for damages that would "necessarily imply" the invalidity of the fact of an inmate's conviction, or "necessarily imply" the invalidity of the length of an inmate's sentence, is not cognizable under § 1983 unless and until the inmate obtains favorable termination of a state, or federal habeas, challenge to his conviction or sentence. Heck v. Humphrey, 512 U.S. 477, 487 (1994); Edwards v. Balisok, 520 U.S. 641, 648 (1997). . . . In the present context, focusing attention on whether petitioner's challenge to the cut-down procedure would *necessarily* prevent Alabama from carrying out its execution both protects against the use of § 1983 to circumvent any limits imposed by the habeas statute and minimizes the extent to which the fact of a prisoner's imminent execution will require differential treatment of his otherwise cognizable § 1983 claims.

The Court also addressed the propriety of a stay of execution in contexts such as this, and emphasized the narrowness of its holding:

Respondents argue that a decision to reverse the judgment of the 11th Circuit would open the floodgates to all manner of method-of-execution challenges, as well as last minute stay requests. But, because we do not here resolve the question of how to treat method-of-execution claims generally, our holding is extremely limited.

Moreover, as our previous decision in Gomez v. United States Dist. Court for Northern Dist. of Cal., 503 U.S. 653 (1992) (per curiam), makes clear, the mere fact that an inmate states a cognizable § 1983 claim does not warrant the entry of a stay as a matter of right. *Gomez* came to us on a motion by the State to vacate a stay entered by an en banc panel of the Court of Appeals for the Ninth Circuit that would have allowed the District Court time to consider the merits of a condemned inmate's last-minute § 1983 action challenging the constitutionality of California's use of the gas chamber. We left open the question whether the inmate's claim was cognizable under § 1983, but vacated the stay nonetheless. The inmate, Robert Alton Harris, who had already filed four unsuccessful federal habeas applications, waited until the 11th hour to file his challenge despite the fact that California's method of execution had been in place for years: "This claim could have been brought more than a decade ago. There is no good reason for this abusive delay, which has been compounded by last-minute attempts to manipulate the judicial process. A court may consider the last-minute nature of an application to stay execution in deciding whether to grant equitable relief."

A stay is an equitable remedy, and "[e]quity must take into consideration the State's strong interest in proceeding with its judgment and ... attempt[s] at manipulation." Thus, before granting a stay, a district court must consider not only the likelihood of success on the merits and the relative harms to the parties, but also the extent to which the inmate has delayed unnecessarily in bringing the claim. Given the State's significant interest in enforcing its criminal judgments, there is a strong equitable presumption against the grant of a stay where a claim could have been brought at such a time as to allow consideration of the merits without requiring entry of a stay.

Finally, the ability to bring a § 1983 claim, rather than a habeas application, does not entirely free inmates from substantive or procedural limitations. The Prison Litigation Reform Act of 1995 (Act) imposes limits on the scope and duration of preliminary and permanent injunctive relief, including a requirement that, before issuing such relief, "[a] court shall give substantial weight to any adverse impact on ... the operation of a criminal justice system caused by the relief." 18 U.S.C. § 3626(a)(1); accord, § 3626(a)(2). It requires that inmates exhaust available state administrative remedies before bringing a § 1983 action challenging the conditions of their confinement. 110 Stat. 1321–71, 42 U.S.C. § 1997e(a) ("No action shall be brought with respect to prison conditions under section 1983 of this title, or any other Federal law, by a prisoner confined in any jail, prison, or other correctional facility until such administrative remedies as are available are exhausted"). The Act mandates that a district court "shall," on its own motion, dismiss "any action brought with respect to prison conditions under section 1983 of this title ... if the court is satisfied that the action is frivolous, malicious, fails to state a claim upon which relief can be granted, or seeks monetary relief from a defendant who is immune from relief." § 1997e(c)(1). Indeed, if the claim is frivolous on its face, a district court may dismiss the suit before the plaintiff has exhausted his state remedies. § 1997e(c)(2).

4. *Res Judicata.* [Here read Note 4 on page 1336.]

Page 1351, add at end of footnote a:

The Supreme Court applied § 1738 to impose issue preclusion in San Remo Hotel, L.P. v. City and County of San Francisco, 545 U.S. __ (2005). The facts are complex, but one issue concerned the effect of Williamson County Regional Planning Comm'n v. Hamilton Bank of Johnson City, 473 U.S. 172 (1985). *Williamson County* held that a takings claim is not ripe for litigation in federal court until a state fails to provide adequate compensation. In the course of state court litigation undertaken to comply with this limitation, the state courts resolved legal issues that were later sought to be asserted in federal court. The victim of the asserted taking argued that an exception to § 1738 should be created to when plaintiffs are forced to litigate in state courts without any realistic opportunity for federal review of their claims. Access to federal district court, it was argued, should be preserved in such a situation.

Relying on *Allen*, *Migra*, and *Kremer*, the Court unanimously rejected the claim:

At base, petitioners' claim amounts to little more than the concern that it is unfair to give preclusive effect to state-court proceedings that are not chosen, but are instead required in order to ripen federal takings claims. Whatever the merits of that concern may be, we are not free to disregard the full faith and credit statute solely to preserve the availability of a federal forum.

Joined by Justices O'Connor, Kennedy, and Thomas, Chief Justice Rehnquist wrote separately. He questioned the soundness of the *Williamson County* holding, even though he joined the Court's opinion. But as that issue had not been addressed in the arguments, he chose to postpone its reconsideration.

*

APPENDIX C

JUDICIAL REVIEW

Page C–10, add to footnote b:

See also Robert J. Reinstein and Mark C. Rahdert, Reconstructing *Marbury*, 57 Ark. L. Rev. 729 (2005), which grounds *Marbury* on rule-of-law considerations and argues for its relevance outside the American legal system.

Page C–10, add to the end of footnote d:

Saikrishna B. Prakash and John C. Yoo, The Origins of Judicial Review, 70 U. Chi. L. Rev. 887 (2003) ("Our goal . . . is to show that the necessary predicate for . . . judicial review . . . is on solid textual, structural, and historical grounds").

†